FLOYD CLYMER - 2025 EDITION
MAICO
250cc-360cc-400cc-450cc-501cc
WORKSHOP MANUAL
1968 to 1978

A Floyd Clymer Publication - 2025 VelocePress.com

PREFACE

TRADEMARKS & COPYRIGHT

Maico® is a registered trademark owned by Axel Kostler. This publication is not sponsored by or endorsed by the trademark owner. We recognize that some words, model names and designations, for example, mentioned herein are the property of the trademark holder. We use them for identification purposes only. This is not an official publication however; it may include non-copyright works of the trademark holder.

INTRODUCTION

Welcome to the world of digital publishing ~ the book you now hold in your hand was printed using the latest state of the art digital technology. The advent of print-on-demand has forever changed the publishing process, never has information been so accessible and it is our hope that this book serves your informational needs for years to come. If this is your first exposure to digital publishing, we hope that you are pleased with the results. Many more titles of interest to the classic automobile and motorcycle enthusiast, collector and restorer are available via our website at www.VelocePress.com. We hope that you find this title as interesting as we do.

NOTE FROM THE PUBLISHER

The information presented is true and complete to the best of our knowledge. All recommendations are made without any guarantees on the part of the author or the publisher, who also disclaim all liability incurred with the use of this information.

INFORMATION ON THE USE OF THIS PUBLICATION

This manual is an invaluable resource for those interested in performing their own maintenance. However, in today's information age we are constantly subject to changes in common practice, new technology, availability of improved materials and increased awareness of chemical toxicity. As such, it is advised that the user consult with an experienced professional prior to undertaking any procedure described herein. While every care has been taken to ensure correctness of information, it is obviously not possible to guarantee complete freedom from errors or omissions or to accept liability arising from such errors or omissions. Therefore, any individual that uses the information contained within, or elects to perform or participate in do-it-yourself repairs or modifications acknowledges that there is a risk factor involved and that the publisher or its associates cannot be held responsible for personal injury or property damage resulting from the use of the information or the outcome of such procedures.

WARNING!

One final word of advice, this publication is intended to be used as a reference guide, and when in doubt the reader should consult with a qualified technician.

CONTENTS

CHAPTER ONE

GENERAL INFORMATION ... 1

    Service hints
    Tools
    Expendable supplies
    Safety hints

CHAPTER TWO

LUBRICATION AND MAINTENANCE ... 4

    Air cleaners
    Transmission oil
    Fork oil
    Control lubrication and adjustment
    Drive chain
    Ignition
    Carburetor
    Engine lubrication
    Carbon removal

CHAPTER THREE

TROUBLESHOOTING ... 14

    Operating requirements
    Starting difficulties
    Poor idling
    Misfiring
    Flat spots
    Power loss
    Overheating
    Backfiring
    Abnormal engine noises
    Piston seizure
    Excessive vibration
    Clutch slip or drag
    Poor handling
    Brake problems
    Lighting problems (Enduros)
    Troubleshooting guide

CHAPTER FOUR

ENGINE ... 18

    Operating principles
    Cylinder head
    Cylinder
    Pistons and rings
    Crankshaft and crankcase
    Servicing, timing, and adjustment

CHAPTER FIVE

TRANSMISSION AND CLUTCH ... 42

    Description
    Clutch servicing
    Kickstarter
    Transmission servicing

CHAPTER SIX

FUEL SYSTEM ... 55

    Carburetor operation
    Carburetor servicing
    Air filter
    Fuel tank

CHAPTER SEVEN

ELECTRICAL SYSTEM 62

    Magneto ignition system   Fault tracing
    Enduro lighting/charging system

CHAPTER EIGHT

FRONT SUSPENSION AND STEERING 71

    Forks   Steering

CHAPTER NINE

REAR SUSPENSION 79

    Swinging arm   Springs and shock absorbers

CHAPTER TEN

WHEELS, TIRES, AND BRAKES 84

    Spokes   Brakes
    Wheel balance   Rear sprocket
    Wheel inspection   Drive chain
    Wheel bearings and seals

CHAPTER ELEVEN

FRAME 93

CHAPTER TWELVE

COMPETITION PREPARATION 94

    General information   Modifications and updating
    Check list   Additional modifications
    Cleaning and inspection

CHAPTER THIRTEEN

USEFUL FORMULAS AND TABLES 104

    Conversion table   Horsepower and torque
    Examples of conversions   Piston speed
    Temperature   Gear ratio
    Piston displacement   Bolt torques
    Compression ratio

APPENDIX 1973 AND LATER 250cc, 400cc, 440cc AND 501cc MODELS . 110

    Parts diagrams with component key   Wiring diagram with lights
    Specifications   Wiring diagram no lights

INDEX 120

CHAPTER ONE

GENERAL INFORMATION

All service operations for late-model Maico motorcycles are presented in this handbook. The information applies to the following models.

Motocross, Enduro, and Gelandesport—1968 through 1975.

250cc	450cc
360cc	501cc
400cc	

Because Maicos are designed principally for racing, changes and improvements are not incorporated by "model year"; they appear continually as minor refinements in order to keep the motorcycles competitive. When you replace a part, take the old one with you so the dealer can match it with a correct new one or in some cases provide a later, improved part.

SERVICE HINTS

Most of the service procedures described can be performed by anyone reasonably handy with tools. It is suggested, however, that you carefully consider your own capabilities before attempting any operation which involves major disassembly of the engine and transmission.

Some operations, for example, require the use of a press. It would be wiser to have them performed by a shop equipped for such work, rather than to try to do the job yourself with makeshift equipment. Other procedures require precision measurements, and unless you have the skills and equipment to make them, it would be better to have a motorcycle shop help in the work.

Repairs can be made faster and easier if the motorcycle is clean before you begin work. There are special cleaners for washing the engine and related parts. Just brush or spray on the solution, let it stand, then rinse it away with water from a garden hose. Clean all oily or greasy parts with cleaning solvent as you remove them. *Never use gasoline as a cleaning agent*. It presents an extreme fire hazard. Always work in a well-ventilated area when using cleaning solvent. Keep a fire extinguisher, rated for gasoline fires, handy just in case.

Special tools are required for some service procedures. These may be purchased through Maico dealers. If you are on good terms with the dealer's service department, you may be able to borrow what you need.

Much of the labor charge for repairs made by dealers is for removal and disassembly of other parts to reach the defective one. It is frequently possible to do all of this yourself, then take the affected part or assembly to the dealer for repair.

Once you decide to tackle a job yourself, read the entire section in this handbook pertaining to it. Study the illustrations and the text until you have a thorough idea of what's involved. If special tools are required, make arrangements to get them before you begin work. It's frustrating to get partway into a job and then discover that you are unable to complete it.

TOOLS

To properly service your motorcycle, you will need an assortment of ordinary hand tools. As a minimum, these include:

1. Combination wrenches (metric)
2. Socket wrenches (metric)
3. Plastic mallet
4. Small hammer
5. Snap ring pliers
6. Slot screwdrivers
7. Impact driver
8. Pliers
9. Feeler gauges
10. Spark plug gauge
11. Spark plug wrench
12. Dial indicator
13. Drift

A tool kit, like the one shown in **Figure 1**, is available through most motorcycle dealers and is suitable for minor servicing.

Electrical system servicing requires a voltmeter, ohmmeter or other device for determining continuity, and a hydrometer for machines equipped with batteries. When selecting a hydrometer, be sure to find one that has numbered graduations from 1.000 to 1.300 rather than color-coded bands.

EXPENDABLE SUPPLIES

Certain expendable supplies are required. These include grease, oil, gasket cement, liquid fastener-locking compound, rags, and cleaning solvent. These items are available at most motorcycle shops and auto supply stores. Distilled water for batteries is available at supermarkets where it is sold for use in steam irons.

SAFETY FIRST

A professional mechanic can work for years and never sustain a serious injury. If you observe a few rules of common sense and safety, you too can enjoy many hours safely servicing your own motorcycle. You can also hurt yourself or damage your motorcycle if you ignore these rules.

1. Never use gasoline as a cleaning solvent.

2. Never smoke or use a torch around flammable liquids, such as cleaning solvent.

3. Never smoke or use a torch in areas where batteries are being charged. Highly explosive hydrogen gas is formed during the charging process. And never arc the terminals of a battery to see if it has a charge; the sparks can ignite the explosive hydrogen as easily as an open flame.

4. If welding or brazing is required on the motorcycle, remove the fuel tank and set it a safe distance away—at least 50 feet.

5. Always use the correct size wrench for turning nuts and bolts, and when a nut is tight, think for a moment what would happen to your hand if the wrench were to slip.

6. Keep your work area clean and uncluttered.

7. Wear safety goggles in all operations involving drilling, grinding, the use of a chisel, or an air hose.

8. Don't use worn tools.

9. Keep a fire extinguisher handy. Be sure it is rated for gasoline and electrical fires.

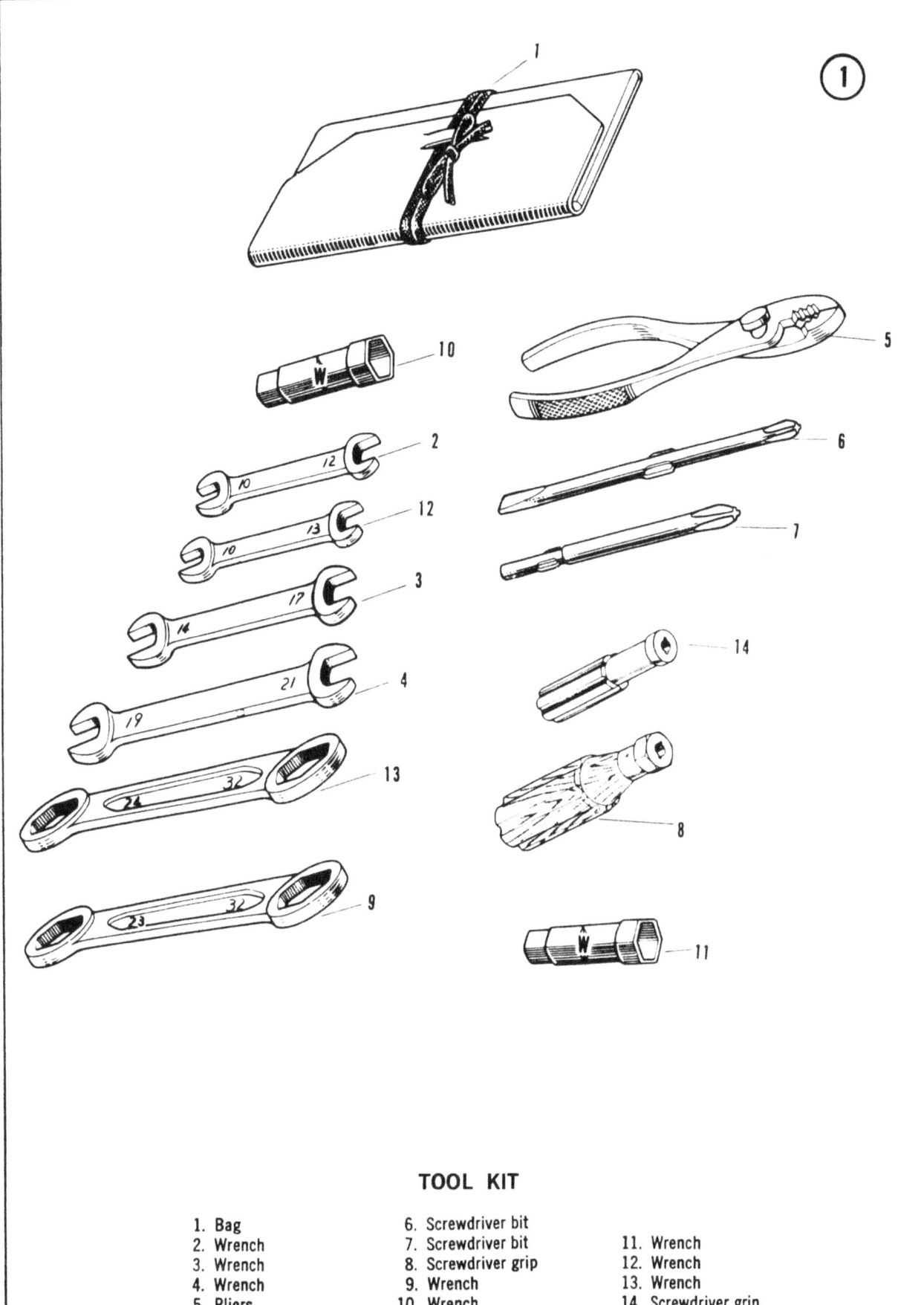

TOOL KIT

1. Bag
2. Wrench
3. Wrench
4. Wrench
5. Pliers
6. Screwdriver bit
7. Screwdriver bit
8. Screwdriver grip
9. Wrench
10. Wrench
11. Wrench
12. Wrench
13. Wrench
14. Screwdriver grip

CHAPTER TWO

LUBRICATION AND MAINTENANCE

To maintain your motorcycle at peak efficiency, the periodic services presented in this chapter should be performed at the intervals indicated.

AIR CLEANER

The air cleaner removes dust and abrasive particles from the air before it enters the engine. Even very fine particles entering the engine will rapidly wear the piston, rings, cylinder, and bearings and clog the small passages in the carburetor. The motorcycle should never be operated with the air cleaner removed, and the filter element should be cleaned frequently, such as at the end of a day of trail riding or after a race.

If you use your motorcycle for motocross racing, it's a good idea to have a second air filter element on hand to replace the first unit between motos; when the filter becomes clogged with dust and dirt the intake flow is restricted resulting in a decrease in engine efficiency.

Servicing

1. Remove the seat from the motorcycle. Unscrew the nut from the top of the mounting stud (**Figure 1**) and remove the air filter element from the air box.
2. If the air filter element is a paper type, blow the dust and dirt out of it, from the inside, using an air hose. Be careful not to rupture the paper. If the element is a foam type, it should be washed first in solvent, then in hot soapy water, rinsed in clear water, and allowed to dry. Oil the foam element with clean engine oil and wring out the excess before reinstalling it.
3. Thoroughly clean the inside of the air box and the connector pipe to the carburetor bell. Lightly grease the sealing surfaces of the filter element.
4. Install the filter element, the sealing ring and the cover plate and tighten the nut securely on the mounting stud. As a precaution against the nut vibrating loose, install a self-locking nut or slip a short length of rubber tubing over the end of the mounting stud. Finally, check to make sure the connector pipe is completely seated around the air box and carburetor intake flanges.

TRANSMISSION OIL

Proper operation and long service life of the clutch and transmission require clean oil. For motorcycles used for trail riding, the oil should be changed about every 500 miles. For motorcycles used in competition, the oil should be changed after every race. Between changes, the oil level should be checked and corrected if necessary.

When the drain plug is removed during an oil change, carefully examine material that has collected on the drain plug magnet (**Figure 2**). It can be an excellent means of detecting potential trouble before serious damage occurs. Fine metal "whiskers" on the magnet are normal but chips from gear teeth, fragments of shifting dogs, or pieces of primary chain side plates are indications of potential serious trouble that should be taken care of immediately.

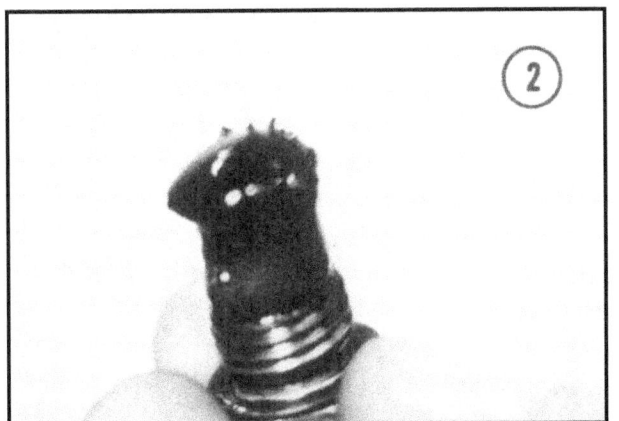

Checking Oil

1. With the motorcycle sitting level, unscrew transmission level plug (**Figure 3**, next page). If oil level is correct, oil will seep out of the hole.

2. If oil level is low, remove transmission fill plug (**Figure 4**, next page) and add a good grade of motorcycle transmission oil, such as Torco MTF, until it begins to seep through the level hole. Then reinstall both the fill and level plugs.

Changing the Oil

1. Start the engine and warm it up. Shut it off and remove the fill plug. Place a drip pan of at least one quart capacity beneath the engine just ahead of the left footrest and remove the drain plug (**Figure 5**). Allow at least 5 minutes for the oil to drain.

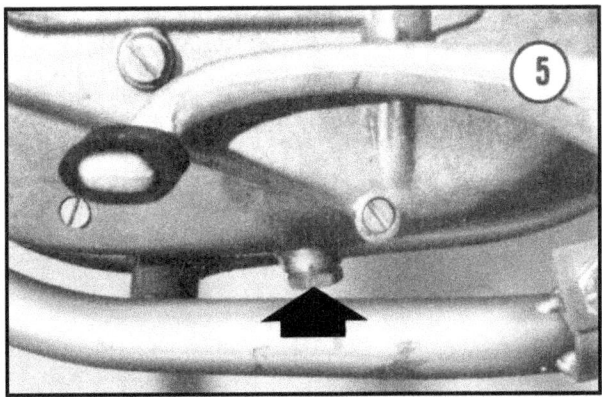

2. Install the drain plug and tighten it securely but not so tight that there is risk of stripping the case threads.

3

4

6

3. Fill the transmission with one quart of a good grade of motorcycle transmission oil. Direct the oil into the filler opening with a funnel to prevent spillage and ensure that the amount is correct. Install and tighten the fill plug.

> NOTE: *Pour the old oil into a discarded plastic bleach bottle, cap it, and put it in the trash.*

DAMPING OIL (FRONT SUSPENSION)

The front suspension requires the correct amount of damping oil in each leg if it is to perform correctly. Damping characteristics depend on oil viscosity, and the handling characteristics of the motorcycle can be altered appreciably by a change from one weight oil to another. The factory recommends a viscosity range from SAE 20 to SAE 50, depending upon temperature, terrain, and rider preference. Only personal experience will enable you to find the weight of oil that is best for your motorcycle. As a rule, the lighter oils are better suited to moderately rough terrain and cooler temperatures while the heavier grades are selected for rough terrain and higher temperatures. Capacity is 6 ounces (200cc) for early forks and 6.5-7 ounces (215-230cc) for late forks.

There is no practical way of topping up the damping oil if some has been lost through a leaky seal; the forks must be drained, flushed, and refilled. If seal leakage is indicated, refer to Chapter Eight and correct the situation before changing the oil.

Oil Changing

1. Working on one fork leg at a time, unscrew the filler cap (**Figure 6**). Place a drip pan beneath the fork leg and unscrew the large bottom plug (**Figure 7**). Allow the fork leg to drain. Flush it with solvent and again allow it to drain very thoroughly.

2. Remove the screw and vent valve from the top cap (**Figure 8**), clean, and reinstall it.

3. Install the bottom plug and fill the fork leg with fresh oil. Install the filler cap and tighten it securely; then service the other fork leg in the same manner.

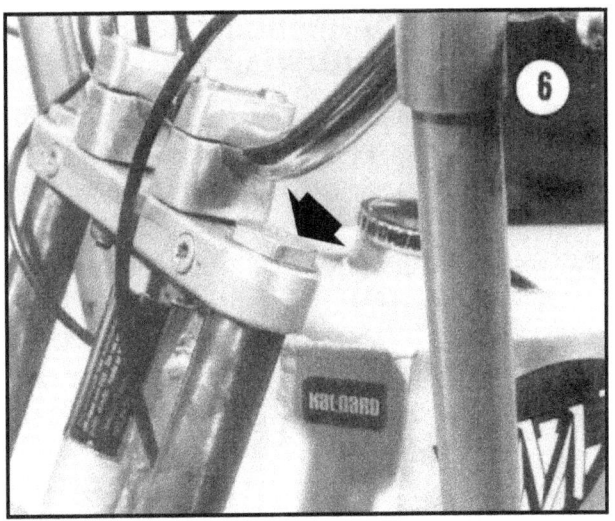

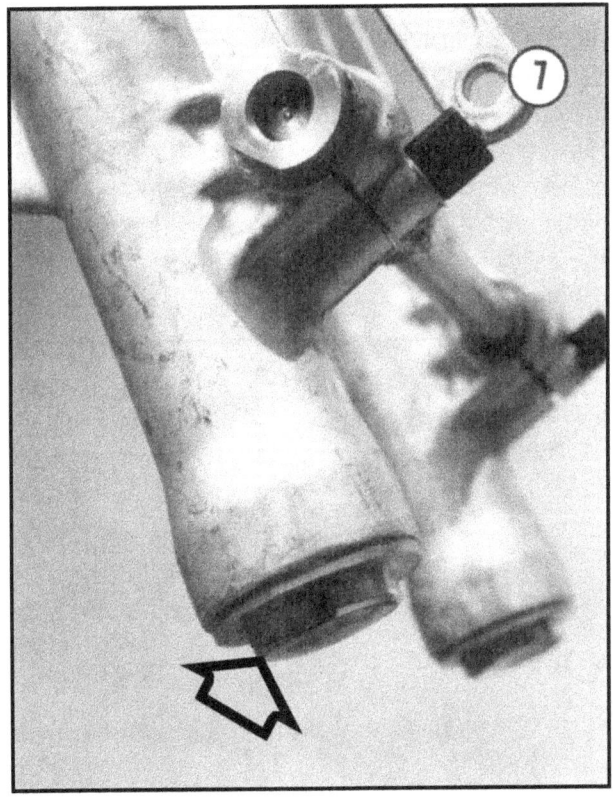

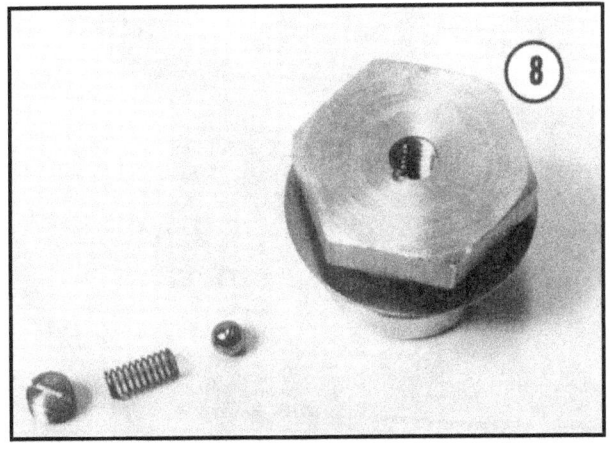

CONTROL LUBRICATION AND ADJUSTMENT

The clutch, throttle, and brake controls should be checked for correct adjustment and the cables lubricated with molybdenum disulfide each time the motorcycle is to be raced or used for a long trail ride. In addition, the control cables should be checked for kinks and signs of wear that could cause the cables to fail or stick. Cables are expendable items and won't last forever under the best of conditions; if one is found to be less than perfect, replace it.

Lubrication

The most positive method of control cable lubrication involves the use of a lubricator like the one shown in **Figure 9**. Disconnect the cable at the control, attach the lubricator, and inject lubricant into the cable sheath until it runs out of the other end. When lubricating a throttle cable with this type of device, the other end of the cable should first be disconnected from the carburetor.

If you do not have access to a lubricator, fashion a funnel from stiff paper and tape it securely to one end of the cable (**Figure 10**). Hold the cable upright and squirt lubricant into the funnel. Work the cable in and out to assist the molybdenum disulfide in migrating down the cable.

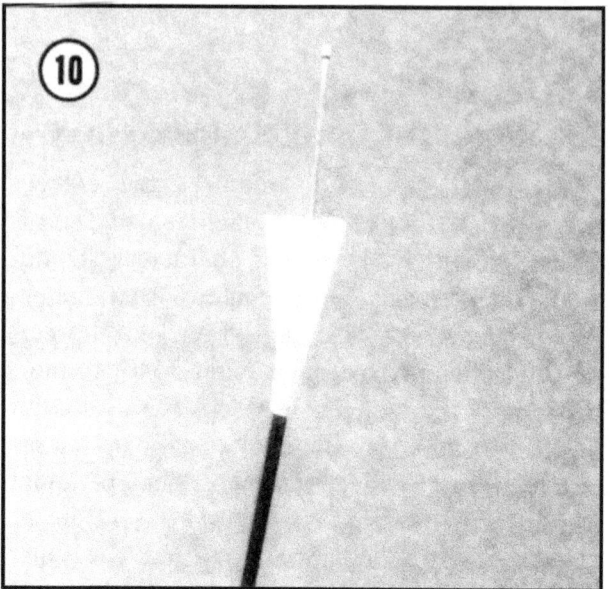

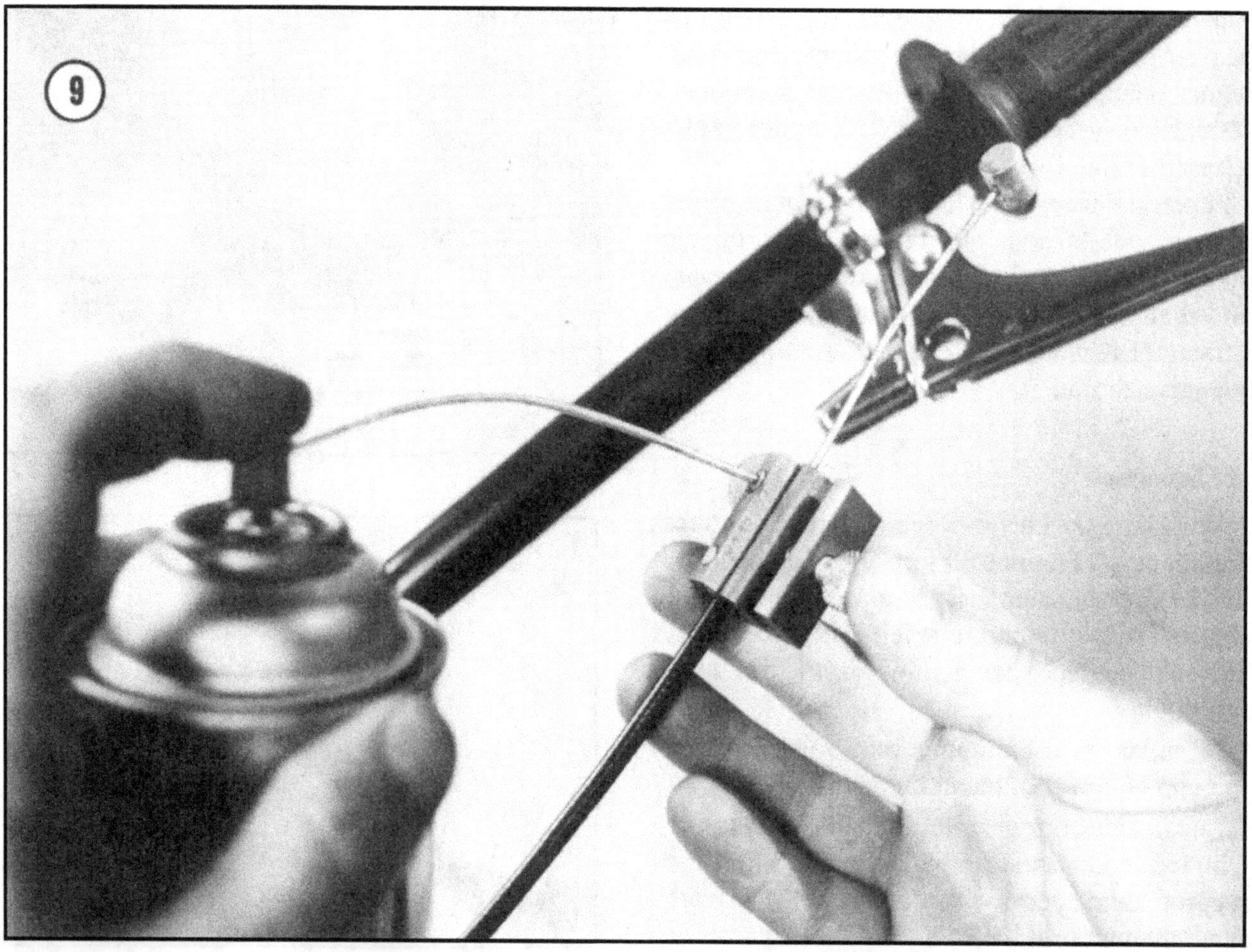

Throttle Adjustment

There should be about 0.039 inch (1.0mm) of end-play in the throttle cable (**Figure 11**). Loosen the locknut, and with the throttle closed, turn the adjuster in or out until the end-play is correct. Tighten locknut, being careful not to turn the adjuster, thus altering end-play. Check the adjustment by opening the throttle fully and allowing it to snap shut. If the adjustment is correct there should be a sharp metallic sound as the slide bottoms out in the carburetor body or against the throttle stop screw.

Clutch Adjustment

The fine adjustment of the clutch cable, made at the hand control (**Figure 12**), should permit about 1/16-1/8 inch (1.6-3.2mm) of free movement of the lever. If this movement can't be obtained with hand adjuster, refer to Chapter Five and carry out primary clutch adjustment.

Brake Adjustment

The brakes are not adjusted by end-play or free pedal play, but rather by feel according to personal preference. If possible, the brakes should be warm when adjusted so that expansion can be compensated for to ensure the brakes will completely release when they are hot. The adjuster for the front brake cable is on the hand control. If the adjustment at the hand control has been used up, loosen the locknut and screw the adjuster in until only a few threads are visible. Loosen the lock bolt on the brake arm (**Figure 13**). Pull the arm off the shaft, rotate it forward 15-20 degrees, and reinstall it. Tighten the lock bolt. Use the hand control adjuster to make the final adjustment.

The only adjustment on the rear brake is the wing nut at the end of the brake rod (**Figure 14**). Again, the adjustment should be made to suit personal preference, but the brake should not be adjusted so tightly that the shoes drag in the drum when the brake is released.

DRIVE CHAIN

The drive chain must be frequently cleaned, lubricated, and adjusted if it is to provide long service life.

Cleaning and Lubricating

1. Disconnect the master link and remove the chain from the motorcycle.

2. Immerse the chain in a pan of cleaning solvent and allow it to soak for about a half hour.

3. Scrub the roller and side plates with a stiff brush and rinse the chain in clean solvent to

carry away loosened grit. Hang up the chain and allow it to dry thoroughly.

4. Lubricate the chain with a good grade of chain lubricant, carefully following the manufacturer's instructions.

5. Reinstall the chain on the motorcycle. Use a new master link clip and install it in the direction shown in **Figure 15**.

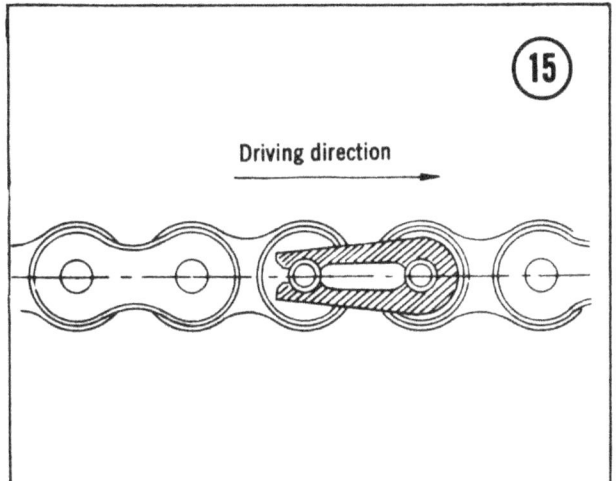

Adjustment

When the drive chain is correctly adjusted it should almost touch the swing arm pivot crossmember (**Figure 16**). When adjusting the chain, check it at several places along its length by rotating the rear wheel; the chain will rarely stretch uniformly and as a result it will be tighter at some places than at others.

> NOTE: *On 1975 models, and on earlier models that have been modified to use forward-mounted spring-shocks, considerably more vertical play is required in the chain to accommodate the increased travel of the swinging arm. Check the travel of the chain with the wheel fully extended and fully compressed to make certain that it is not too tight at either extreme.*

1. Loosen the bolts on both ends of the brake anchor (**Figure 17**).

2. Loosen the brake adjustment wing nut a couple of turns.

3. Loosen the rear axle nut (**Figure 18**).

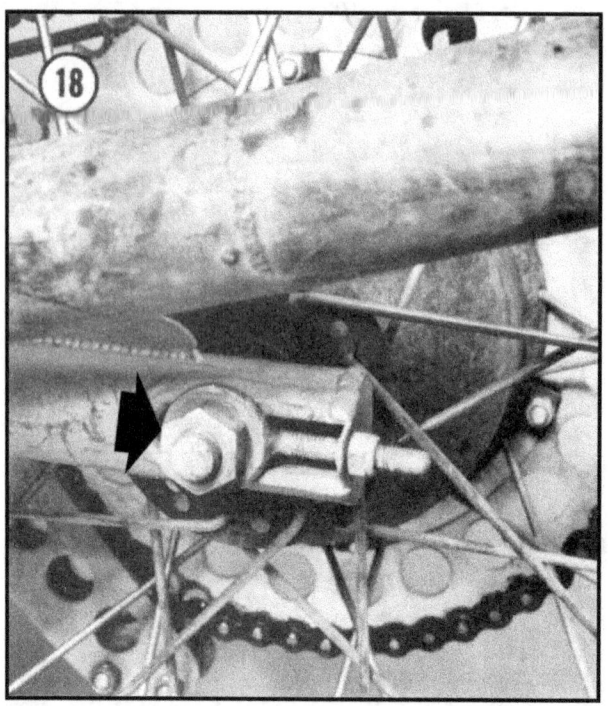

4. Turn the adjuster nuts (**Figure 19**) in or out equally until the adjustment is correct.

5. Check the alignment of the wheel in the swing arm and the chain on the sprocket by sighting along the top of the chain from the rear of the motorcycle (**Figure 20**). There should be no lateral bend in the chain. If the wheel is cocked to the right, align it by loosening the left adjuster and tightening the right. If it is cocked to the left, loosen the right adjuster and tighten the left.

When the wheel, chain, and sprocket are correctly aligned, recheck the vertical play of the chain and adjust it if necessary, turning both adjuster nuts equally. Tighten the locknuts.

IGNITION

The ignition timing and contact breaker condition should be checked every time the motorcycle is raced or prior to a long trail ride. Major service of the ignition and the detailed timing procedure are presented in Chapter Seven.

CARBURETOR

The carburetor should be removed, disassembled, cleaned and adjusted at the same

Table 1   FUEL AND OIL MIXTURES

Fuel (U.S. Gallons)	Oz.	(cc)
0.5	3.2	96
1.0	6.4	192
1.5	9.6	288
2.0	12.8	384
2.5	16.0	480
5.0	32.0	960

interval the ignition is serviced—prior to each race or long trail ride. Carburetor servicing and adjustment is presented in Chapter Six.

ENGINE LUBRICATION

Maico engines are lubricated by oil mixed with the fuel. Use a good grade of two-stroke engine oil (SAE 50), in a 5-percent solution. Mix the oil and gasoline thoroughly in a separate container before pouring it into the motorcycle's fuel tank. Always measure the quantities carefully—don't guess.

The factory does not recommend the use of 2-stroke oils that are to be mixed in solutions of 25- or 40-to-1; these solutions are considered too lean to provide adequate lubrication.

Table 1 lists the quantities of oil and gasoline for a 5-percent (20:1) oil/fuel mixture.

CARBON REMOVAL

Carbon builds up quickly in the combustion chamber, on the piston crown, and in the exhaust port of a 2-stroke engine. The carbon deposits will increase the compression ratio but rather than provide an increase in performance, they will cause overheating and preignition which may result in engine damage.

To remove carbon from the engine, it's necessary to remove the cylinder head, cylinder, piston, and exhaust system, as described in Chapter Four. For engines used in competition, the carbon should be removed after every 3 or 4 races. For engines used in trail riding, carbon should be removed at about 1,000-mile intervals.

If the carbon is removed at these intervals, and if a specially compounded 2-stroke oil is used in the proportions recommended in Table 1, the carbon deposits will rarely amount to more than a thick, soft film which can be removed with solvent and a soft wire brush. However, if hard deposits have formed, they should be carefully scraped off with a soft metal scraper, such as a piece of aluminum or wood that has had one end rounded and smoothed; hard metal scrapers can easily gouge the piston and combustion chamber causing burrs which will create hot spots during engine operation.

CHAPTER THREE

TROUBLESHOOTING

Diagnosing motorcycle ills is relatively simple if you use orderly procedures and keep a few basic principles in mind.

Never assume anything. Don't overlook the obvious. If you are riding along and the engine suddenly quits, check the easiest, most accessible problem spots first. Is there gasoline in the tank? Is the gas petcock in the ON or RESERVE position? Has a spark plug wire fallen off? Check the ignition switch. Sometimes the weight of keys on a key ring may turn the ignition off suddenly.

If nothing obvious turns up in a cursory check, look a little further. Learning to recognize and describe symptoms will make repairs easier for you or a mechanic at a shop. Describe problems accurately and fully. Saying that "it won't run" isn't the same as saying "it quit at high speed and wouldn't start," or that "it sat in my garage for 3 months and then wouldn't start."

Gather as many symptoms together as possible to aid in diagnosis. Note whether the engine lost power gradually or all at once, what color smoke (if any) came from the exhaust, and so on. Remember that the more complicated a machine is, the easier it is to troubleshoot because symptoms point to specific problems.

You don't need fancy equipment or complicated test gear to determine whether repairs can be attempted at home. A few simple checks could save a large repair bill and time lost while the bike sits in a dealer's service department. On the other hand, be realistic and don't attempt repairs beyond your abilities. Service departments tend to charge heavily for putting together a disassembled engine that may have been abused. Some won't even take on such a job—so use common sense, and don't get in over your head.

OPERATING REQUIREMENTS

An engine needs 3 basics to run properly: correct gas/air mixture, compression, and a spark at the right time. If one or more are missing, the engine won't run. The electrical system is the weakest link of the 3. More problems result from electrical breakdowns than from any other source. Keep that in mind before you begin tampering with carburetor adjustments and related procedures.

If a bike has been sitting for any length of time and refuses to start, check the battery if the machine is so equipped, for a charged condition first, and then look to the gasoline delivery system. This includes the tank, fuel petcock, line, and the carburetor. Rust may have formed in the tank, obstructing fuel flow. Gasoline deposits may have gummed up carburetor jets and air passages. Gasoline tends to lose its potency after standing for long periods. Condensation may contaminate it with water. Drain old gas and try starting with a fresh tankful.

Compression, or the lack of it, usually enters the picture only in the case of older machines. Worn or broken pistons, rings, and cylinder bores could prevent starting. Generally a gradual power loss and harder and harder starting will be readily apparent in this case.

STARTING DIFFICULTIES

Check gas flow first. Remove the gas cap and look into the tank. If gas is present, pull off a fuel line at the carburetor and see if gas flows freely. If none comes out, the fuel tap may be shut off, blocked by rust or foreign matter, or the fuel line may be stopped up or kinked. If the carburetor is getting usable fuel, turn to the electrical system next.

Check that the battery is charged by turning on the lights or by beeping the horn. Refer to your owner's manual for starting procedures with a dead battery. Have the battery recharged if necessary.

Pull off the spark plug cap, remove the spark plug, and reconnect the cap. Lay the plug against the cylinder head so its base makes a good connection, and turn the engine over with the kickstarter. A fat, blue spark should jump across the electrodes. If there is no spark, or a weak one, you have electrical system trouble. Check for a defective plug by replacing it with a known good one. Don't assume a plug is good just because it's new.

Once the plug has been cleared of guilt, but there's still no spark, start backtracking through the system. If the contact at the end of the spark plug wire can be exposed, it can be held about 1/8 inch from the head while the engine is turned over to check for a spark. Remember to hold the wire only by its insulation to avoid a nasty shock. If the plug wires are dirty, greasy, or wet, wrap a rag around them so you don't get shocked. If you do feel a shock or see sparks along the wire, clean or replace the wire and/or its connections.

If there's no spark at the plug wire, look for loose connections at the coil and battery. If all seems in order there, check next for oily or dirty contact points. Clean points with electrical contact cleaner, or a strip of paper. On battery ignition models, with the ignition switch turned on, open and close the points manually with a screwdriver.

No spark at the points with this test indicates a failure in the ignition system. Refer to Chapter Seven (Electrical System) for checkout procedures for the entire system and individual components. Refer to the same chapter for checking and setting ignition timing.

Note that spark plugs of an incorrect heat range (too cold) may cause hard starting. Set the gap to specifications. If you have just ridden through a puddle or washed the bike and it won't start, dry off the plug and plug wire. Remove the magneto cover and dry the magneto. Water may have entered the carburetor and fouled the fuel, but a wet plug and wire or a wet magneto are the more likely problems.

If a healthy spark occurs at the right time, and there is adequate gas flow to the carburetor, check the carburetor itself. Make sure all jets and air passages are clean, check the float level, and adjust it if necessary. Shake the float to check for gasoline inside it, and replace or repair it as indicated. Check that the carburetor is mounted snugly, and no air is leaking past the mounting flange. Check for a clogged air filter.

Compression may be checked in the field by turning the kickstarter by hand and noting that an adequate resistance is felt, or by removing the spark plug and placing a finger over the plug hole and feeling for pressure.

An accurate compression check gives a good idea of the condition of the basic working parts of the engine. To perform this test, you need a compression gauge. The motor should be warm.

1. Remove the spark plug from the cylinder and clean out any dirt or grease.

2. Insert the tip of the gauge into the hole, making sure it's seated correctly.

3. Open the throttle all the way.

4. Crank the engine several times and record the highest pressure reading on the gauge. If the compression is extremely low (100 psi or less), it's likely that a ring is broken or there is a hole in the piston. If the reading is only slightly below normal (120-140 psi), ring or cylinder wear is likely.

POOR IDLING

Poor idling may be caused by incorrect carburetor adjustment, incorrect timing, or ignition system defects. Check the gas cap vent for an obstruction. Also check for loose carburetor mounting bolts or a poor carburetor flange gasket.

MISFIRING

Misfiring can be caused by a weak spark or dirty plugs. Check for fuel contamination. Run the machine at night or in a darkened garage to check for spark leaks along the plug wires and under the spark plug cap. If misfiring occurs only at certain throttle settings, refer to the carburetor chapter for the specific carburetor circuits involved. Misfiring under heavy load, as when climbing hills or accelerating, is usually caused by bad spark plugs.

FLAT SPOTS

If the engine seems to die momentarily when the throttle is opened and then recovers, check for a dirty main jet and needle jet in the carburetor, water in the fuel, or an excessively lean or rich mixture.

POWER LOSS

Poor condition of rings, piston, or cylinder will cause a lack of power and speed. Ignition timing should be checked.

OVERHEATING

If the engine seems to run too hot all the time, be sure you are not idling it for long periods. Air-cooled engines are not designed to operate at a standstill for any length of time. Spark plugs of the wrong heat range can burn pistons. An excessively lean gas mixture may cause overheating. Check ignition timing. Don't ride in too high a gear. Broken or worn rings may permit compression gases to leak past them, heating heads and cylinders excessively. Check the oil level and use the proper grade lubricants. Check for air leaks at the base gasket or intake manifold.

BACKFIRING

Check that the timing is not advanced too far. Check the fuel for contamination.

ENGINE NOISES

Experience is needed to diagnose accurately in this area. Noises are hard to differentiate and harder yet to describe. Deep knocking noises usually mean main bearing failure. A slapping noise generally comes from a loose piston. A light knocking noise during acceleration may be a bad connecting rod bearing. Pinging, which sounds like marbles being shaken in a tin can, is caused by the ignition advanced too far or gasoline with too low an octane rating. Pinging should be corrected immediately or piston damage will result. Compression leaks at the head/cylinder joint will sound like a rapid on and off squeal.

PISTON SEIZURE

Piston seizure is caused by incorrect piston clearances when fitted, fitting rings with improper end gap, too thin an oil being used, incorrect spark plug heat range, or incorrect ignition timing. Overheating from any cause may result in seizure.

EXCESSIVE VIBRATION

Excessive vibration may be caused by loose motor mounts, worn engine or transmission bearings, loose wheels, worn swinging arm bushings, a generally poor running engine, broken or cracked frame, or one that has been damaged in a collision or spill. Also see *Poor Handling*.

CLUTCH SLIP OR DRAG

Clutch slip may be due to worn plates, improper adjustment, or glazed plates, old springs, or the wrong oil. A dragging clutch could result from damaged or bent plates, improper adjustment, the wrong oil, or excessive clutch spring pressure.

POOR HANDLING

Poor handling may be caused by improper tire pressures, a damaged frame or swinging arm, worn shocks or front forks, weak fork springs, a bent or broken steering stem, misaligned wheels, loose or missing spokes, worn tires, bent handlebars, worn wheel bearings, or dragging brakes.

BRAKE PROBLEMS

Sticking brakes may be caused by broken or weak return springs, improper cable or rod adjustment, or dry pivot and cam bushings. Grabbing brakes may be caused by greasy linings (which must be replaced). Brake grab may also be due to out-of-round drums or linings which have broken loose from the brake shoes. Glazed linings will cause loss of stopping power.

LIGHTING PROBLEMS
(ENDURO MODELS)

Bulbs which continuously burn out may be caused by excessive vibration, loose connections that permit sudden current surges, poor battery connections, or installation of wrong bulb.

A dead battery or one which discharges quickly may be caused by a faulty generator or rectifier. Check for loose or corroded terminals. Shorted battery cells or broken terminals will keep a battery from charging. Low water level will decrease a battery's capacity. A battery left uncharged after installation will sulphate, rendering it useless.

A majority of light and horn or other electrical accessory problems are caused by loose or corroded ground conncetions. Check those first ,and then substitute known good units for easier troubleshooting.

TROUBLESHOOTING GUIDE

The following summarizes the troubleshooting process. Use it to outline possible problem areas, then refer to the specific chapter or section involved.

Loss of Power

1. *Poor compression*—Check piston rings and cylinder, cylinder head gasket, and crankcase leaks.

2. *Overheated engine*—Check lubricating oil supply, air leaks, ignition timing, clogged cooling fins, and carbon in combustion chamber.

3. *Improper mixture* — Check for dirty air cleaner, restricted fuel flow—jets, clogged gas cap vent holes.

Gearshifting Difficulties

1. *Clutch*—Check clutch adjustment, clutch springs, friction plates, steel plates, and oil quantity and type.

2. *Transmission*—Check oil quantity and type, oil grade, gearshift mechanism adjustment, return spring, and gear change forks.

Brake Troubles

1. *Poor brakes* — Check brake adjustment, brake drum out-of-round, oil or water on brake linings, and loose brake linkage or cables.

2. *Noisy brakes*—Check for worn or scratched linings, scratched brake drums, and dirt in brakes.

3. *Unadjustable brakes*—Check for worn linings, drums, and brake cams.

4. *Miscellaneous*—Check for dragging brakes, tight wheel bearings, defective chain, and clogged exhaust system.

Steering Problems

1. *Hard steering*—Check steering head bearings, steering stem head, and correct tire pressures.

2. *Pulls to one side*—Check for worn swinging arm bushings, bent swinging arm, bent steering head, bent frame, and front and rear wheel alignment.

3. *Shimmy*—Check for improper drive chain adjustment, loose or missing spokes, deformed wheel rims, worn wheel bearings, and improper wheel balance.

CHAPTER FOUR

ENGINE

Removal, disassembly, service, and reassembly of the engine are covered in this chapter. The procedures are presented in the sequence that would be employed to totally dismantle the engine, beginning with the cylinder head and continuing on through disassembly of the crankshaft assembly. However, each major area is complete, from disassembly, through inspection and reassembly to ensure that the procedures require a minimum of interpretation and cross referencing.

Routine engine-related lubrication and maintenance are covered in Chapter Two. Support systems such as fuel and ignition are covered in Chapters Two, Six, and Seven.

OPERATING PRINCIPLES

During this discussion on 2-stroke operating principles, assume that the crankshaft is rotating counterclockwise. In **Figure 1**, as the piston travels downward, a transfer port (A) between the crankcase and the cylinder is uncovered. The exhaust gases leave the cylinder through the exhaust port (B), which is also opened by the downward movement of the piston. A fresh fuel-air charge, which has previously been compressed slightly, travels from the crankcase (C) to the cylinder through the transfer port (A) as

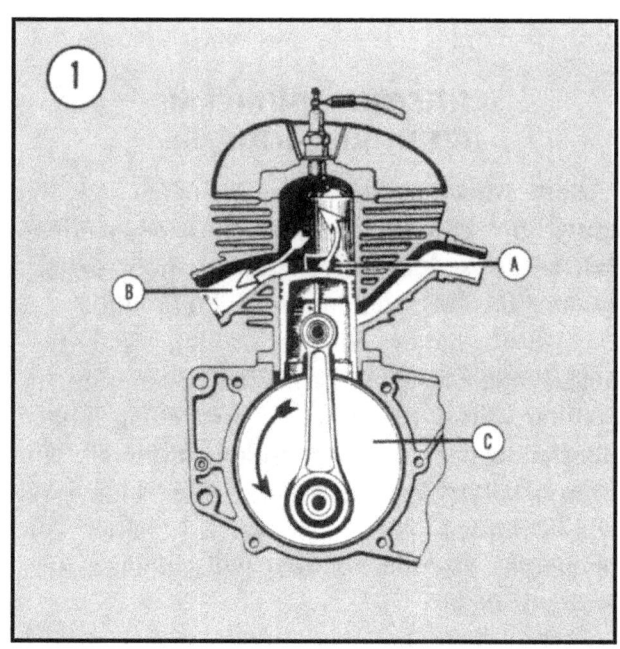

the port opens. Since the incoming charge is under pressure, it rushes into the cylinder quickly and helps to expel the exhaust gases from the previous cycle.

Figure 2 illustrates the next phase of the cycle. As the crankshaft continues to rotate, the piston moves upward, closing the exhaust and transfer ports. As the piston continues upward, the air/fuel mixture in the cylinder is compressed. Notice also that a low pressure area is created in the crankcase at the same time. Further upward

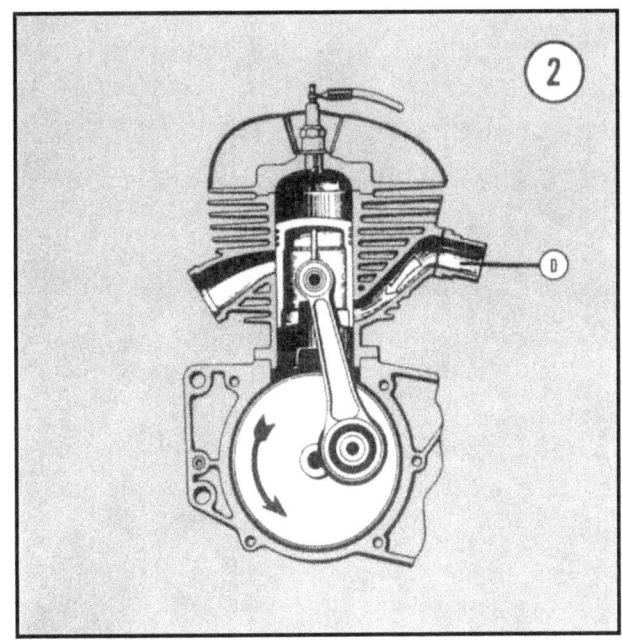

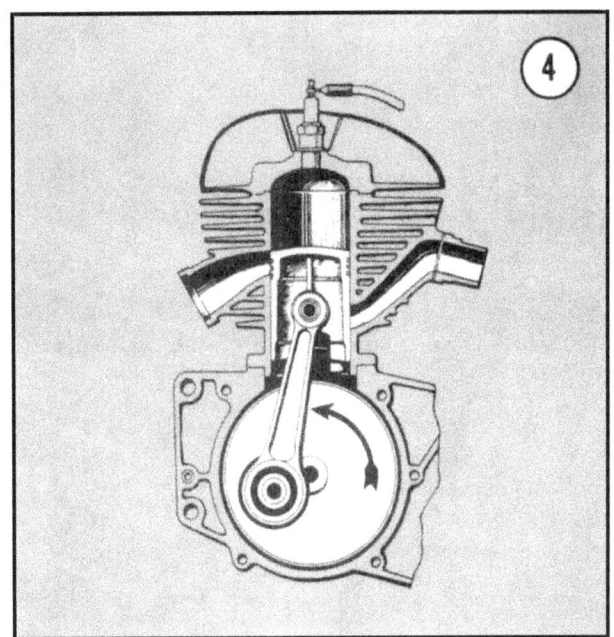

movement of the piston uncovers the intake port (D). A fresh fuel-air charge is then drawn into the crankcase through the intake port because of the low pressure created by the upward piston movement.

The third phase is shown in **Figure 3**. As the piston approaches top dead center, the spark plug fires, igniting the compressed mixture. The piston is then driven downward by the expanding gases.

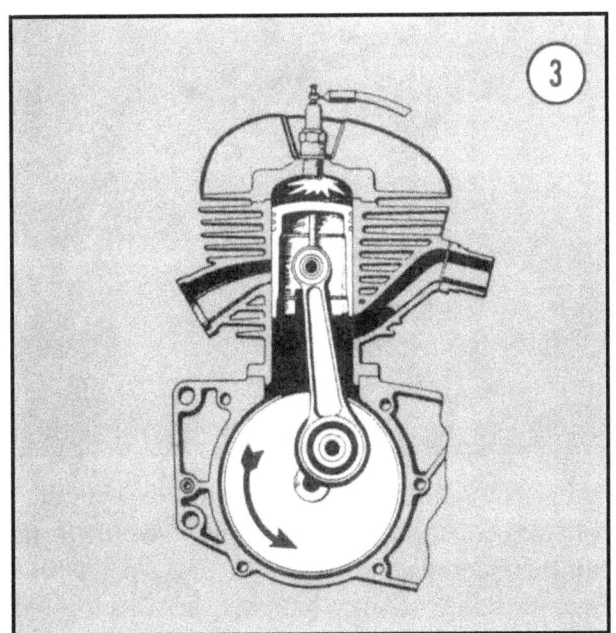

When the top of the piston uncovers the exhaust port, the fourth phase begins, as shown in **Figure 4**. The exhaust gases leave the cylinder through the exhaust port. As the piston continues downward, the intake port is closed and the mixture in the crankcase is compressed in preparation for the next cycle.

It can be seen from the foregoing discussion that every downward stroke of the piston is a power stroke.

CYLINDER HEAD

Maico cylinder heads are cast from lightweight aluminum alloy in 2 fin patterns—vertical (**Figure 5**) and radial, or sunburst (**Figure 6**). Periodically the head should be removed and carbon deposits wiped and scraped away before they have had a chance to build up and adversely alter engine performance.

Removal

Thoroughly clean the outside of the engine and adjacent areas with solvent or a good grade of engine cleaner. Flush away dirt and grime with water and thoroughly dry the engine.

To avoid possible distortion of the cylinder head, remove it only when the engine is completely cool.

1. If the engine is installed in the motorcycle, shut off the fuel tap, disconnect the line, and remove the fuel tank from the motorcycle. Unplug the high tension lead from the spark plug and unscrew it from the cylinder head.

2. Disconnect the cylinder head yoke from the frame (**Figure 7**).

3. Loosen and remove the cylinder head nuts in a crisscross pattern, turning each one a half-turn at a time until all 4 have been loosened 2 or 3 full turns. Then unscrew them completely and remove the head yoke.

4. Lift the cylinder head off the through-studs,

taking care not to drop washers into the cylinder. If necessary, tap around the bottom of the head with a soft mallet to loosen it; never pry it off, because doing so may damage the fins or the sealing surface.

Removing Carbon Deposits

Wipe the carbon deposits out of the combustion chamber with a clean rag soaked in solvent.

If hard deposits have formed, they may be carefully scraped loose using a piece of aluminum that has been rounded and smoothed on one end. Wrap a portion of the scraper with tape to prevent damage to your hand. Never use a hard metal scraper. Small burrs resulting from gouges in the combustion chamber will create hot spots which will cause preignition and heat erosion of the head and piston. Gouges in the sealing surface will result in an improper seal of the combustion chamber.

After removing the carbon, thoroughly clean the head in solvent. Carefully clean the spark plug bore with a fine wire brush and blow out carbon particles and dirt with an air hose.

Remove the head gasket and clean the top of the cylinder. Check the condition of the gasket and if it's excessively compressed replace it.

Installation

1. Set the gasket in place on top of the cylinder. On radial fin models, lightly coat the gasket with grease and set it in the head. Set the head in place over the through-studs, install the washers, and screw the nuts on finger-tight.

2. Tighten the nuts in a criss cross pattern to the correct torque shown in **Table 1**. Rotate the crankshaft to move the piston up and down in the cylinder after tightening each nut.

Table 1   CYLINDER HEAD TORQUE SETTINGS

Model	Torque
250cc, 360cc, 400cc, 450cc	18-20 ft.-lb. (2.5-2.8 mkg)
501cc	25 ft.lb. (3.5 mkg)

3. Install the cylinder head steady and tighten the nuts to 18-20 ft.-lb. (2.5-2.8 mkg).

4. Install the spark plug and connect the high-tension lead. Install the fuel tank and connect the fuel line.

CYLINDER

The cylinder is 2-piece construction consisting of an aluminum alloy cylinder and an interference-fitted steel liner. The liner will accommodate 5 to 6 overbores and in most cases is good for the life of the motorcycle. However, if the liner is severely damaged by ring seizure or other malfunction, it can be replaced. This is a job for an expert; the interference fit of the liner in the cylinder requires the use of a large hydraulic press and skillful handling of the 2 pieces to ensure correct alignment of the ports. For ference, should the liner require replacement, the new line should be turned to an interference fit with the cylinder of 0.004-0.006 in. (0.1-0.15mm).

Removal

1. Remove the cylinder head as described earlier. Refer to Chapter Six and remove the carburetor.

2. Remove the exhaust system by disconnecting the springs at the cylinder (**Figure 8**), removing the chamber mounting bolt (**Figure 9**), and disconnecting the strut (**Figure 10**).

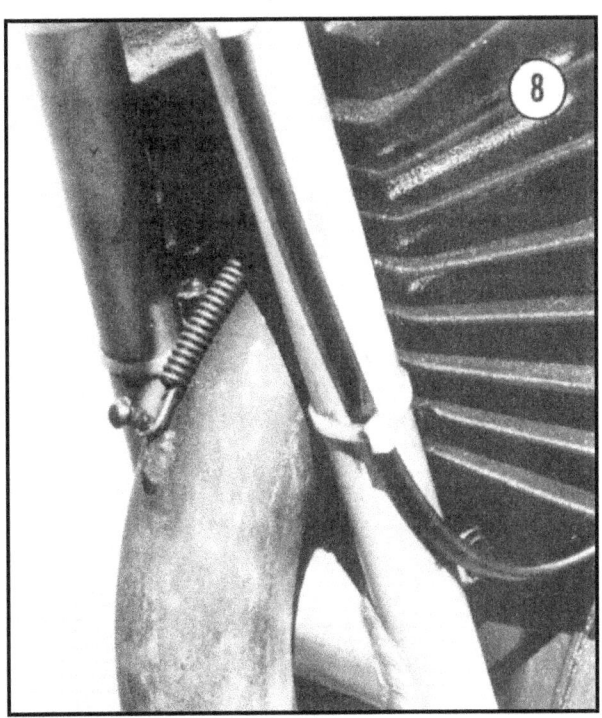

3. Disconnect the compression release cable at the hand control. Slide a tube-type spark plug wrench over the cable and onto the compression release (**Figure 11**, page 23). Unscrew the release from the cylinder.

4. On square barrel models, if the cylinder is being removed with the engine installed in the motorcycle, it's necessary to remove the 4 through-studs before the cylinder can be re-

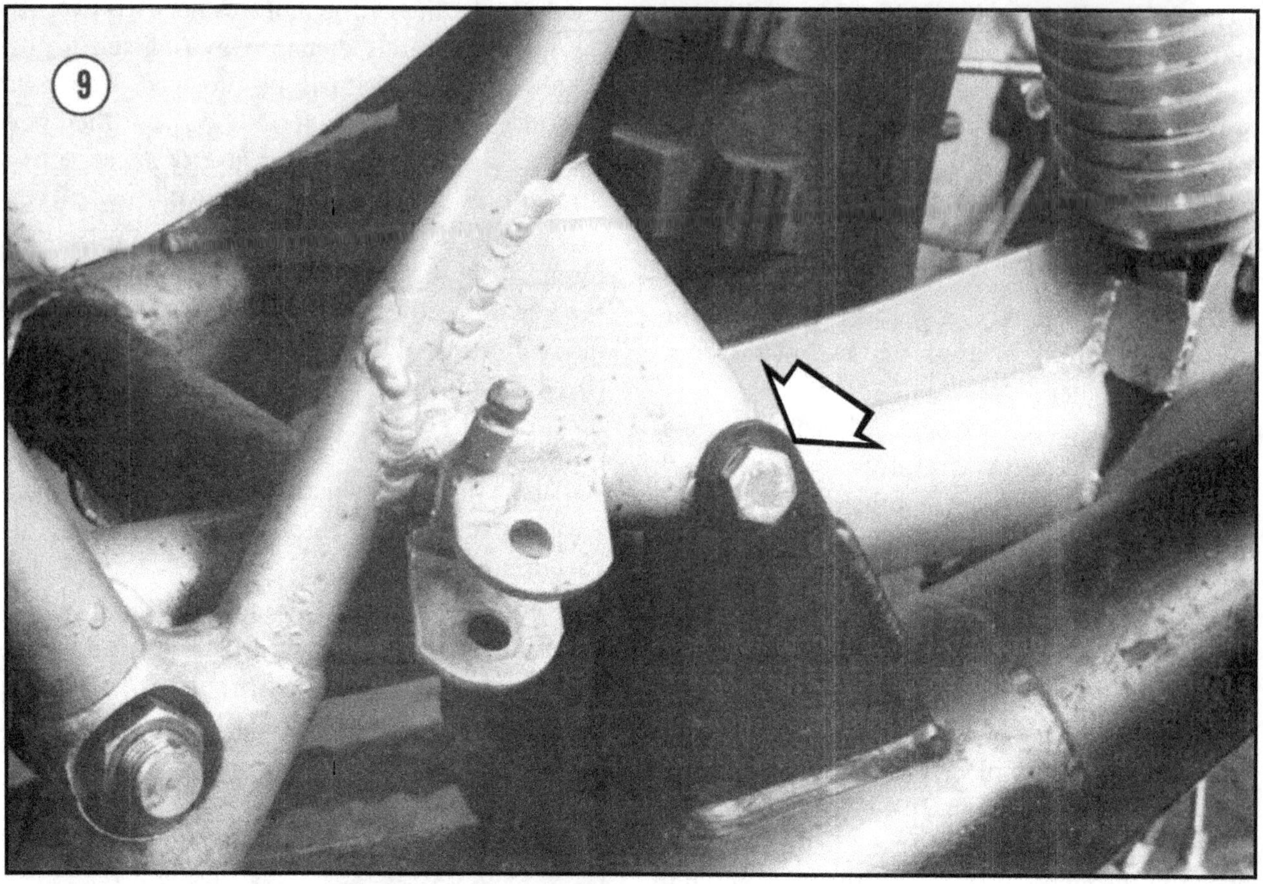

22

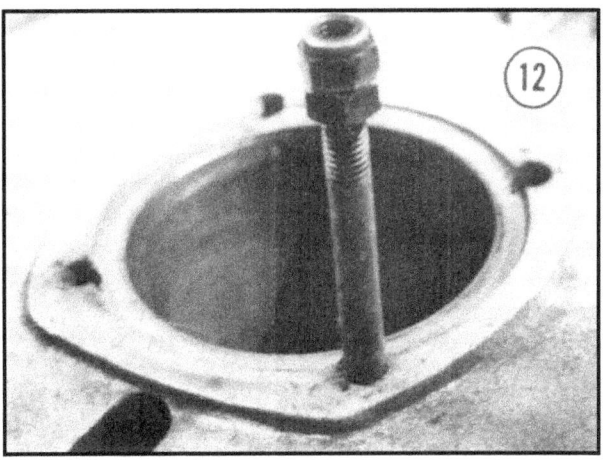

moved. Double nut each stud in turn, locking the top nut securely with the bottom nut. Then unscrew the stud by turning the bottom nut with an open-end wrench (**Figure 12**). On radial fin models, unscrew the 4 cylinder base nuts (**Figure 13**).

5. When the studs have been removed, rotate the crankshaft to bring the piston to the bottom of its stroke and lift the cylinder off. Don't rotate the cylinder as you lift it; this could break the rings.

Inspection

Measure cylinder wall wear at 3 depths within the cylinder. Use a cylinder gauge or inside micrometer, as shown in **Figure 14**. Measure parallel and at a right angle to the crankshaft at the locations shown in **Figure 15**. If taper or

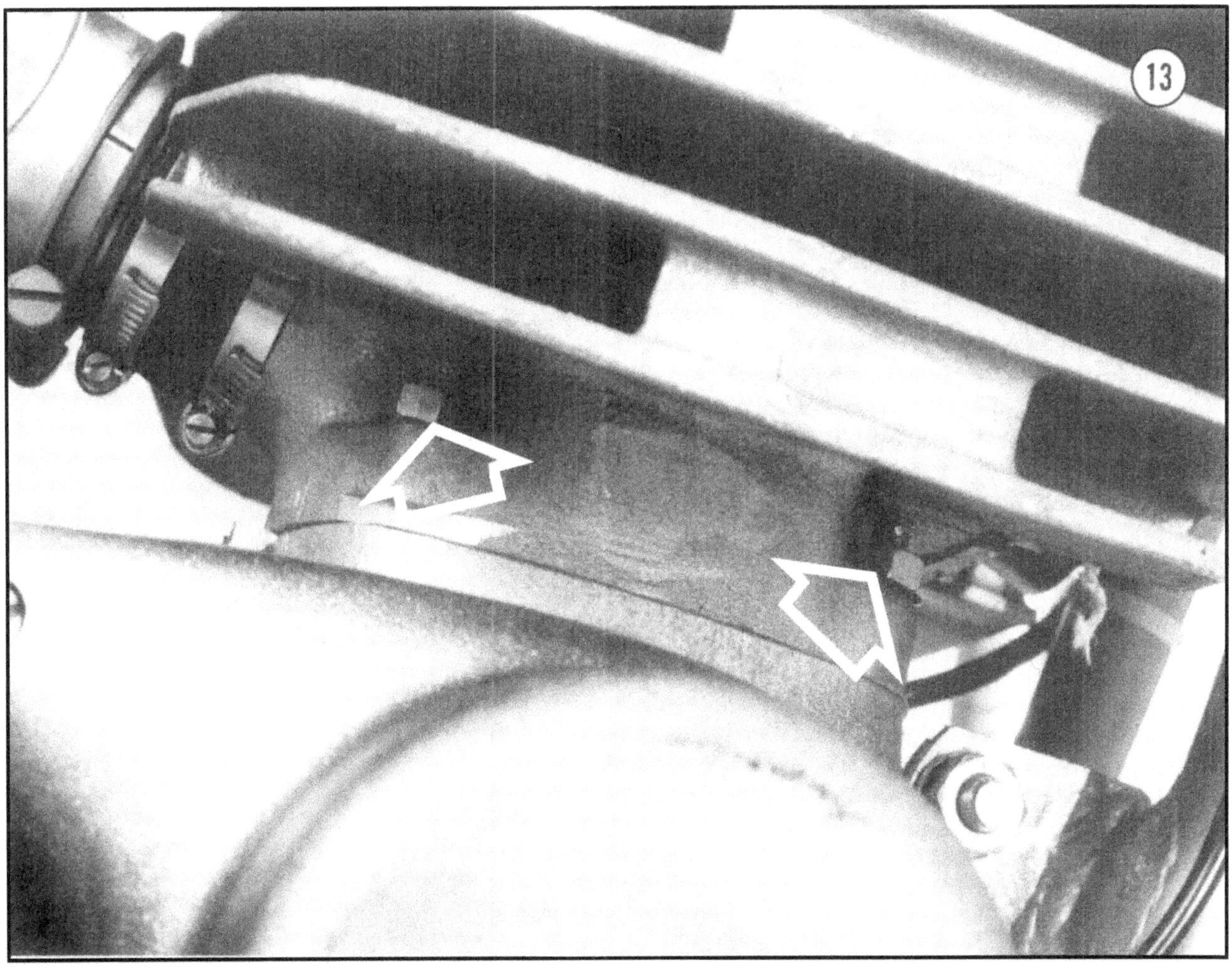

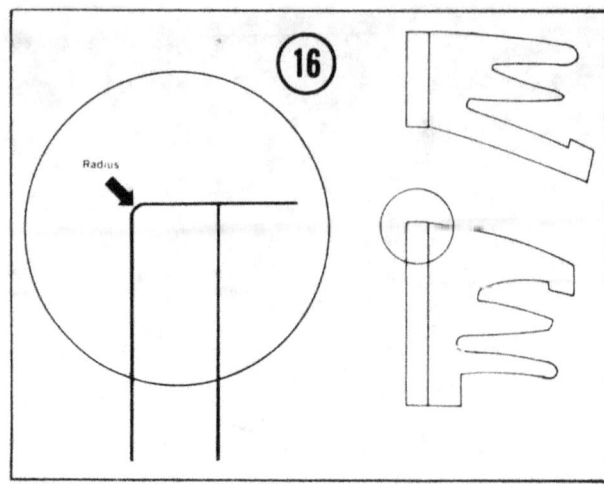

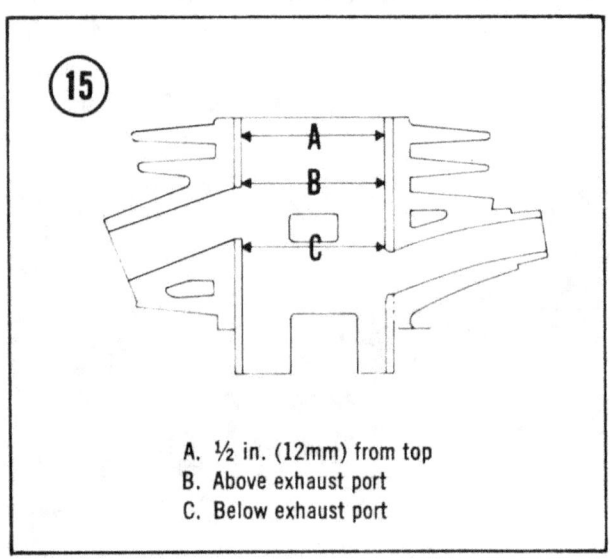

A. ½ in. (12mm) from top
B. Above exhaust port
C. Below exhaust port

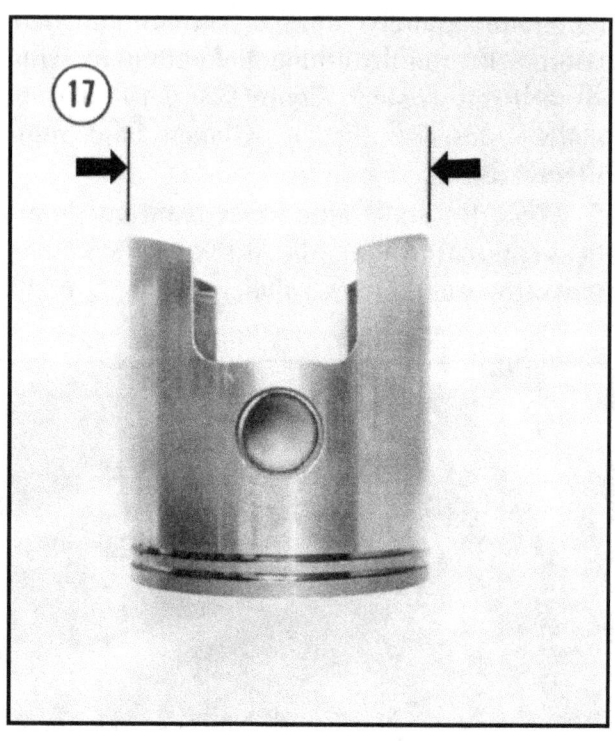

out-of-round exceed 0.006 inch (0.15mm) rebore and hone the cylinder to the next oversize.

After boring, radius the edges of the transfer, intake, and exhaust ports (**Figure 16**) to prevent the sharp edges from snagging the rings.

Have the new piston on hand prior to reboring the cylinder so that it may be measured and the cylinder bored to provide the required piston-to-cylinder clearance. See **Tables 2 and 3**.

Measure the piston just above the bottom of the skirt and at a right angle to the pin bosses (**Figure 17**). Add the result to the desired clearance to determine the final overbore size of the cylinder.

To check the clearance of a run-in piston and bore, measure the piston and cylinder as described above and subtract the piston dimension from the cylinder dimension. If the clearance exceeds 0.006 in. (0.15mm), the cylinder should be rebored to the next oversize and a new piston fitted.

CAUTION
*Because Maico wrist pins are fitted low in the piston, the wear pattern in the cylinder tends to become barrel-shaped (**Figure 18**). This condition accelerates ring wear. If this condition exists and only the rings are replaced, they will wear rapidly. If "barreling" is even slightly evident, rebore the cylinder to the next oversize and fit a new piston.*

Table 2   PISTON OVERSIZES

	250cc	360cc	400cc	450cc	501cc
Standard	66.99mm	76.95mm	76.95mm	81.92mm	91.52mm
1st Oversize	67.11mm	77.10mm	77.10mm	82.07mm	91.67mm
2nd Oversize	67.26mm	77.25mm	77.25mm	82.22mm	91.82mm
3rd Oversize	67.41mm	77.40mm	77.40mm	82.37mm	91.97mm
4th Oversize	67.56mm	77.55mm	77.55mm	none	none
5th Oversize	67.71mm	77.70mm	77.70mm	none	none
6th Oversize	67.96mm	77.85mm	77.85mm	none	none

Table 3   PISTON-TO-CYLINDER CLEARANCE

Displacement	Clearance
250cc, 360cc, 400cc	0.002 inch (0.05mm)
450cc	0.0035 inch (0.089mm)
501cc	0.0025 inch (0.06mm)

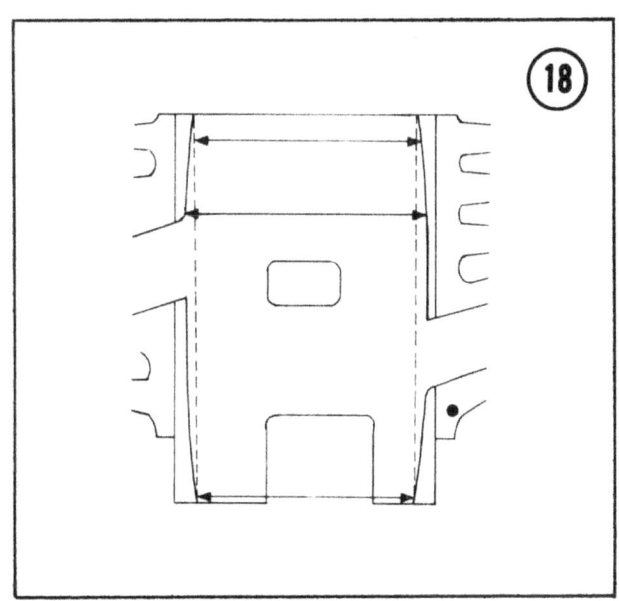

Ring measurement and clearance are covered under *Piston Inspection*.

Installation

1. Install a new cylinder base gasket on the top of the crankcase.

2. Place a wood block beneath the piston (**Figure 19**).

NOTE: *The block can be made from a piece of scrap lumber or plywood cut to the dimensions shown in* **Figure 20.**

3. Make sure the rings are seated in the grooves and correctly lined up with the locating pins in the ring grooves (see **Figure 21**).

4. Oil the cylinder bore and start the cylinder

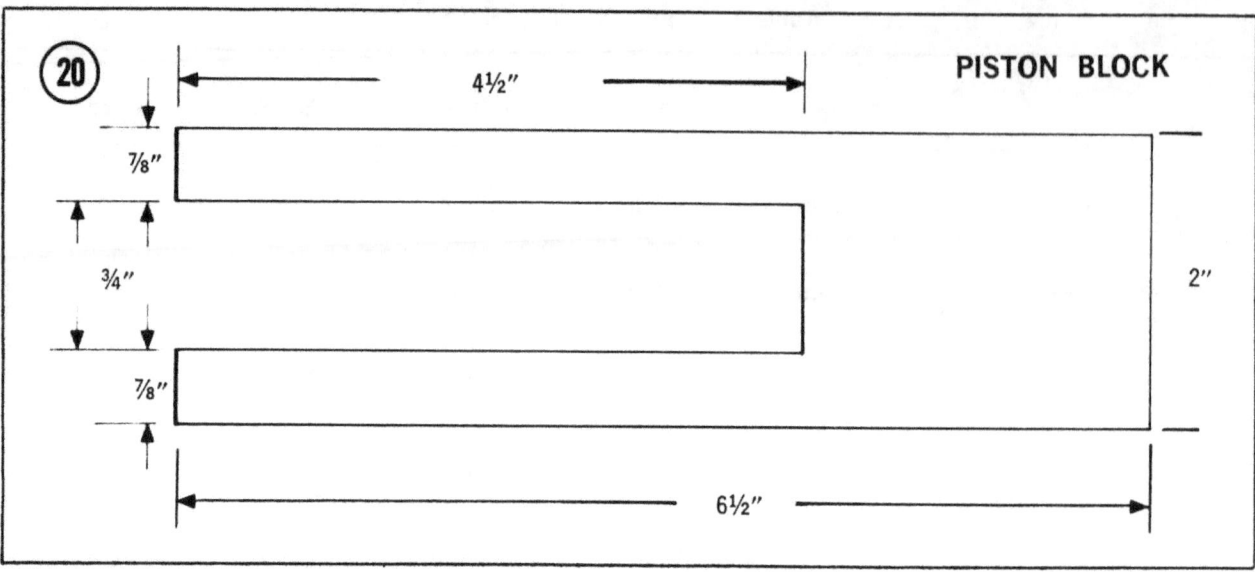

PISTON BLOCK

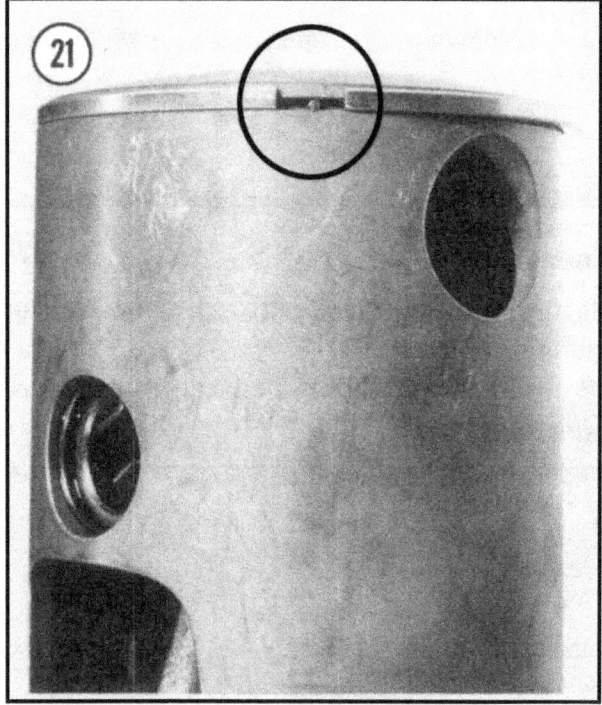

onto the piston. Make sure the cylinder is correctly positioned—intake to the rear.

> NOTE: *It's a good idea to have someone assist in installing the barrel to ensure that the rings remain aligned with the pins.*

5. Carefully slide cylinder down over the rings.

6. Remove the wood block and push the cylinder all the way down onto the crankcase.

7. Thoroughly clean the threads of the through-studs. Double nut each stud in turn and screw it tightly into the crankcase by applying an open-end wrench to the top nut.

8. Install cylinder head as discussed previously.

PISTON AND RINGS

Maico pistons (**Figures 22 and 23**) are made of aluminum alloy. The wrist pin is press fitted and retained in the piston with 2 wire clips. A caged needle bearing is used on the small end of the connecting rod.

Removal

Allow the engine to cool completely to prevent distortion of the cylinder head upon removal. Then remove the head and the cylinder as described previously.

1. Stuff a clean, lint-free rag into the top of the crankcase and place a wood block beneath the

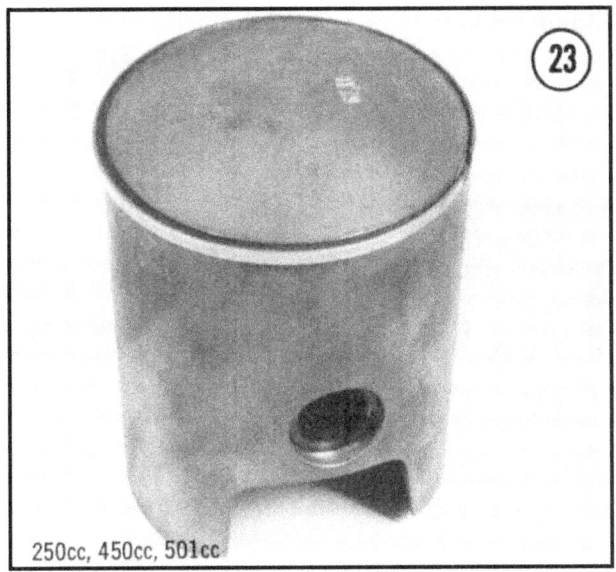

250cc, 450cc, 501cc

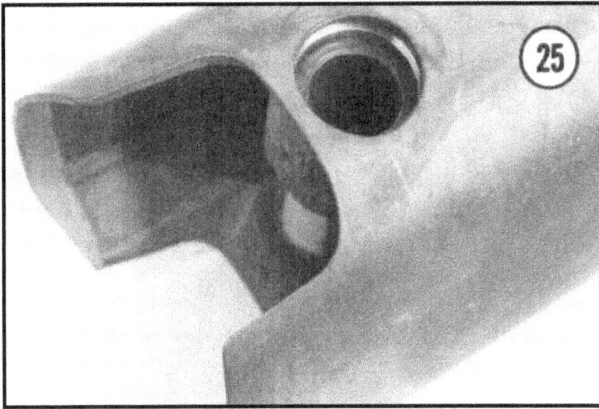

piston. Remove the clips from both sides of the piston (**Figure 24**).

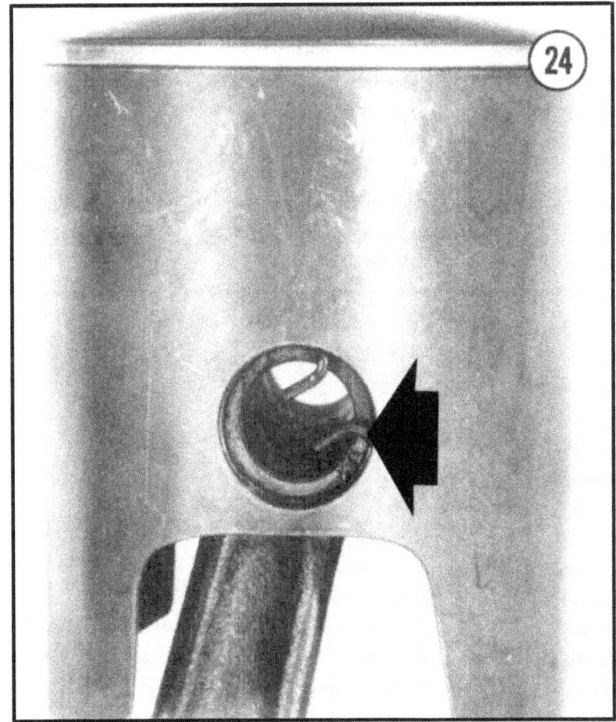

2. Push the pin out of the piston with a pin extractor. Be careful not to damage the rings.

3. Remove the piston and the needle bearing assembly from the connecting rod.

Inspection

Examine the piston carefully for hairline cracks at the top edges of the transfer cutaways (**Figure 25**). If any cracks are found, replace the piston. Check the ring lands for chips or breaks on the edges. Check the ring locating pin for wear. Replace the piston if there is any doubt about its condition.

Remove the rings from the piston by spreading the top ring with a thumb on each end, as shown in **Figure 26**. Remove the ring from the top of the piston and repeat the procedure for removing the secondary ring.

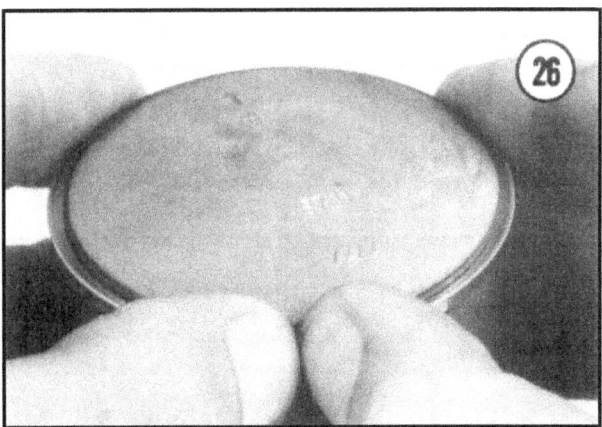

Clean the carbon from the top of the piston with a rag soaked in solvent. If the carbon deposits are hard, scrape them loose with a piece of aluminum that has been rounded on one end. Clean the carbon and gum from the ring grooves with a broken ring or a groove cleaner. Any deposits left in the grooves will prevent the rings from seating correctly and may very likely result in piston seizure.

Check the top of the piston for erosion of the metal and replace it if any is found. Erosion of the piston crown is very often caused by an extremely lean fuel/air mixture. This condition should be corrected immediately after a new piston has been installed and the engine reassembled.

Check the skirt of the piston for brown varnish deposits. More than a slight amount is evidence of worn or sticking rings which should be replaced. Also check the skirt for galling and abrasion—a common symptom of piston seizure. If light galling is present, smooth the affected area with No. 400 emery paper or a fine oilstone. However, if galling is severe or if the piston is deeply scored, replace it.

Measure the piston for clearance in the cylinder as described earlier. Replace the piston and rebore the cylinder as described if the clearance is excessive. Measure the end gap of the rings as shown in **Figure 27**. Insert the ring about one inch (25mm) into the cylinder, squaring it up by pushing it into position with the head of the piston. The end gap should be 0.006-0.010 in. (0.15-0.25mm) per inch of piston diameter for both rings. If the gap exceeds 0.016 in. (0.4mm), replace the rings as a set. Check the end gap of new rings in the same manner.

Clean the needle bearing assembly in solvent and dry it thoroughly. With a magnifying glass, examine the bearing assembly for cracks at the corners of the bearing slots, and also on the needles themselves (see **Figure 28**). If any are found, replace the bearing. This bearing should be replaced routinely when piston is replaced.

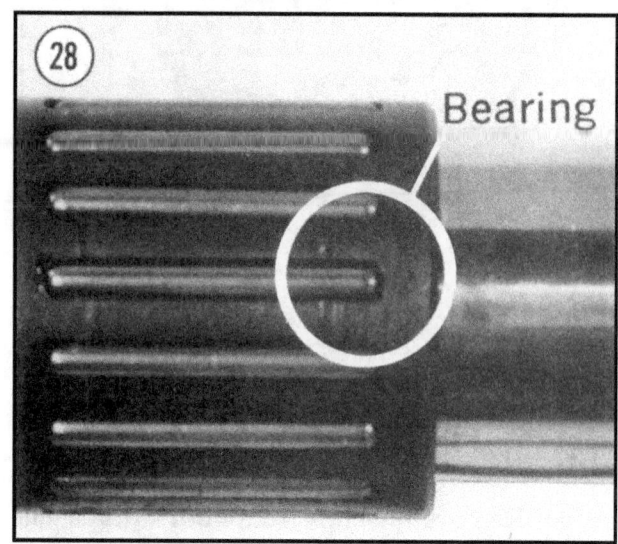

Installation

1. Lightly oil the bearing and reinstall it in the upper end of the connecting rod. Install a new pin retainer clip in one side of the piston. Make sure the clip is completely seated in the groove.

2. Place the slotted wood block over the top of the crankcase and set the piston on the top of the

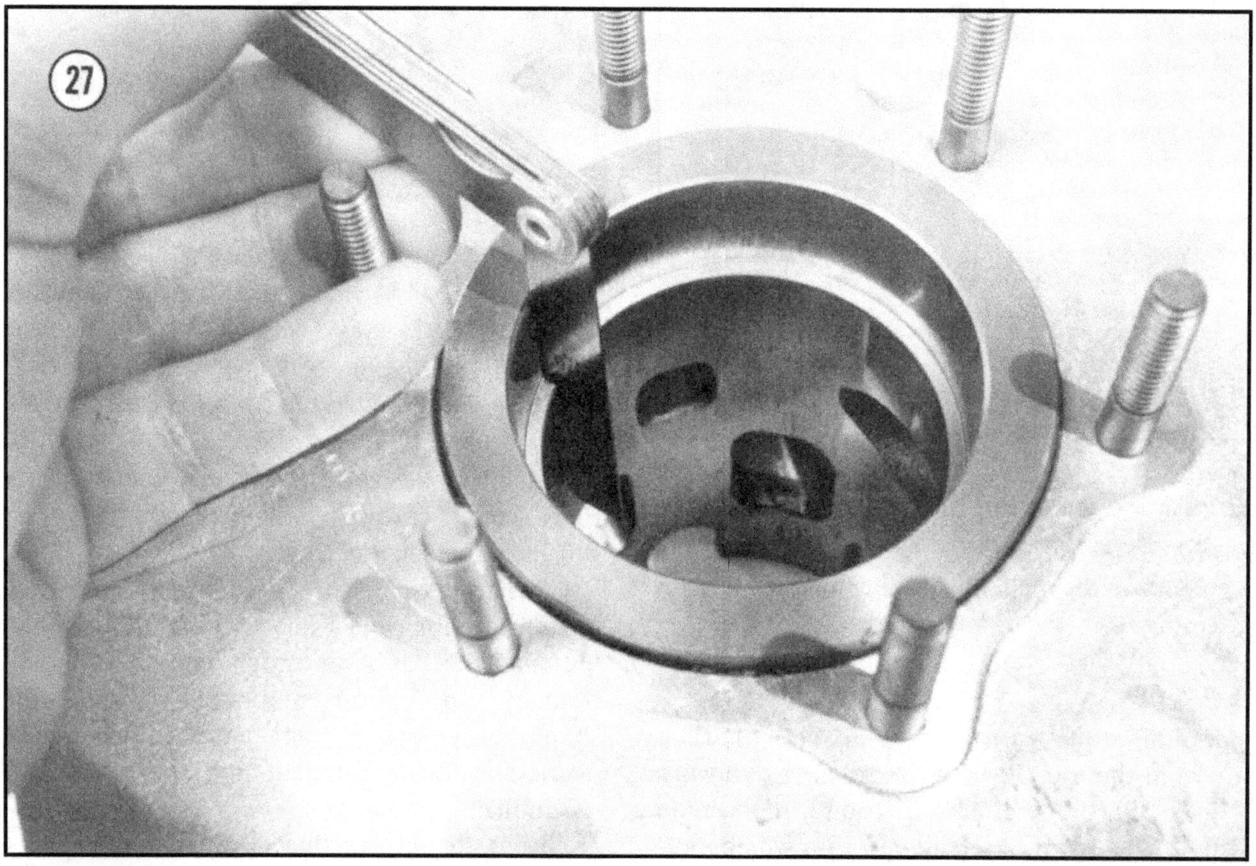

rod. The arrow on the top of the piston must point forward.

> NOTE: *The block can be made from a piece of scrap lumber or plywood cut to the dimensions shown in Figure 20.*

3. Lightly oil the pin and start it into the piston. Set the pin remover/installer tool in place.

4. Align the pin bosses in the piston with the connecting rod and press the pin into the piston by turning the installer bolt clockwise. Stop when the far end of the pin has reached the retainer clip. Remove the installer.

5. Install a new clip in the other side of the piston. Make sure both clips are completely seated in their grooves by rotating them slightly with the flat of a screwdriver.

6. Check the installation by rocking the piston back and forth around the pin axis and from side-to-side to slide along the axis. It should rotate freely back and forth but not rock from side-to-side.

7. Install the rings—first the bottom one, then the top—by carefully spreading the ends of the ring with the thumbs and slipping the ring over the top of the piston. Make sure the rings seat completely in the grooves, all the way around the circumference, and the ends are aligned with the locating pins.

8. Install the cylinder and cylinder head and reassemble the remaining components as described previously.

If the rings were replaced, or if the cylinder was rebored and a new piston installed, the engine must be run in at moderate speeds and loads for no less than 2 hours. Don't exceed 75 percent of normally allowable rpm during run in. After the first half hour, remove the spark plug and check its condition. The electrode should be dry and clean and the color of the insulation should be light to medium tan. If the insulation is white (indicating a too lean fuel/air mixture) or if it is dark and oily (indicating a too rich fuel/air mixture ratio), correct the condition with a jet change; both incorrect conditions produce excessive engine heat and can lead to damage of the rings, piston, and cylinder before they have had a chance to seat in.

CRANKSHAFT AND CRANKCASE

The crankshaft assembly is made up of 2 full-circle flywheels pressed together on a hollow crankpin. The connecting rod big-end bearing on the crankpin is a needle bearing assembly. The crankshaft assembly is supported in 2 roller bearing assemblies, one on the drive (left) side and one on the ignition (right) side.

The 2-piece crankcase splits vertically along the centerline of the connecting rod. Disassembly, or splitting, of the crankcase yields access to both the crankshaft and the transmission. Refer to the exploded master drawing (**Figure 29**, next page) for relationship of the crankcase and crankshaft components.

The procedure which follows is presented as a complete, step-by-step major lower-end rebuild that would be followed if an engine is to be completely reconditioned. However, if you're replacing a known failed part, the disassembly need be carried out only until the failed part is accessible; there's no need to disassemble the engine beyond that point so long as you know the remaining components are in good condition and that they were not affected by the failed part.

Removal

Before the crankcase can be split, the engine must be removed from the motorcycle. Prior to beginning work, thoroughly clean, rinse, and dry the motorcycle, paying particular attention to the engine.

The engine may be removed from the motorcycle intact; however, removing the kickstarter, magneto rotor, and loosening the countershaft sprocket nut can be done beforehand to make the job easier.

1. Remove the kickstarter (**Figure 30**), and the footrests (**Figures 31 and 32**).

2. Place a drip pan beneath the engine on the left side and unscrew the drain plug. Allow several minutes for the oil to drain.

3. Refer to Chapter Six and remove the carburetor. Refer to the cylinder removal section in this chapter and remove the exhaust system, and to the cylinder head section and remove the fuel tank. If the motorcycle is equipped with an external frame-mounted coil, note the locations of the leads, identify them with strips of tape, and

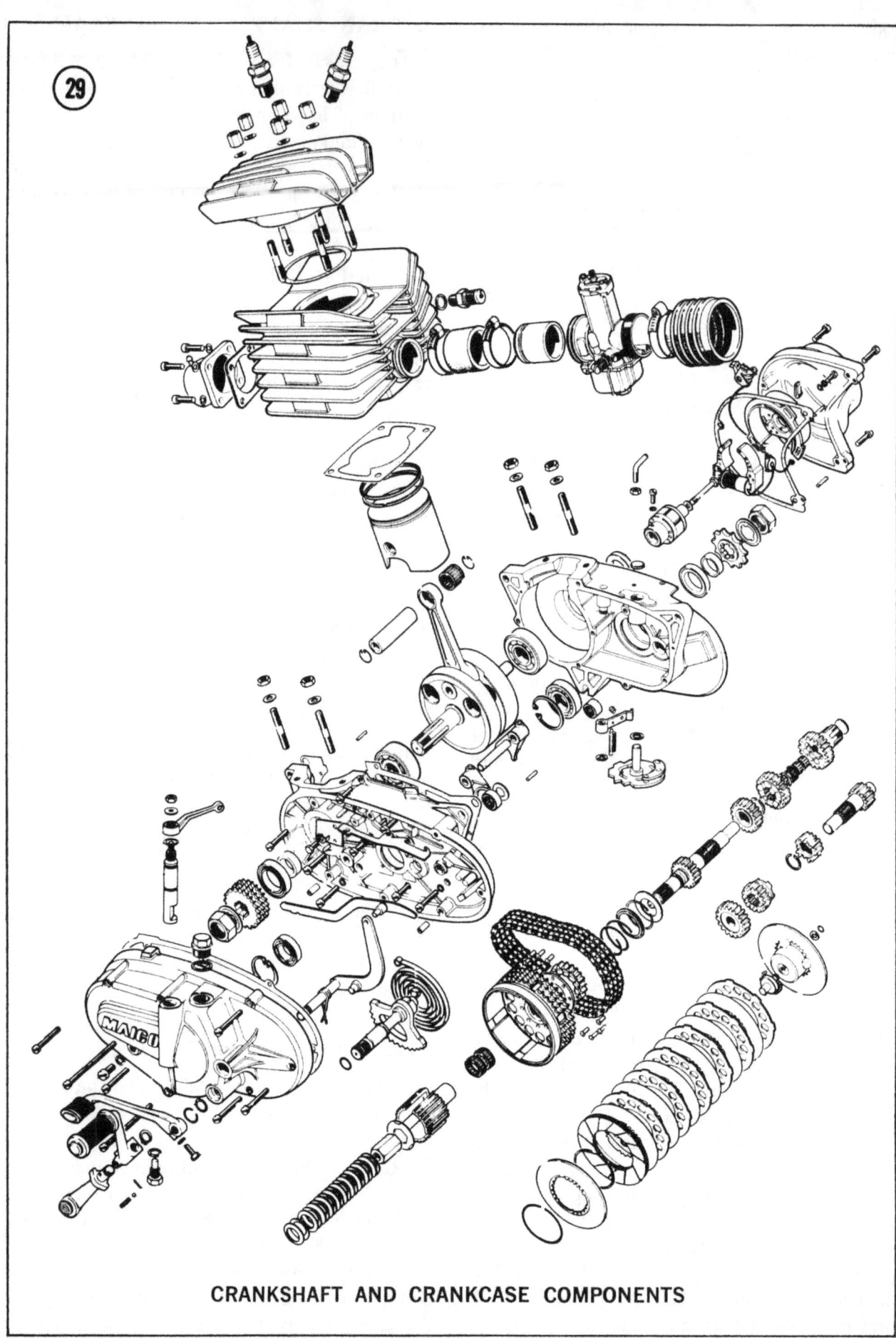

CRANKSHAFT AND CRANKCASE COMPONENTS

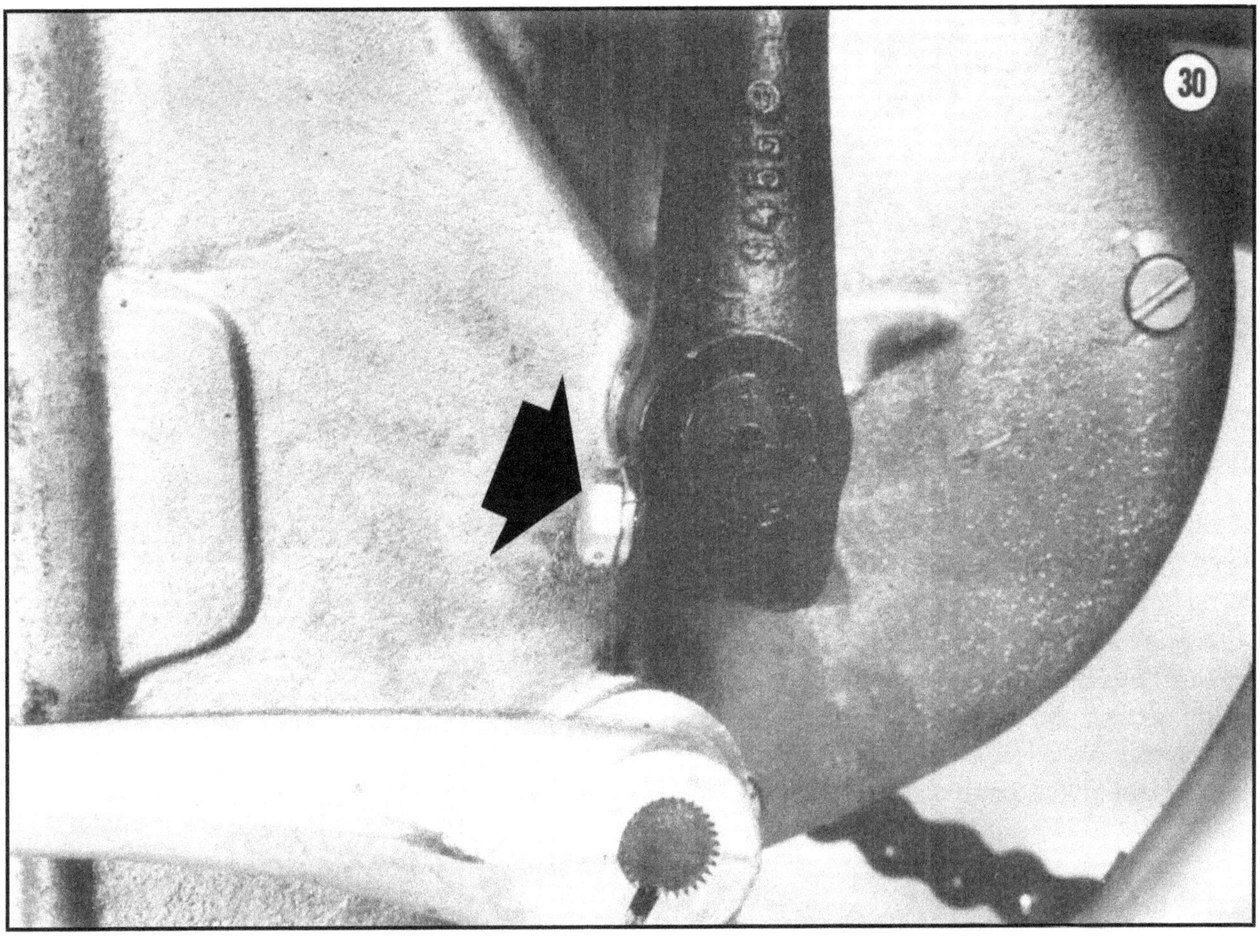

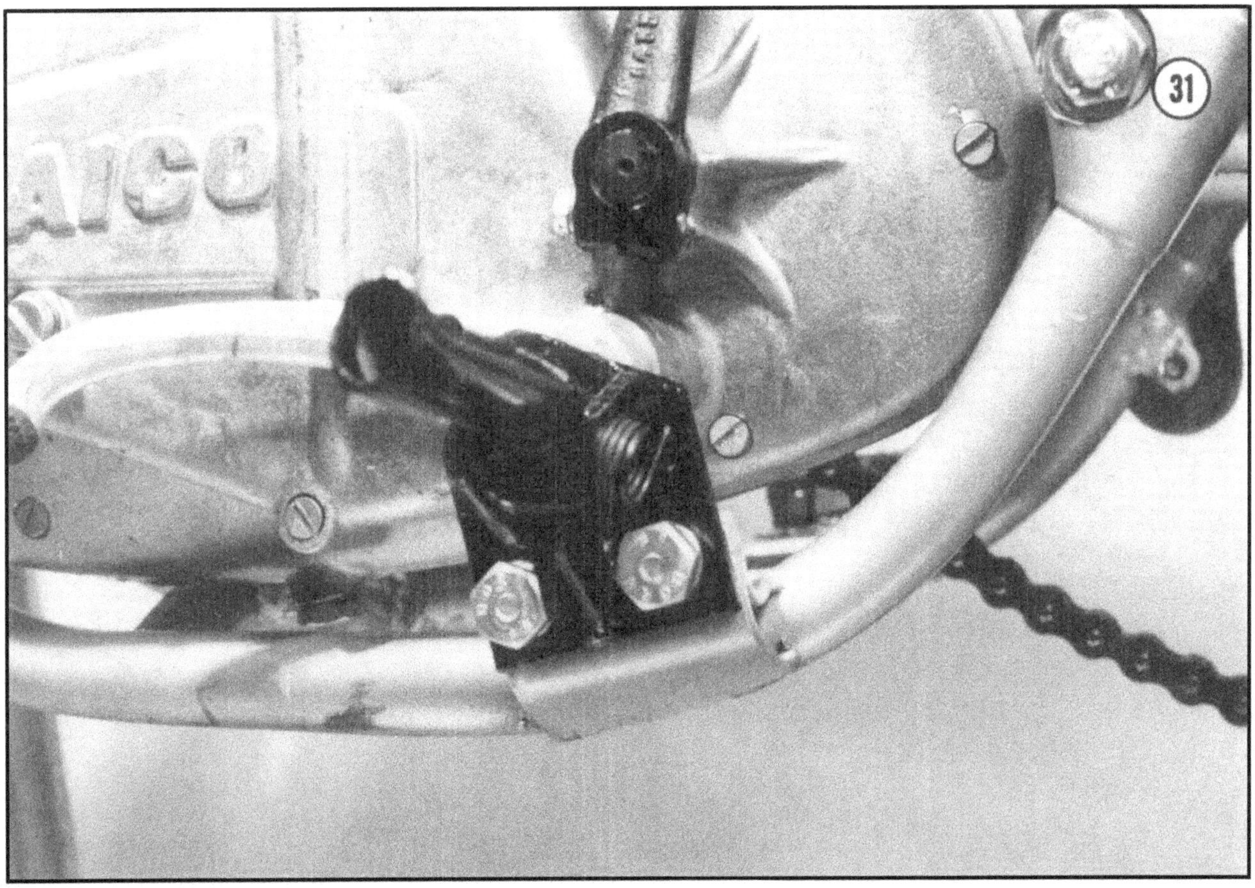

31

disconnect them. Also disconnect the wiring loom from the frame. Disconnect the clutch cable from the clutch arm (**Figure 33**).

4. Straighten the tab washer on the countershaft sprocket nut (**Figure 34**). Depress the rear brake pedal to lock the wheel and unscrew the nut. Disconnect the chain at the master link and remove it from the countershaft sprocket. Remove the tab washer, countershaft sprocket, and ring spacer.

5. Remove the right engine cover (**Figure 35**). Unscrew the 3 screws which hold the magneto stator (**Figure 36**). Carefully pry the rubber grommet out of the case and pull out the ignition leads (**Figure 37**). Remove the stator from the engine and set it aside.

6. Loosen the setscrew in the rotor collar and unscrew the magneto bolt (**Figure 38**). With a suitable puller, such as a slide hammer, remove the rotor from the shaft. Set the rotor inside the stator, wrap the assembly in clean newspaper, and set it out of the way.

7. Remove the cylinder head yoke.

8. Remove the compression release as described under *Cylinder Removal*.

9. Remove the front engine bolt (**Figure 39**) and the rear engine bolt (**Figure 40**). Loosen the bottom bolt (**Figure 41**).

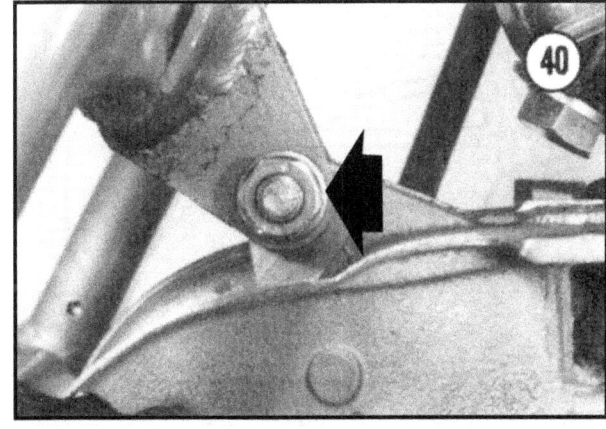

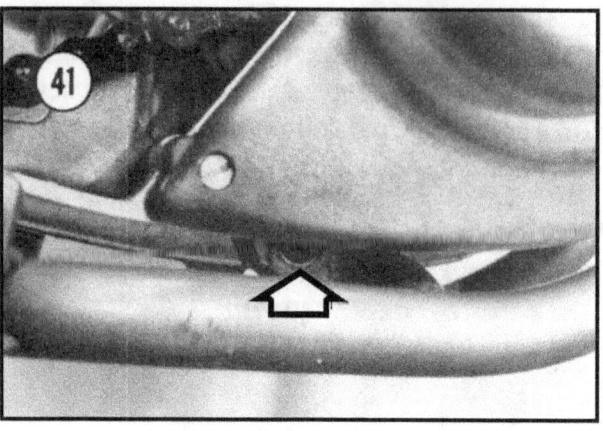

10. Lift the engine by the cylinder and move it rearward. Continue to lift while tilting it back and remove from frame (**Figure 42**).

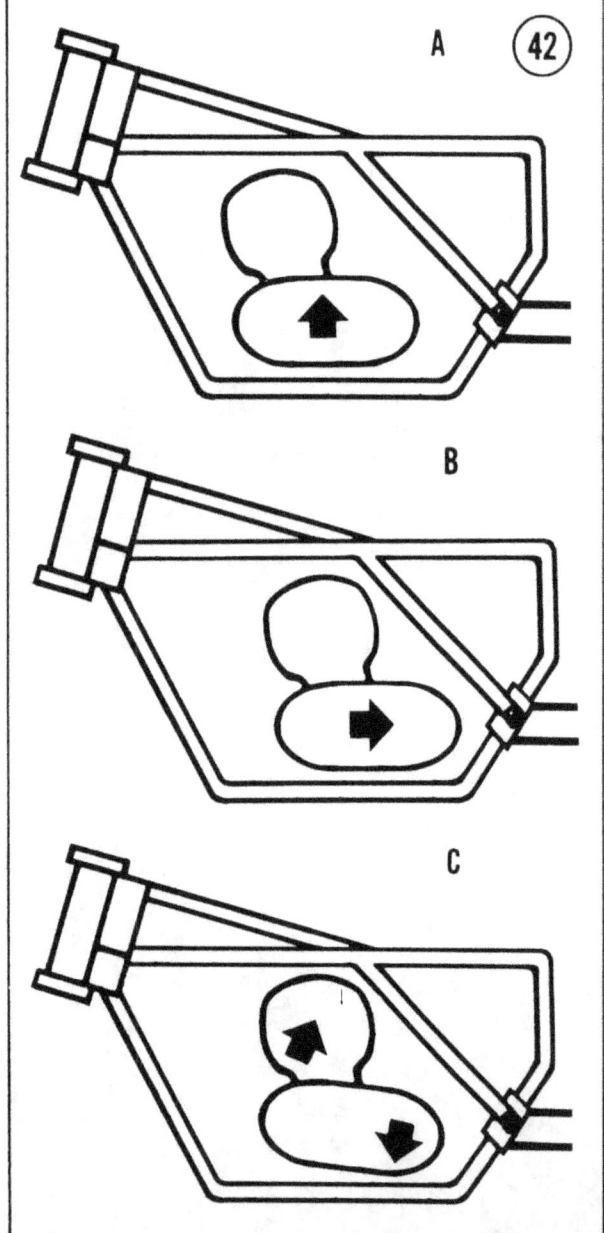

Disassembly

1. Remove the cylinder head, cylinder, and piston—referring to the earlier procedures in this chapter. With the engine removed from the motorcycle, it's not necessary to remove the head/cylinder through-studs.

2. Prevent the connecting rod from hitting the case by slipping a length of innertube or heavy rubber band over one of the right-side through-studs, through the small end of the rod, and over the other right-side through-stud. Rotate the crankshaft to bring the rod to the lowest position and slip the rubber band down the studs. The tension of the rubber band should be sufficient to prevent the rod from moving back and forth but not so tight to create side loading on the rod and bearing.

3. Set the engine on its right side (**Figure 43**). If you don't have an engine holding fixture, an inexpensive work block like the one shown in **Figure 44** can be made from 2 x 4-inch wood.

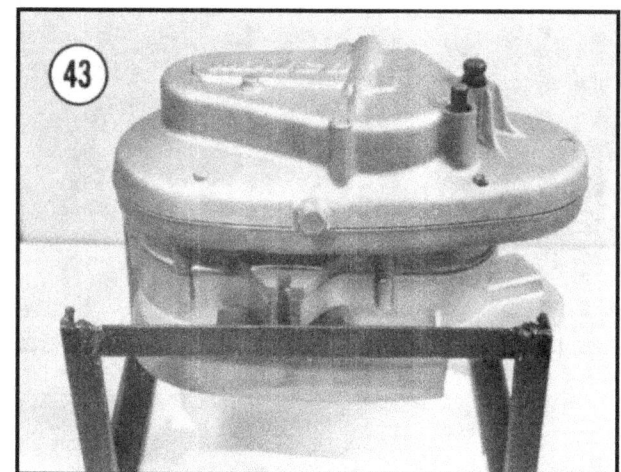

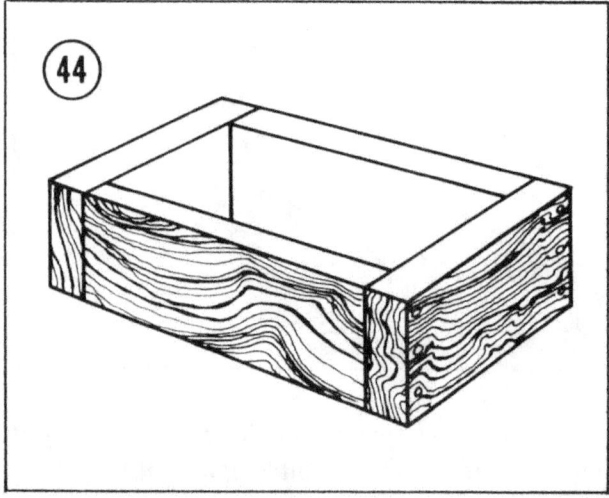

4. Remove the 7 screws from the clutch-side cover (**Figure 45**) and pull the cover straight up and off the engine.

5. Refer to Chapter Five and remove the clutch.

6. Straighten the lock tab on the engine sprocket nut (**Figure 46**). Insert a long drift or small bar through the piston pin hole in the connecting rod and rotate the crankshaft counterclockwise (viewed from the left side of the engine) to bring the bar in contact with 2 blocks of wood set over the top of the crankcase (**Figure 47**). Unscrew the engine sprocket nut and remove it and the lockwasher.

7. Remove the sprocket from the crankshaft with a puller and lift out the spacer ring (**Figure 48**).

8. Straighten the tab washer on the shift linkage cover plate bolt and unscrew the bolt and remove the cover plate and the linkage pull bar (**Figure 49**).

9. Fold a shop rag into several thicknesses and wrap it around the kickstarter shaft (**Figure 50**) to protect your hand. Pull up on the shaft and allow the spring to unwind.

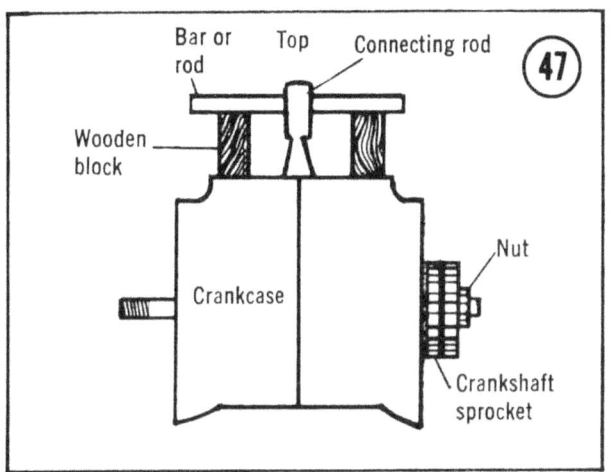

48

49

WARNING
Keep your free hand out of the way when you release the spring tension, and never attempt to remove the kickstarter mechanism without the protection of the shop rag.

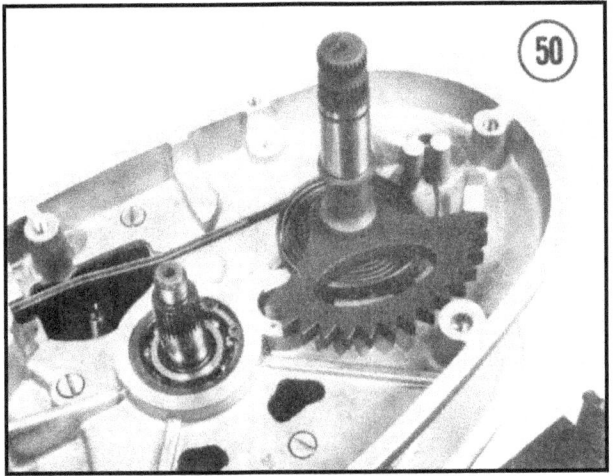

10. Disconnect the return spring from the ratchet hook (**Figure 51**) and remove the hook.

11. Unscrew the 8 crankcase screws. On early 250 and 360 models, all of the screws are located inside the left engine cover. On late 250, 400, and 501 models, 7 screws are located inside the cover and one is located outside at rear of crankcase opening (**Figure 52**).

12. Tap along the mating line for the crankcase halves and carefully pull the left-hand case half up and off the right case half (**Figure 53**).

13. Pull the crankshaft assembly out of the right case half.

NOTE: *If the crankshaft assembly is the item to be inspected and repaired, the transmission gearset and remaining gearshift mechanism need not be removed from the right half of the crankcase. However, if the crankshaft main bearings are to be replaced, refer to Chapter Five and disassemble the transmission.*

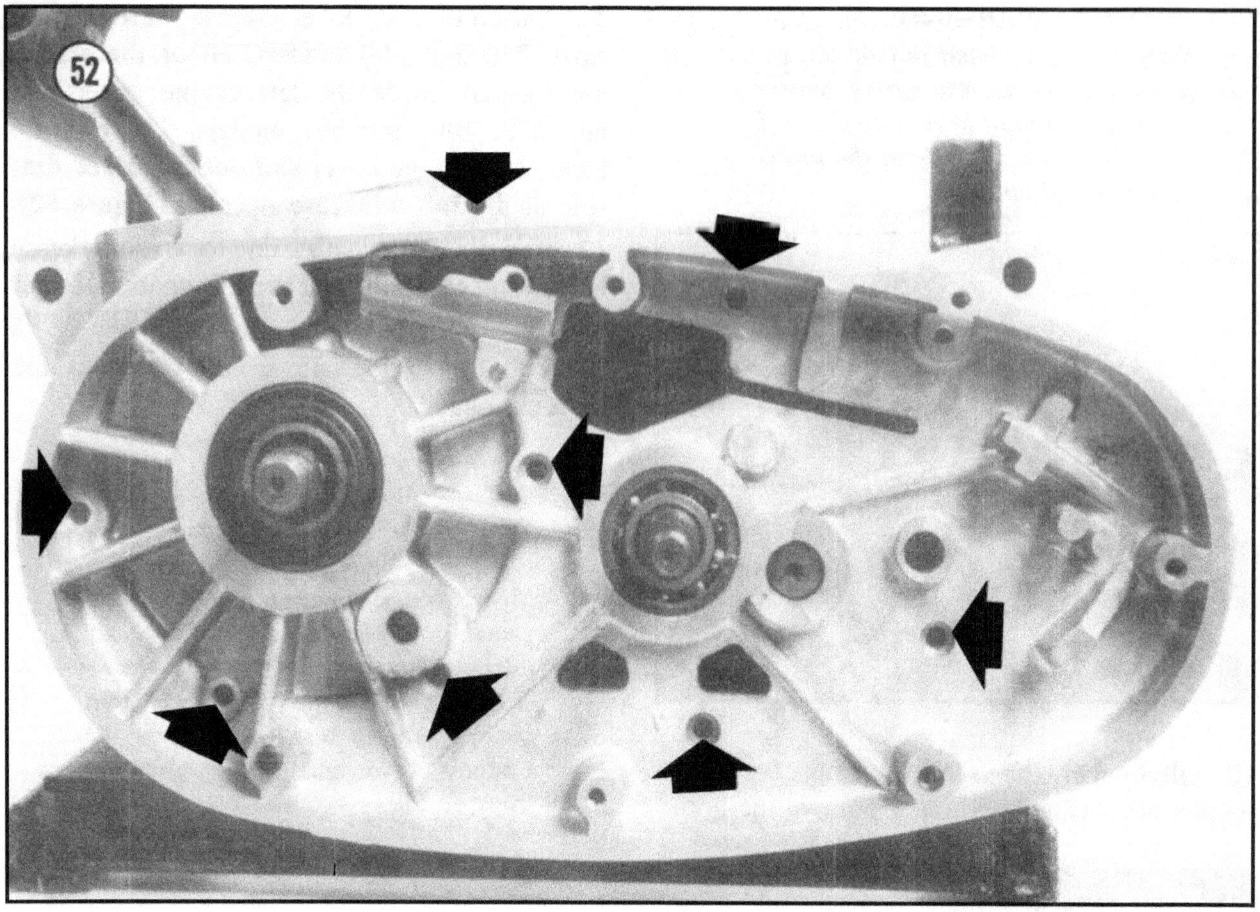
52

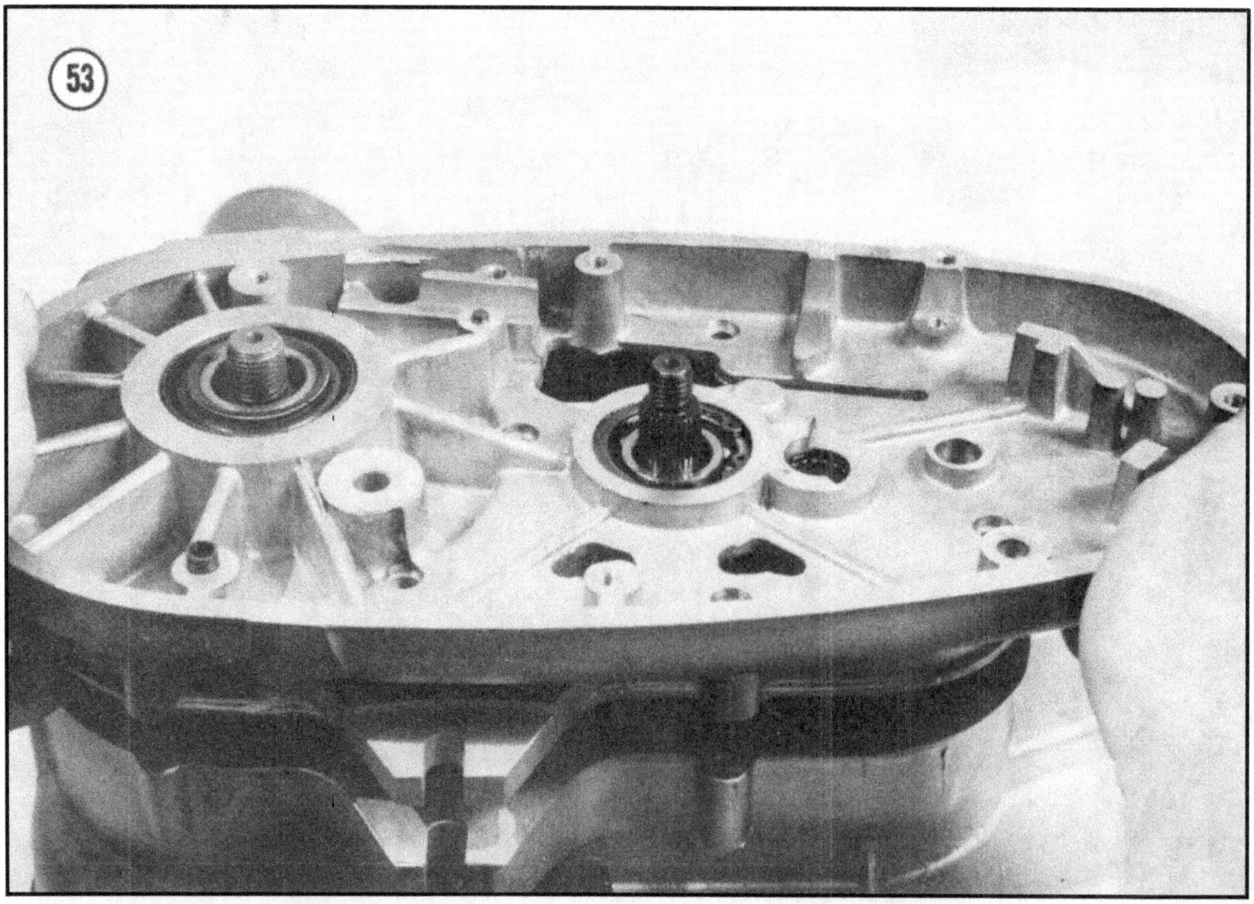
53

At this point of disassembly, major service can be performed on the crankcase assembly. Crankshaft and transmission seals and bearings can be removed and installed and all critical inspections can be performed.

14. The crankshaft seals should be replaced routinely each time the crankcase and crankshaft are disassembled. Heat the cases in an oven to 250° F and carefully pry the seals out of the seal bores. On 250, 360, and 400 square-barrel models, the seals are located inboard of each main bearing, and on 501 and radial models they are located outside the main bearings.

Inspection

Check the crankcase halves for cracks or fractures in the stiffening webs, around the bearing bosses, and at threaded holes. While the likelihood of such damage is rare, it should be checked for, and particularly so following a catastrophic malfunction (i.e., piston breakage, bearing failure, gear breakage) or after a collision or hard spill in which the engine suffers external damage.

If cracks or fractures are found, they should be repaired immediately by a reputable shop experienced in and equipped to perform repairs on precision aluminum castings.

Check the condition of the connecting rod big end bearing by supporting the crankshaft horizontally with the crankpin in the 12 o'clock position.

> NOTE: *This check is most easily performed with the crankshaft installed in the crankcase.*

Grasp the connecting rod firmly and pull up on it. Tap sharply on the top of the rod with your free hand. If the bearing and crankpin are in good condition, there should be no movement felt in the rod. If movement is felt, or if there is a sharp, metallic click, the bearing may be unserviceable and should be replaced. This is a job which should be entrusted to a shop equipped with a press capable of separating and reassembling the crank halves and the pin.

If the condition of the connecting rod big end bearing is satisfactory, check the side play of the connecting rod with the crank halves using a flat feeler gauge (**Figure 54**). The side play should be 0.020-0.024 inch (0.51-0.60mm).

> NOTE: *If the side play is greater than 0.024 inch (0.60mm) and it can be seen that the connecting rod has worn into the flywheels, measure the distance across the wheels (**Figure 55**). If the distance is 2.475-2.490 inch (62.82-63.20mm), side play slightly greater than 0.024 inch is acceptable. If, however, the distance across the wheels is not within the dimensions specified, or is uneven around the circumference of the wheels, the alignment of the wheels should be checked and corrected by a shop equipped with a press.*

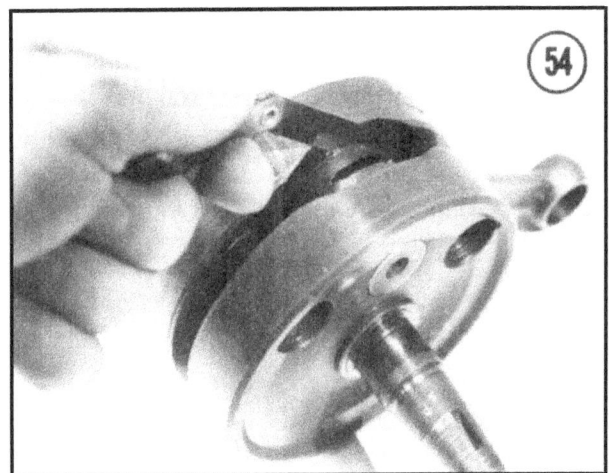

If alignment of the flywheels is in question, support the crankshaft assembly on knife edges and check the alignment with a dial indicator (**Figure 56**). The maximum allowable misalignment is 0.002 inch (0.050mm) measured at the end of the magneto-side shaft. If the misalignment is greater than this, the flywheel halves

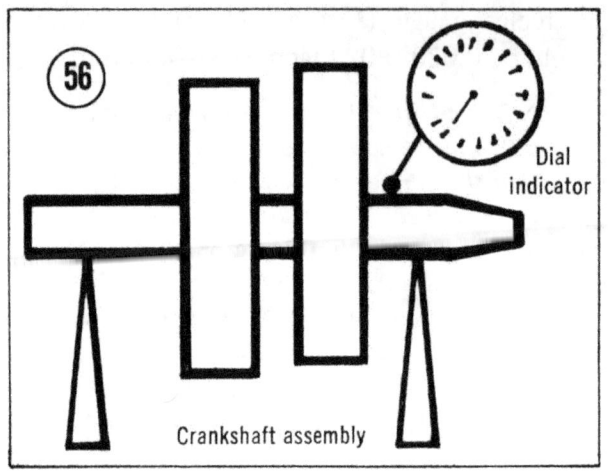

should be realigned in a press. Once again, this is a job for an expert.

Check the crankshaft and transmission bearings for pitting, galling and wear. Rotate the bearings by hand and feel for roughness and play. They should turn smoothly and evenly and there should be no apparent radial play. If any bearing is found faulty in any way, replace it.

Bearing Replacement

Crankshaft and transmission main bearings are installed with a slight interference fit which requires that the case half being serviced be heated uniformly to about 250° F.

CAUTION
Heating should be done in an oven and not with a torch; it's virtually impossible to obtain the required overall and uniform heating with a torch, and the likelihood of warping the case is great.

When the cases are adequately heated, the bearings should release from their bores when the case is rapped sharply on a soft wood surface. The new bearing must be installed immediately, while the case is still hot. It must be completely seated in the bore, against the machined shoulder (**Figure 57**).

If a serviceable transmission bearing was dislodged when the old crankshaft bearing was removed, reinstall it immediately and then install the crankshaft bearing.

Assembly

1. Refer to Chapter Five and assemble the transmission.
2. Fit the complete crankshaft assembly into the right-side case.
3. Coat the mating surfaces of both crankcase halves with light grease and install a new gasket over the alignment dowels in the right case half (**Figure 58**). Check to make sure that any spacers or shims that were removed during disassembly have been installed.

4. Position the left crankcase half over the crankshaft and transmission shafts and push it firmly and evenly down until it contacts the right case half. Install the shifting ratchet hook (Figure 51) and connect the return spring.
5. Screw the 8 screws into the crankcase and tighten them in the pattern shown in **Figure 59** to 5.8-7.25 ft.-lb. (0.8-1.0 mkg).
6. Continue assembly by following the disassembly steps in reverse. When assembling the clutch, pay particular attention to the instructions in Chapter Five. Refer to **Table 4** for the correct torque values of the nuts and bolts listed.

Table 4   TORQUE VALUES

Fastener	Torque
Engine sprocket nut	43-55 ft.-lb. (5.95-7.65 mkg)
Clutch hub nut	36 ft.-lb. (5 mkg)
Magneto rotor bolt	12 ft.-lb. (1.7 mkg)
Cylinder head nuts	
250, 360, 400cc	18-20 ft.-lb. (2.5-2.8 mkg)
501cc	25 ft.-lb. (3.5 mkg)
Engine mounting bolts	
Front and bottom	25 ft.-lb. (3.5 mkg)
Rear	37 ft.-lb. (5.2 mkg)
Countershaft sprocket nut	48-60 ft.-lb. (6.8-8.5 mkg)

SERVICE, TIMING, AND ADJUSTMENT

When assembly and installation of the engine in the motorcycle are complete, fill the transmission with oil as described in Chapter Two. Before installing the ignition cover, refer to Chapter Seven and time the ignition. Refer to Chapter Six and adjust the carburetor and to Chapter Two and adjust the controls.

CHAPTER FIVE

TRANSMISSION AND CLUTCH

The Maico transmission is a 4-speed type offered in close-ratio motocross versions, and a wide-ratio cross-country version. Service to all types is identical. A typical gearset is shown in **Figure 1**. The relationship of the gears and shifting forks is shown in **Figure 2**. The relationship of the shifting forks and camplate is shown in **Figure 3**. Four basic clutches have been used in late-model Maicos. They are similar in construction but the type, number, and relationship of the components differ. When replacing clutch components, take the old ones to your dealer so they can be matched with the correct new ones.

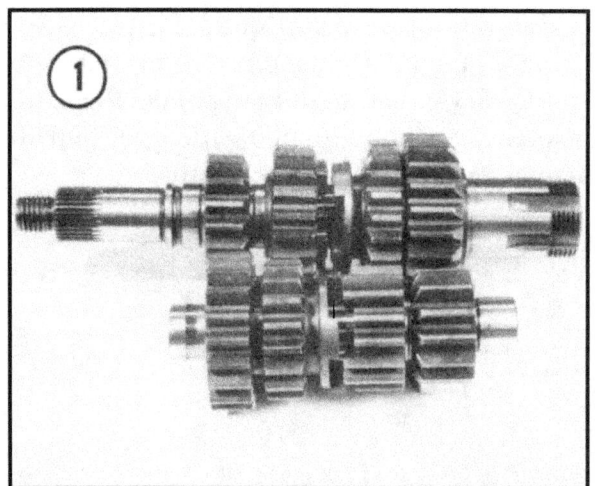

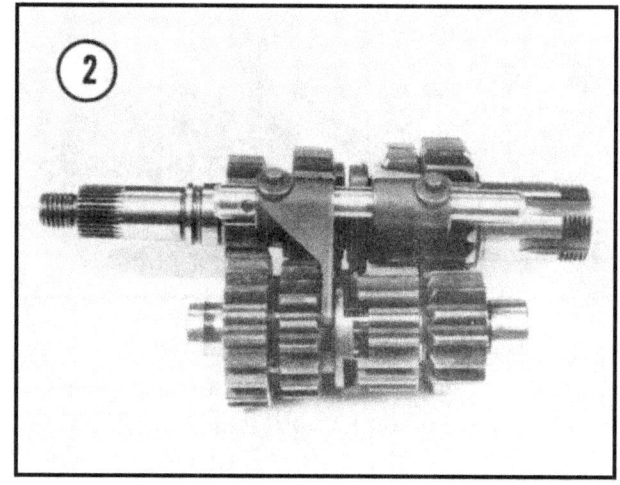

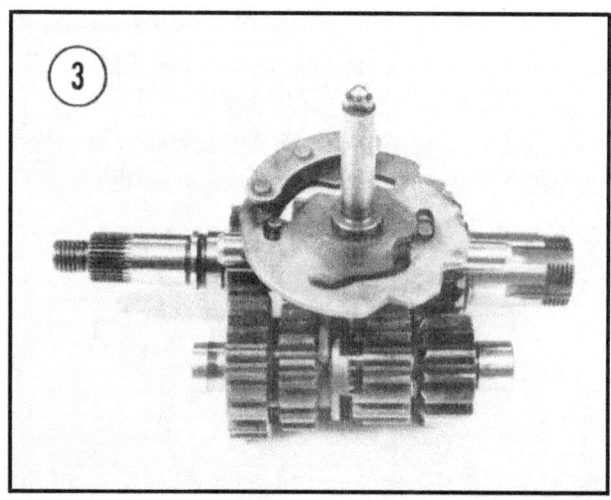

CLUTCH

The clutch may be removed, serviced, installed, and adjusted with the engine in the motorcycle. It's recommended that the motorcycle be laid on its right side so that the transmission oil isn't lost and that installation of the clutch spring stack is made easier. Close the fuel tap on the gas tank, disconnect the fuel line to the carburetor and remove the tank. Pull the transmission vent hose out of the case and turn it 180 degrees to prevent the oil from running out, then lay the motorcycle on its right side.

Removal

1. Loosen the clutch adjuster at the handlebar and disconnect the cable from the clutch arm and the left case (**Figure 4**).

2. Remove the kickstarter pedal and the left footrest.

3. Remove the 7 screws from the cover (**Figure 5**) and lift it straight up and off the engine.

4. Install a puller on the clutch body (**Figure 6**), compress the pressure plate, and remove the snap rings (**Figure 7**). Unscrew the puller bolt to relax the clutch springs and remove the puller.

5. Lift the guide and plate stack out together (**Figure 8**). Remove the top plate and note the direction of the oil slinger grooves in the fiber plate (**Figure 9**, page 45). Also note which side is up. Grooved plates must be installed in ex-

actly the same direction for the oil to be correctly distributed in the clutch. Remove all of the plates from the stack.

6. Remove the spring segments and note their arrangement (**Figure 10**). Also note the location of the washer so that it may be installed in the same manner.

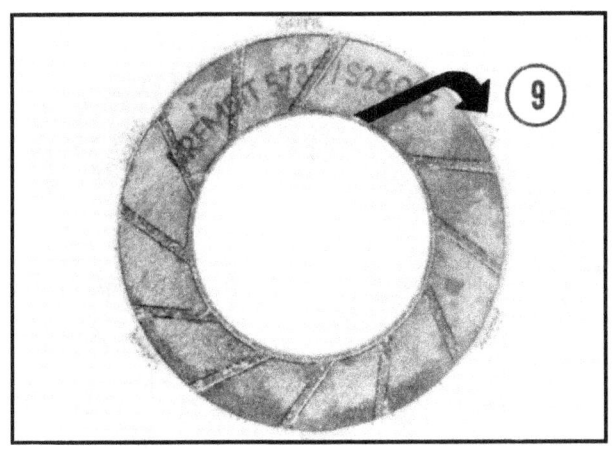

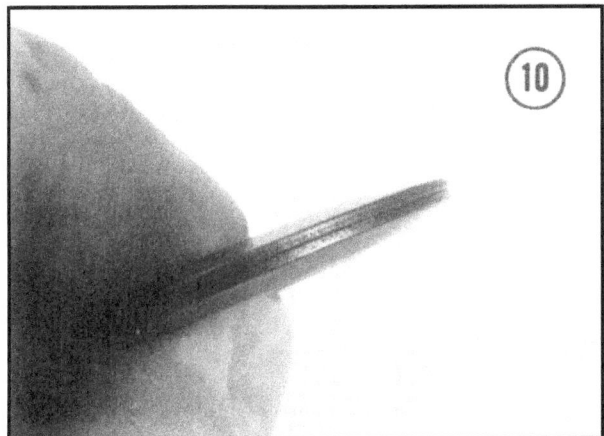

NOTE: *It's not necessary to remove the clutch hub or the basket (Figure 11) unless they are damaged or their splines are worn requiring replacement of one or both pieces. In such case, carry out the next 4 steps.*

1. Hub   2. Basket

7. On 250, 360, and 400 models, remove the lock tab washer from the clutch hub nut (**Figure 12**). On 501 and radial models, the clutch hub nut is secured with Loctite.

8. Set the clutch hub holding fixture over the clutch hub and rest the fixture arm against the kickstarter shaft (**Figure 13**).

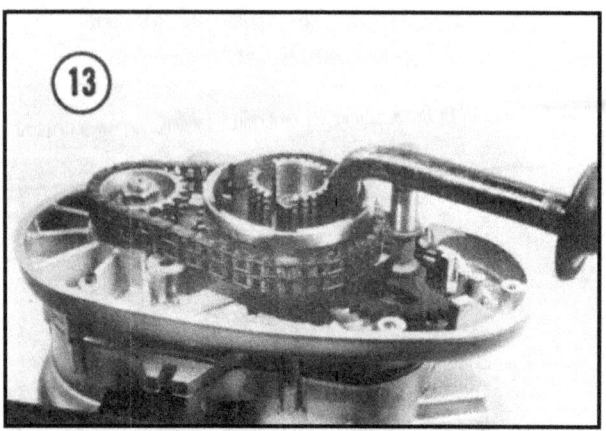

NOTE: *A suitable fixture can be made by brazing a 5-inch length of ⅜-inch diameter steel rod or handlebar segment to an old internally splined clutch plate.*

9. Unscrew the clutch hub nut (**Figure 14**) and remove the hub and the bushing behind it.

10. Lift up the clutch basket and remove it from the primary chain (**Figure 15**). Remove the thrust washer from behind basket (**Figure 16**).

Inspection

Place each of the clutch plates on a smooth, level surface such as a surface plate or a panel of glass and check for warpage. Warped plates should be replaced with new plates; they can't be effectively straightened.

Examine the plates for galling or grooves. The friction material on fiber plates should be of

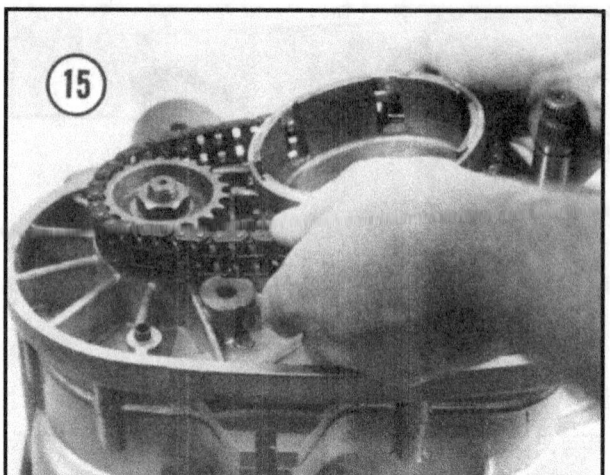

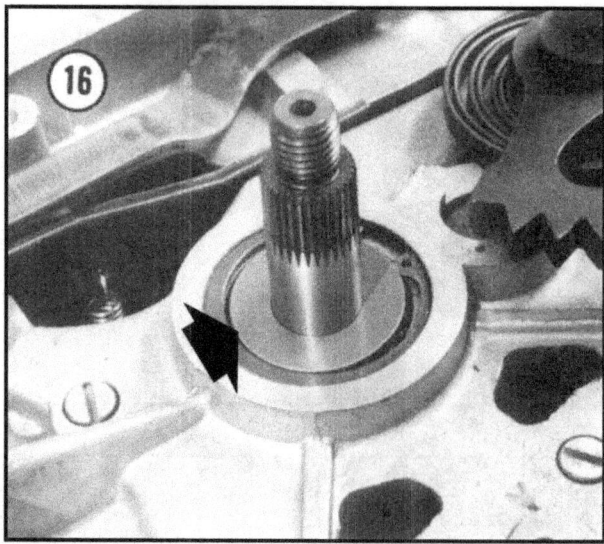

uniform thickness on both sides and there should be no evidence of burning. See **Table 1**. If the plates are less than satisfactory on these points, replace them.

Table 1   STEEL CLUTCH SERVICE LIMITS

Plate	New Thickness	Replacement Thickness
Fiber (1)	0.150 in. (3.8mm)	0.145 in. (3.68mm)
Driven (6)	0.050 in. (1.27mm)	0.045 in. (1.14mm)
Driving (6)	0.085 in. (2.16mm)	0.080 in. (2.03mm)

If the clutch is an all-steel type (one fiber plate), measure each of the plates and replace them if they are worn beyond the service limit. See Table 1.

Measure each spring segment with a caliper. A new segment is 0.075 in. (1.9mm) (**Figure 17**). A segment should be replaced when it is 0.070 in. (1.78mm) or less.

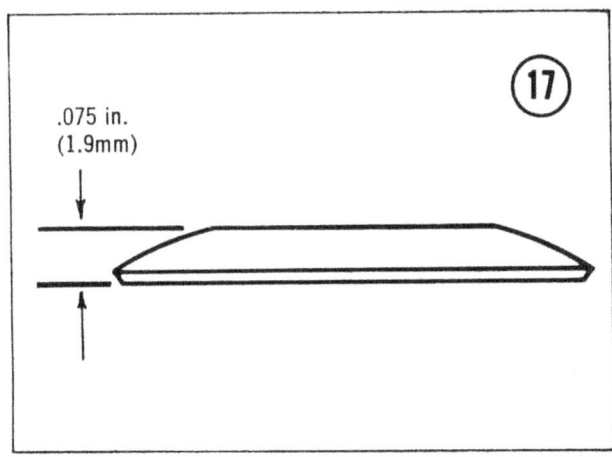

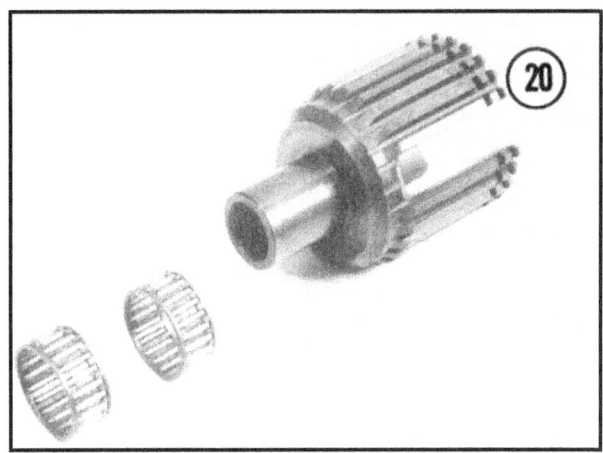

Check the condition of the thrust washer that fits behind the clutch basket. It should be flat and smooth. If it's bent or grooved, replace it.

Check the throwout bearing for worn or damaged races and balls (**Figure 18**) and replace them if necessary. There should be 14 ball bearings in the assembly.

Check the bushing or bearing that fits between the bore in the basket and the hub shaft (**Figures 19 and 20**). Replace it if it's worn, galled, or grooved.

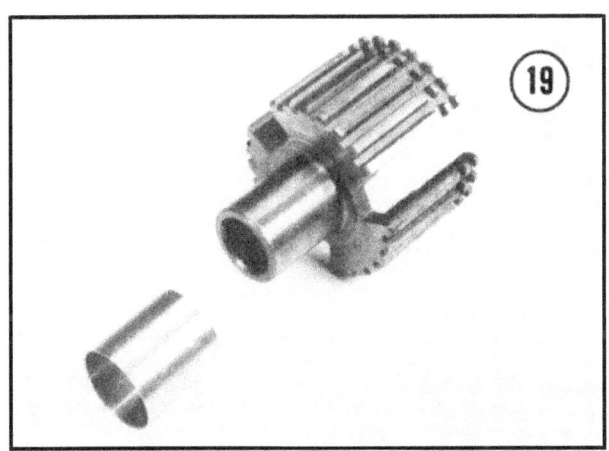

Assembly

1. Set the thrust washer in place on the transmission shaft. Engage the sprocket teeth of the clutch basket with the primary drive chain and set the basket in place on the shaft.

2. Install the heavy washer on the clutch hub shaft and fit the bushing. Install the hub in the basket.

CAUTION
Thoroughly clean the threads on the transmission shaft and in the clutch hub nut with contact cleaner or acetone. Apply Loctite to the threads on the shaft and screw on the nut. Set the hub holding fixture in place and tighten the nut to 30 ft.-lb. (5 mkg). These steps are very important; if the clutch hub nut comes loose, the transmission and clutch will be severely damaged.

On all models except the 501, set the lock tab washer in place over the nut.

3. Stack the springs in the order and pattern shown in **Table 2** and set them in place in the clutch hub (**Figure 21**).

4. Set the washer on top of the clutch spring stack. Line up the cutouts in the clutch plate guide with the segments in the hub and install the guide (**Figure 22**).

5. For all clutches, first install a driving plate (**Figure 23**) and then a driven plate (**Figure 24**), continuing to alternate them until they are all installed. All fiber plates, including the single fiber plate used beneath the terminal plate in the steel clutch, must be installed with their oil grooves pointing clockwise (Figure 9).

Table 2   CLUTCH SPRING STACKING

Model and Type	No.	Pattern
250 and 360cc (Fiber)	18	))(())(())(())(())
	20	(())(())(())(())(())
250 and 400cc (Steel)	20	(())(())(())(())(())
400 and 501cc (Fiber, early)*	20	()()()()()()()()()()
400, 450 and 501cc (Fiber, late)**	18	()()()()()()()()()
	20	()()()()()()()()()()

*Most 1971 models   **All 1972 models and later

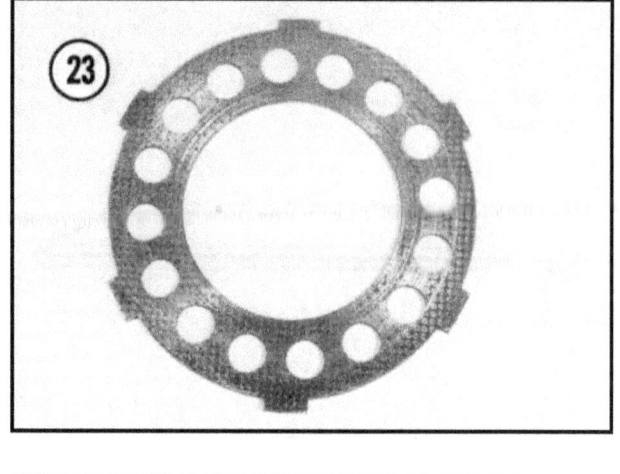

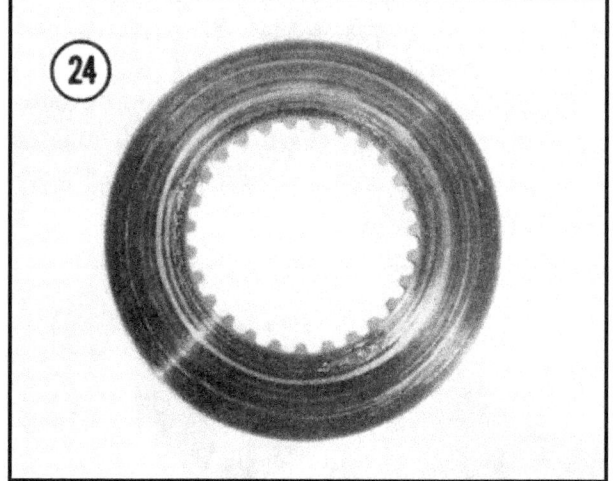

CAUTION
*The first 2 driven plates have machined recesses (**Figure 25**) that must be lined up with the stiffeners in the hub. If these plates are not installed correctly, the clutch will not engage.*

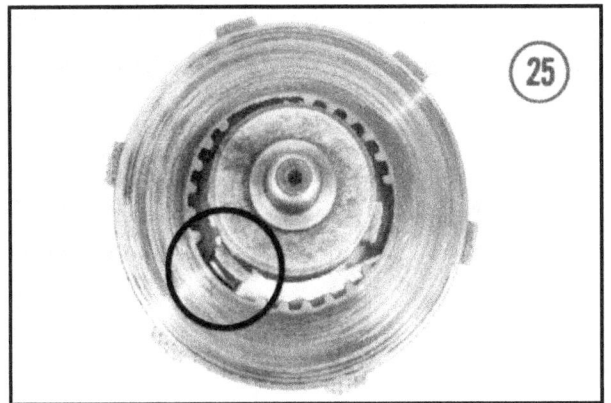

6. Install the terminal plate. On late 400, 450, and 501 models, the machined band on the terminal plate must face out (**Figure 26**).

7. Install the clutch puller tool and compress the guide. Install the snap rings. Make sure they are completely seated all around their grooves before removing the puller.

8. Lightly grease the mating surface of the case and the left cover and set a new gasket in place over the alignment dowels.

9. Make sure the return spring on the gear selector crank straddles the post on the crank and the post in the cover (**Figure 27**).

10. Set the cover in place, making sure the post in the gear selector linkage pull bar engages the hole in the gear selector crank (**Figure 28**).

11. Install the screws in the cover and tighten them in the pattern shown (**Figure 29**).

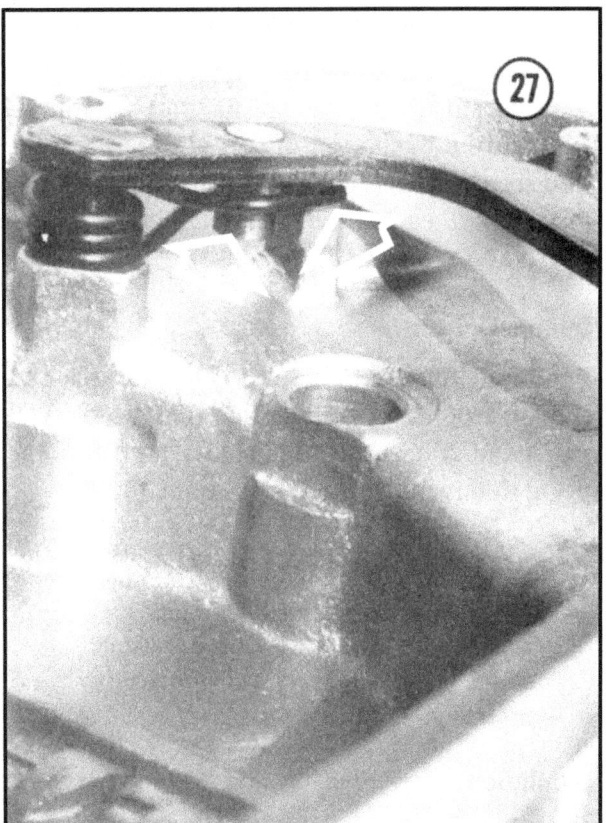

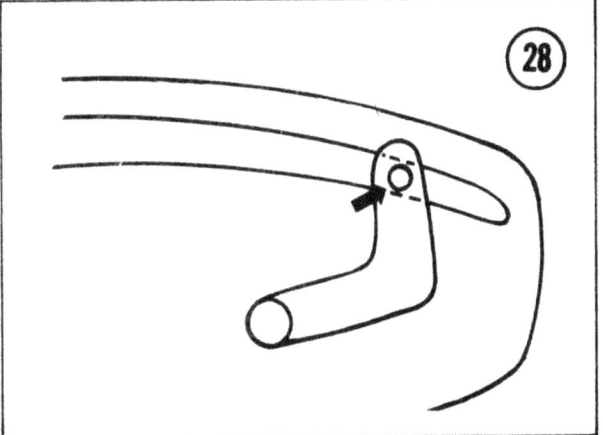

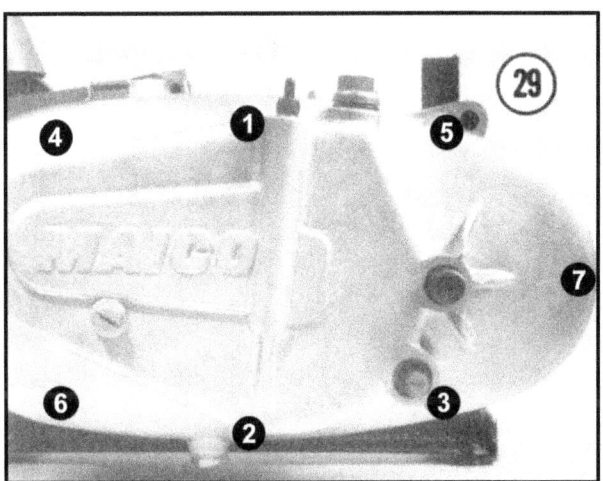

KICKSTARTER

Service of the kickstarter assembly is limited to replacement of the spring and quadrant, although the likelihood of this is remote. It's a good idea to check the O-ring seal on the kickstarter shaft each time the outer cover is removed and replace it if nicked.

Removal

Fold a shop rag into several thicknesses and wrap it around the kickstarter shaft to protect your hand. Pull up on the shaft and allow the spring to unwind.

> **WARNING**
> *Keep your free hand out of the way when you release the spring tension, and never attempt removal without the protection of a shop rag.*

Installation

Set the end of the spring between the 2 posts (**Figure 30**). Carefully wind the starter 3 complete turns using the kickstarter lever as a handle. Push the starter shaft all the way down to lock it in place.

TRANSMISSION

Service of the transmission requires that the engine be removed from the motorcycle and the crankcase "split." Refer to Chapter Four, *Crankshaft and Crankcase Disassembly*, and carry out Steps 1 through 11. If only the transmission is being worked on, there's no need to remove the crankshaft assembly from the right case half.

Disassembly

1. Remove the first sliding gear from the countershaft (**Figure 31**). Check to see if it is shimmed. Some models are fitted with shims (**Figure 32**) which set the first gear clearance of 0.012 inch (0.3mm).

> **CAUTION**
> *If these shims are omitted during reassembly, the transmission will not function correctly. Also, it's possible to engage 2 gears at a time, resulting in severe transmission damage.*

2. Remove the shifting fork spindle (**Figure 33**).
3. Remove the countershaft and countershaft shifting fork (**Figure 34**).

4. Remove the main shaft (**Figure 35**) and the main shaft shifting fork and gear (**Figure 36**).

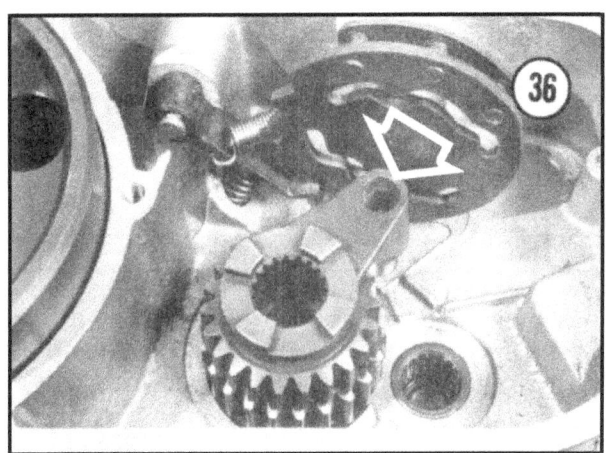

5. Turn the case half over and tap the output sleeve gear (**Figure 37**) out of the case with a soft mallet.

6. Turn the case over to the original position and remove the shifting cam (**Figure 38**). On some models there is a washer between the camplate and the pivot boss in the case. This should be collected and set on the spindle until the

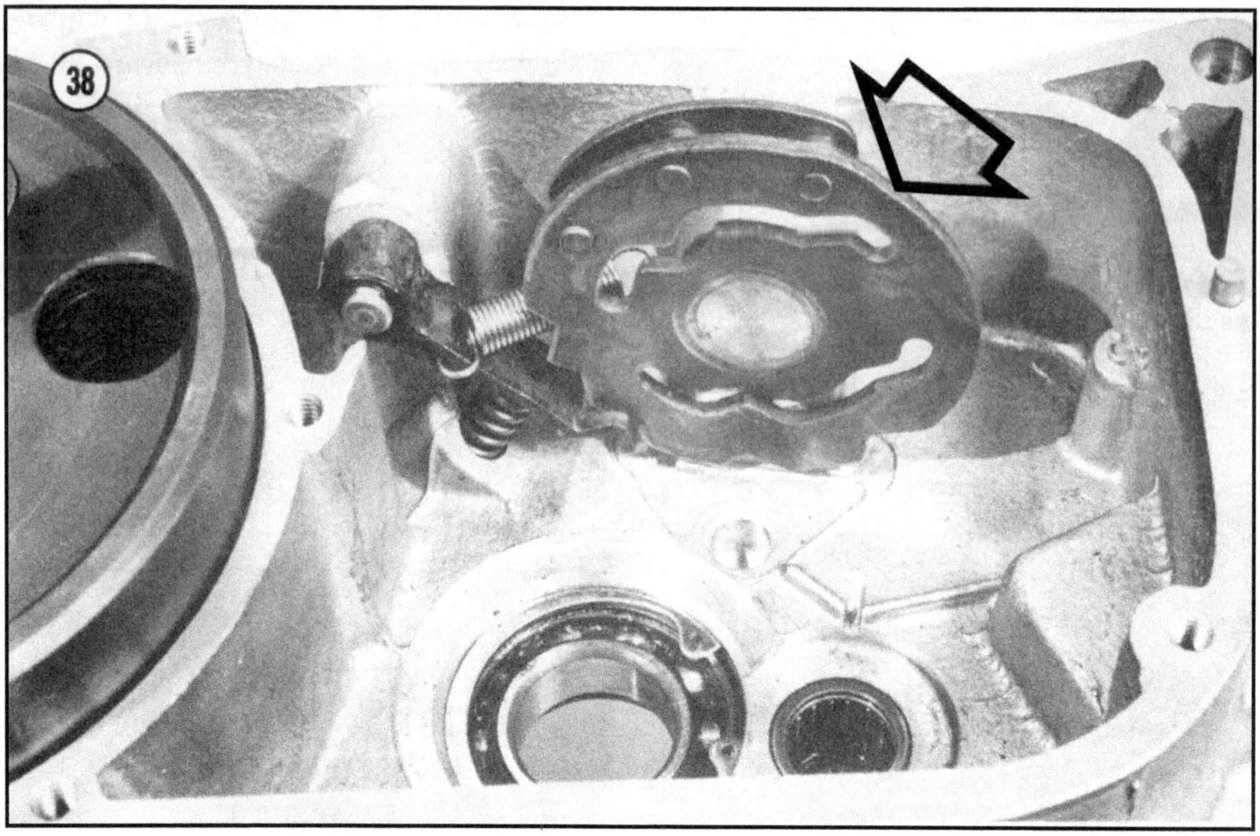

transmission is reassembled. Remove the O-ring from the top of the cam spindle boss (**Figure 39**).

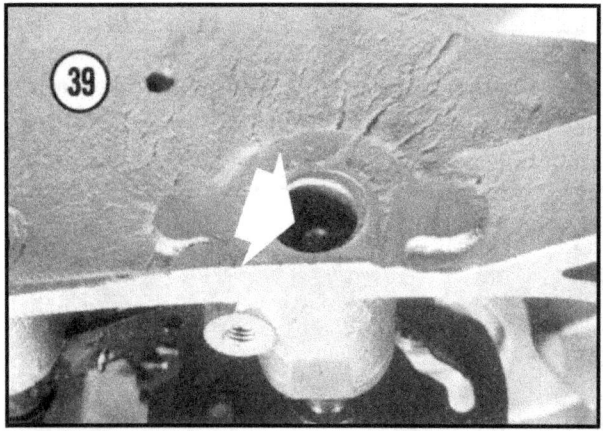

Inspection

Clean and dry all the parts thoroughly and inspect them for excessive wear. Burrs, pitting, or roughness on the teeth of a gear will cause wear on the mating gear. Defective gears should be replaced, and it's a good idea to replace the mating gear even though it may not show as much wear or damage.

Minor roughness can be cleaned up with an oilstone but there's little point in wasting time attempting to remove deep scars.

Carefully check the engagement dogs. If they are chipped, worn, or missing, the affected gear must be replaced.

Inspect the shifting forks for wear, damage, and bending. The forks should be perpendicular to the shaft.

If possible, the runout of each transmission shaft should be checked. Mount the shaft being checked in a lathe, on V-blocks, or some other suitable centering device. Place a dial indicator so that its plunger contacts a constant surface nearest the center of the shaft. Rotate the shaft and record the extremes of the dial readings. The shaft should be replaced if the runout exceeds 0.0016 inch (0.04mm).

Rotate the main shaft ball bearing assemblies by hand and check for roughness, noise, and radial play. Any bearing that is suspect should be replaced by tapping it out after the circlip has been removed (**Figures 40 and 41**). Line up the new bearing squarely with its bore and carefully tap it into place using a bearing driver or suitably sized socket set on the outer race. Don't apply any force to the inner race of the new bearing.

Examine the countershaft and sleeve gear bearing cages for cracks at the corners of the

53

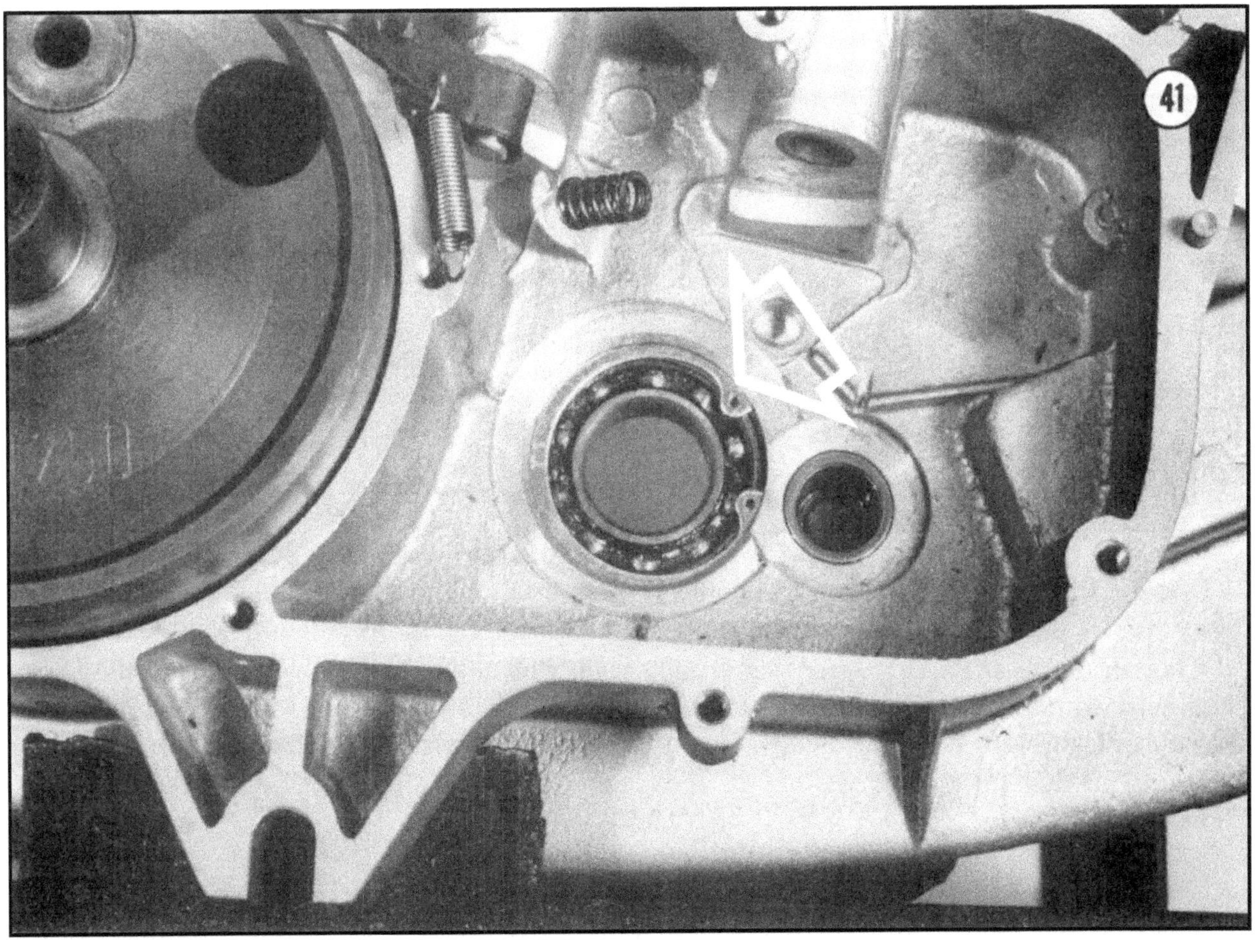

needle slots (**Figure 42**) and inspect the needles themselves for cracking and wear. Replace any bearing that is less than perfect.

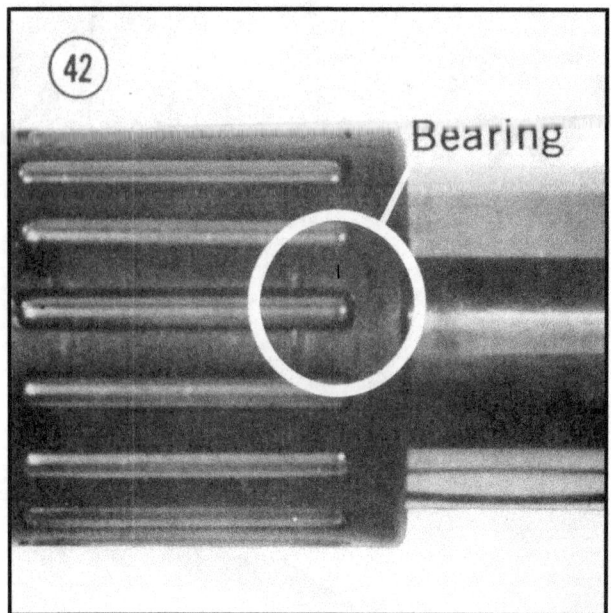

Assembly

1. Assemble the transmission by reversing the disassembly steps. Before installing the camplate, make sure the detent spring is in place (**Figure 43**).

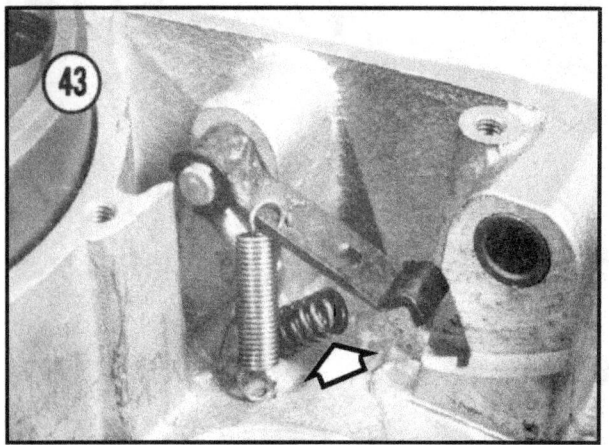

2. Grease the main shaft bearings and oil all of the needle bearings, gears, and both shafts.

3. After installing the sleeve gear, set the 3 bearings and the spacer in place in the order shown in **Figure 44**.

4. **Figures 45 and 46** are provided as reference for gear locations.

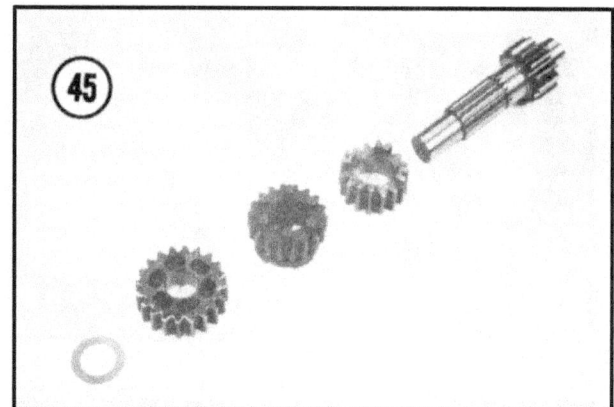

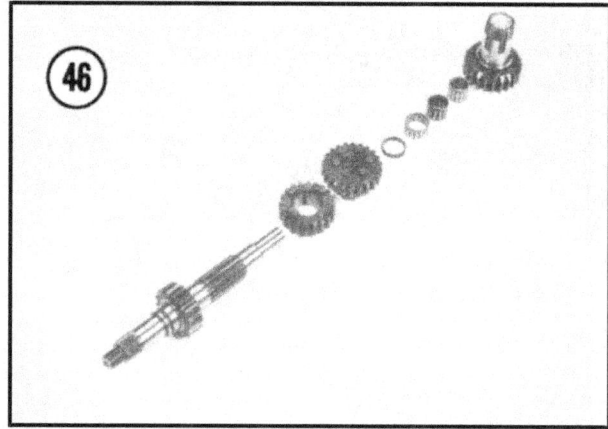

5. Refer to Chapter Four and assemble the crankcase halves. Refer to the clutch section in this chapter and install and assemble the clutch and the primary drive and install the outer cover.

6. Fill the transmission with oil and adjust the clutch as described in Chapter Two.

CHAPTER SIX

FUEL SYSTEM

For correct operation, a gasoline engine must be supplied with fuel and air mixed in proper proportions by weight. A mixture in which there is an excess of fuel is said to be rich. A lean mixture is one which contains an insufficient amount of fuel. It is the function of the carburetor to supply the correct fuel/air mixture to the engine under all operating conditions.

Maico engines are equipped with Bing carburetors. The carburetor incorporates 3 subsystems; fuel feed, main control, and idling.

CARBURETOR OPERATION

The Bing carburetor is shown in exploded view in **Figure 1**. This illustration will be helpful in identifying individual components and their relationships.

Fuel Feed System

The fuel feed system consists of the float chamber, float, and needle valve. When fuel flowing into the float chamber reaches the correct operating level it lifts the float which raises the valve needle into the valve, cutting off the flow of fuel from the fuel tank.

As the engine consumes fuel, the level in the float chamber drops, causing the float to drop which lowers the valve needle and allows additional fuel to enter the float chamber. The needle serves only as a level regulator; it cannot positively shut off the fuel flow to the carburetor. Because of the likelihood of small particles becoming lodged between the needle and its seat and holding the valve open permitting a continuous flow of fuel into the float chamber, it's important that the fuel tap on the tank be closed when the engine is shut off and the motorcycle allowed to stand.

The float chamber incorporates a tickler which can be used to depress the float and allow the chamber to fill completely for cold-engine starts. The tickler tube and a hole in the top of the float chamber serve as atmospheric vents for the float chamber. If the vent hole becomes clogged, the tickler tube will act as a vent although the engine will experience fuel starvation until the vent hole is unblocked.

Main Control System

The main control system consists of the air control slide, needle, needle jet, mixing tube, and main jet. The amount of air drawn through the carburetor and into the engine is controlled by the air slide. As the slide is lifted the air flow through the carburetor increases creating a vacuum in the carburetor bore. The vacuum siphons fuel from the float chamber through the

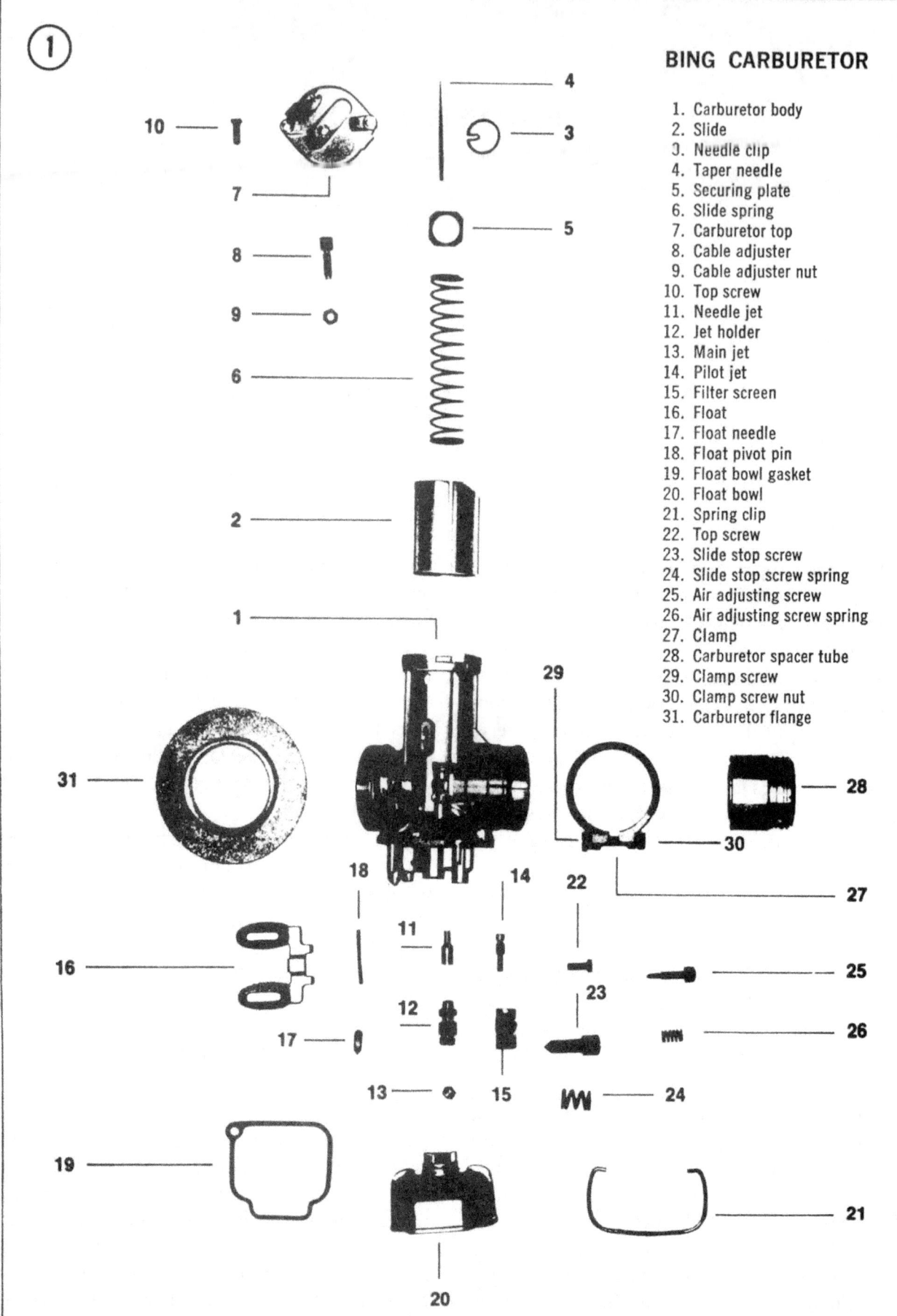

jets where it is mixed with the incoming air. A portion of the incoming air is routed into the mixing tube where it helps to atomize the fuel passing through the jets and into the main chamber.

At partial throttle settings (from ¼ to ¾ opening), fuel flow is controlled by the needle and needle jet. As the tapered needle is lifted in the needle jet, the effective flow area of the jet is increased to permit an increase of fuel flow into the incoming air stream.

At full throttle, the needle and needle jet are completely open, permitting the main jet to flow fuel at its full capacity.

Idling System

The idling system consists of an idling jet, adjustable air flow screen, and adjustable throttle stop screw.

With the air control slide closed, the vacuum in the main chamber is too low to siphon fuel through the needle jet. Air flow through the primary air hole in the bottom of the carburetor air intake passes by the air adjustment screw and through a drill-way to the idling jet where it siphons fuel from the float chamber. The main air flow through the carburetor intake mixes with the fuel from the idling jet and the resulting air/fuel mixture is consumed by the engine.

Correct idling mixture is important to efficient engine operation and it must be achieved through careful adjustment of both the slide stop position and the amount of air flow to the idling jet.

CARBURETOR SERVICING

Major carburetor service intervals depend on use. A carburetor on a motorcycle that is used principally for trail riding will usually not require attention for several hundred miles. At the extreme, for a motorcycle that is used weekly in rigorous competition, the carburetor should be serviced more frequently to ensure it is always in top working order.

The disassembly, inspection, service, and reassembly procedures presented require that the carburetor be removed from the engine. The adjustments are carried out with the carburetor installed.

Removal and Disassembly

1. Shut off the fuel taps and disconnect the line at the carburetor.

2. Remove the cover screws (**Figure 2**) and pull out the spring, slide, and needle assembly. Note the position of the retaining plate with regard to the notches on the needle and disassemble the cable, spring, cap, needle, and slide.

3. Loosen the screws in the clamping bands (**Figure 3**). Slide the intake bellows off the carburetor and remove the carburetor from engine.

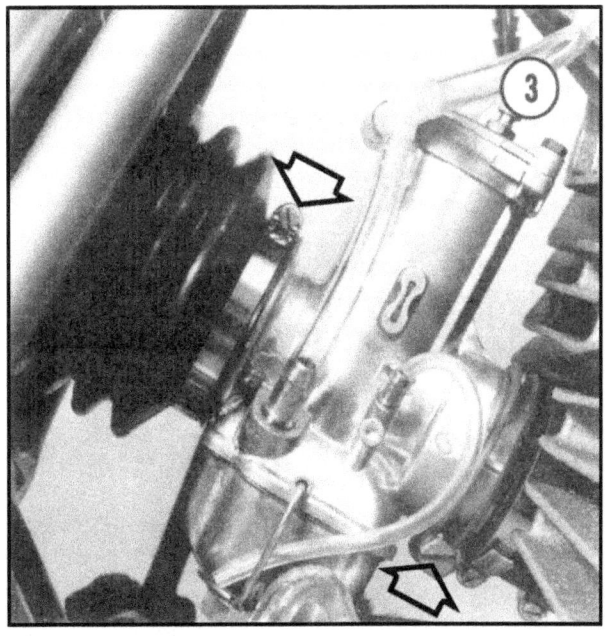

4. Unscrew the air adjusting screw and throttle stop screw (**Figure 4**).

5. Press the float chamber retaining clip forward

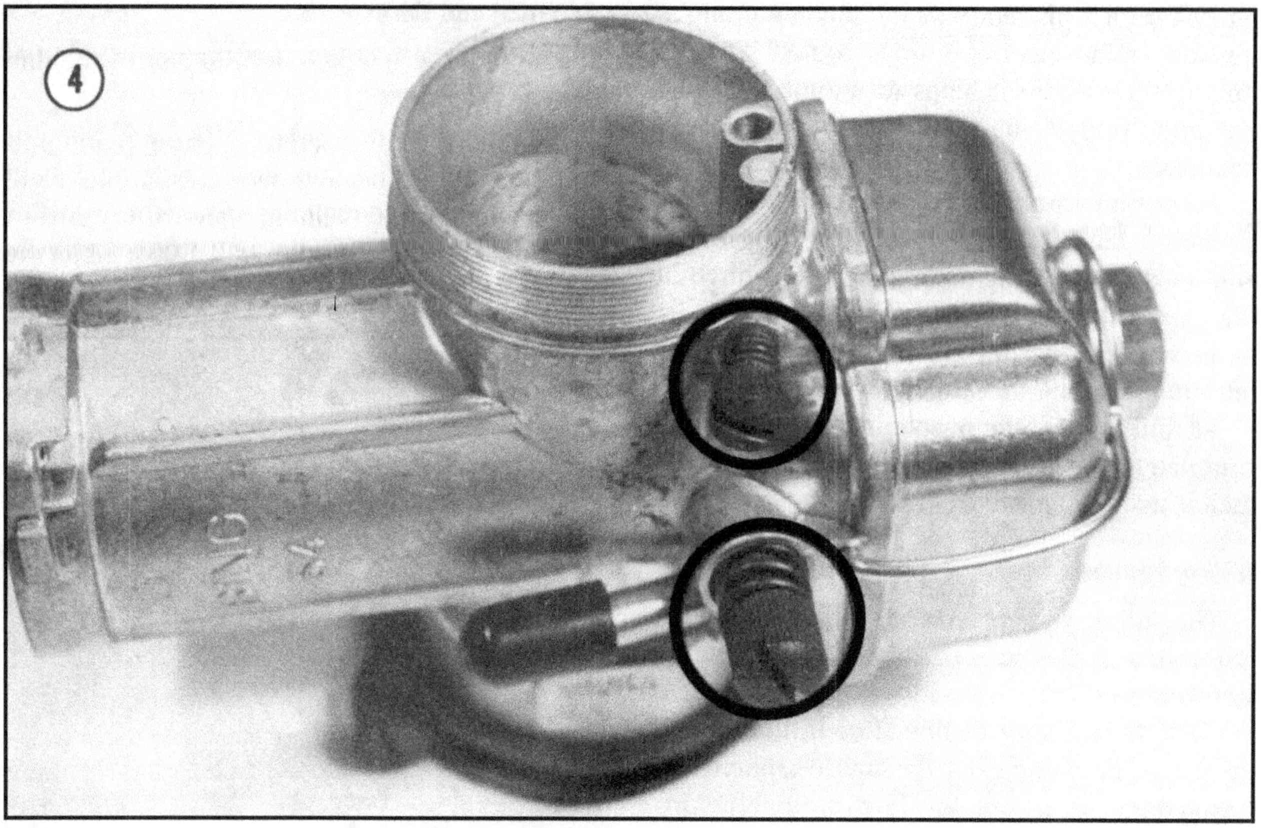

with your thumbs and remove the float chamber (**Figure 5**).

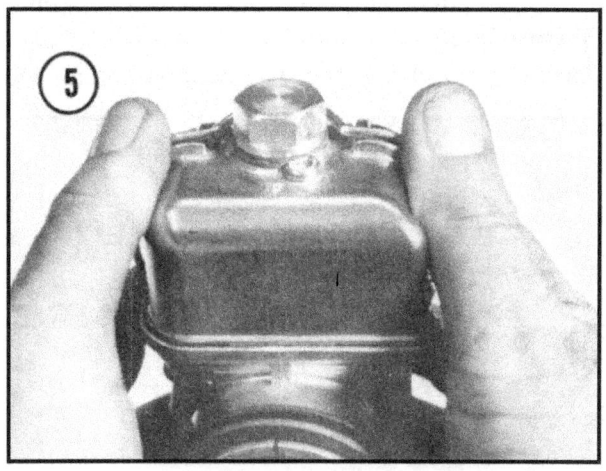

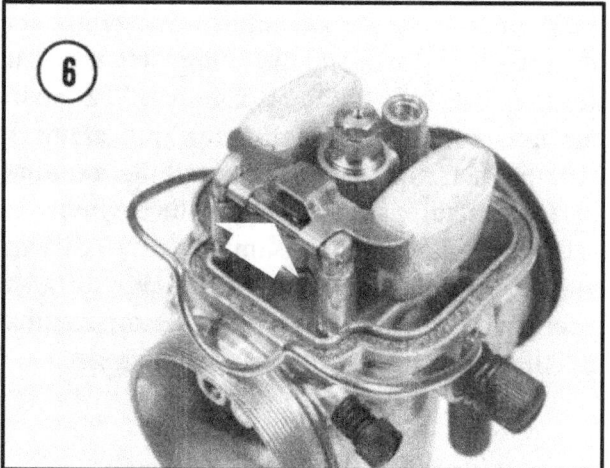

6. Slide the float hinge pin out to the side with a pair of needle-nose pliers and remove the float and needle valve (**Figure 6**).

7. Unscrew the main jet, mixing tube, and idling jet, noting their locations for reference during reassembly (**Figure 7**).

8. Unscrew the fuel hose nipple (**Figure 8**).

Cleaning and Inspection

1. Thoroughly clean and dry all parts. If a special carburetor cleaning solution is used, the float, top-cap, O-ring, and gaskets should be omitted from the bath and cleaned separately in common solvent.

2. Blow out all the passages and jets with compressed air. Don't use wire to clean any of the orifices; wire will enlarge them.

3. Check the cone of the float needle and replace it if it is scored or pitted. Also, the spring-loaded ball in the bottom of the needle should move freely in and out of its bore.

4. If the float is all brass, shake it to determine if there is any fuel in it. If there is, replace it with a new float.

5. Check the slide for scoring and galling, and if it's excessive, replace the slide.

6. Check the top-cap O-ring and replace it if it's damaged or shows signs of deterioration.

Reassembly

The carburetor is assembled by reversing the order of disassembly. The jets should be tight but be careful not to strip the threads. The float chamber gasket and the sealing ring on the fuel hose nipple should be replaced with new ones.

With the float needle valve and float reinstalled, check the float level by inverting the carburetor on a level surface. With the needle fully seated in the valve bore, the bottom of the float should be parallel to the mating surface of the float chamber as shown in **Figure 9**. The ball in the bottom of the float needle should not be compressed into the needle. If necessary, the float level can be corrected by carefully bending the brass tab on the float.

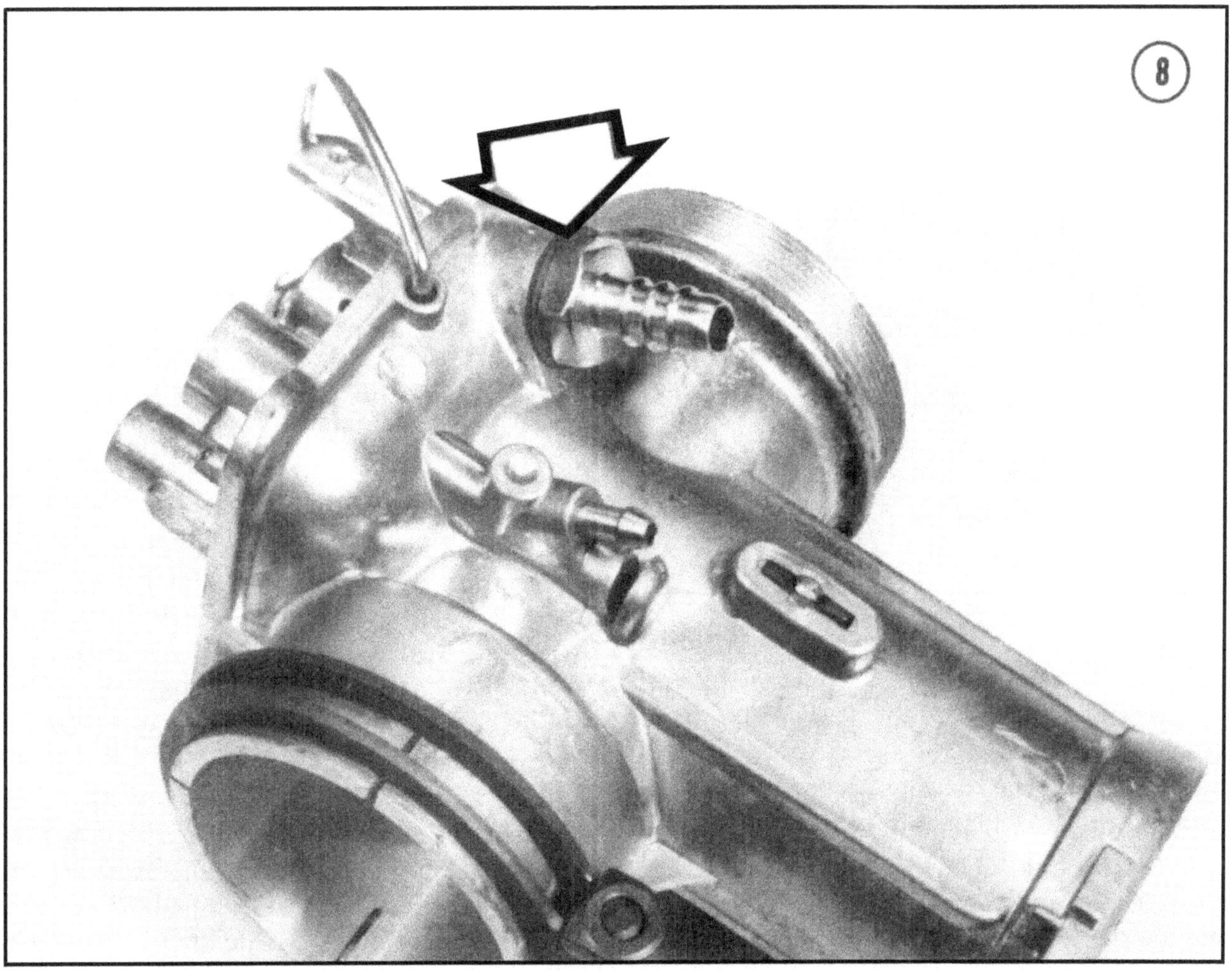

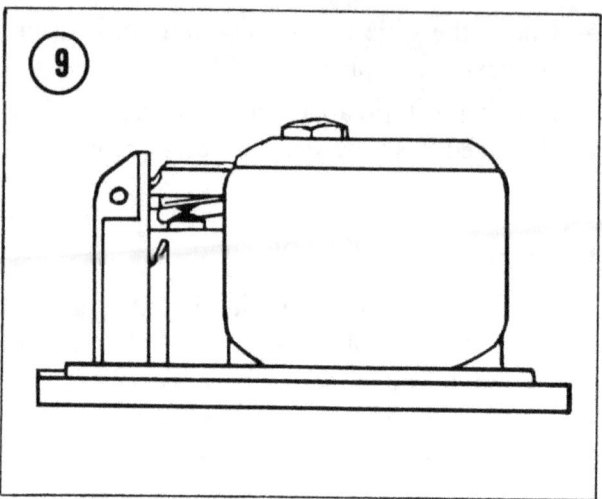

NOTE: *Late-model carburetors are fitted with an anti-surge screen at the bottom of the main jet (Figure 10). This device entraps gas around the main jet to prevent fuel starvation and surging when the motorcycle is operated at moderate and high speeds over undulating terrain. It's recommended that the screen be fitted in place of the flat washer on the main jet of earlier carburetors.*

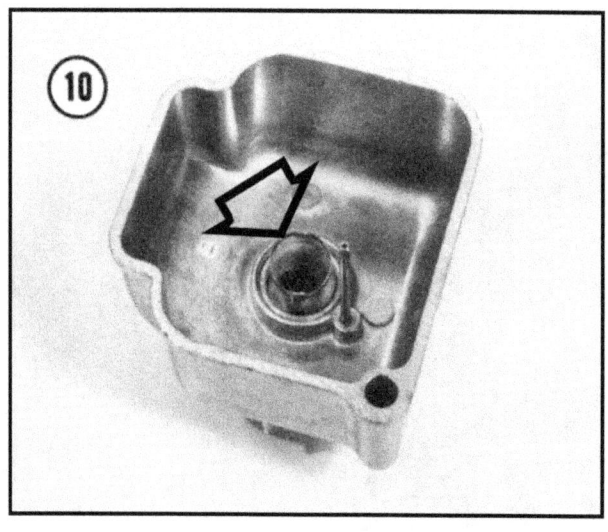

When installing the slide assembly in the carburetor body, make sure the needle is seated in the needle jet and that the movement of the slide with cap and ring installed is smooth throughout the length of the slide's travel.

Reinstall the carburetor on the engine, reconnect the control cable and fuel line, and reconnect intake bellows between the carburetor and air cleaner.

Carburetor Adjustment

Carburetor adjustments should be made with the engine warmed up to operating temperature.

1. Adjust the free-play in the throttle cable by turning the adjuster screw on the top of the carburetor in or out until the cable sheath can be pulled out of the carburetor top about 0.039 inch (1.0mm).

2. With the engine running, screw in the throttle stop screw (**Figure 11**) until engine speed increases slightly with throttle completely closed.

3. Screw in the air adjustment screw (**Figure 12**) until the engine falters and then screw it out until the engine begins to run smoothly (about ½ turn). The basic settings should be 1½-2 turns out from the point at which the screw bottoms.

4. Slowly unscrew the throttle stop screw to bring the engine to its lowest idle speed. For competition use it's recommended that very little or no idling occur with the throttle closed.

AIR FILTER

There are 2 basic types of air filters used on Maico-engine motorcycles—micronic paper element and oil-wetted foam. Service on both units is presented in Chapter Two.

FUEL TANK

The fuel tank should be removed from the motorcycle and cleaned after every 3 or 4 races or each couple of months. Close the fuel tap and disconnect the line at the carburetor. Remove the tank from the motorcycle and discard the fuel that is in it. Pour about a pint of clean fuel (without oil) into the tank, install the cap, slosh the fuel around for about a minute, and pour it out.

Remove the fuel taps from the tank, disassemble them and clean them in gasoline. Check the gaskets on the taps and replace them if they are damaged or excessively compressed. Reassemble the taps and install them in the tank. Reinstall the tank on the motorcycle and connect the fuel lines. Partially fill the tank with fresh fuel/oil mixture and check for leaks around the tap and at the line connections. Tighten tap if necessary.

61

CHAPTER SEVEN

ELECTRICAL SYSTEM

Two basic systems are used on Maico engines: an ignition only magneto, and a magneto-generator with charging and lighting coils. Both types are flywheel-mounted systems with mechanical contact breakers. This chapter includes repair and replacement procedures for both systems.

MAGNETO IGNITION SYSTEM

A magneto is a mechanically driven alternating current generator which produces the electrical enegry required to fire the spark plug. On models equipped with lights, additional coils in the magneto produce the energy required to charge the battery and power the lights.

Magneto Operation

Figure 1 illustrates a typical contact-breaker magneto ignition system. As the flywheel rotates, magnets located in the flywheel move past a stationary ignition source coil inducing a current in the coil. A contact breaker, controlled by a cam attached to the crankshaft, opens at the precise instant the piston reaches its firing position. The energy produced in the source coil is then discharged to the primary side of the high-voltage ignition coil where it is increased, or stepped up to a voltage high enough to jump the gap between the spark plug electrodes.

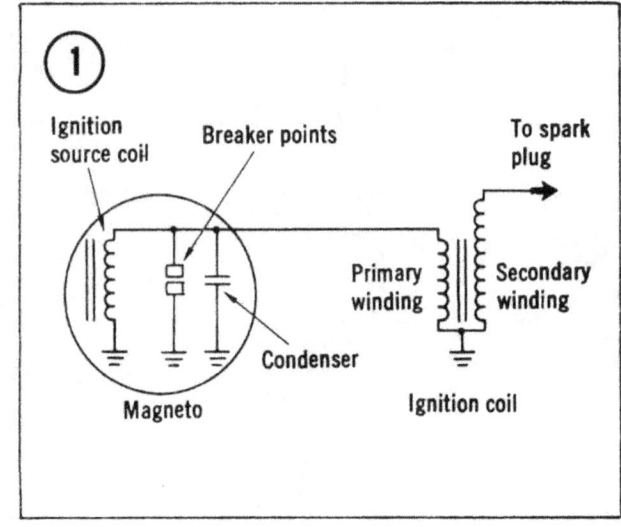

Breaker Points

The contact breaker for Maico ignition systems is shown in **Figure 2**. During normal operation, the contact surfaces of the points gradually burn and erode away. If the points are not badly pitted, they can be dressed with a few strokes from a point file. Never use sandpaper or emery cloth for dressing the contacts; for maximum efficiency, the contact surfaces must be flat and parallel, and sandpaper will round off the edges of the contacts and create the sort of condition you are attempting to correct (see **Figure 3**). If a few strokes won't correct the contact surfaces, replace the breaker assembly.

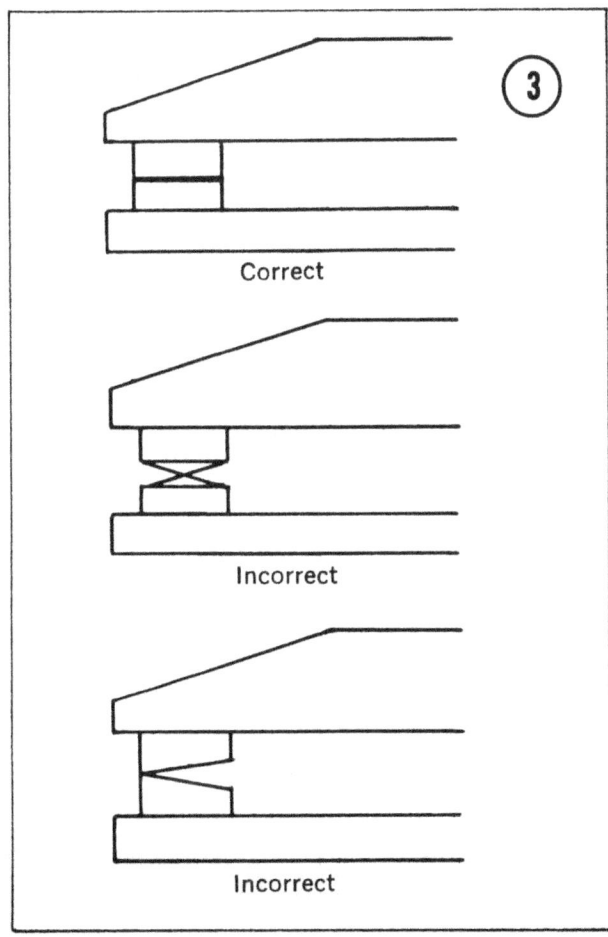

NOTE: *Always remove the contact breaker assembly before dressing the contacts. The time spent removing, reinstalling, and adjusting the points is preferable to risking small particles finding their way into the magneto.*

Oil or dirt may get on the contacts, creating electrical resistance in them or resulting in their failure. These conditions can be caused by a defective crankshaft seal, incorrect breaker cam lubricant, or dirt getting into the magneto when the outer cover is removed. To correct any of these conditions, remove the contact breaker assembly and dress the contacts, clean the assembly in contact cleaner, lacquer thinner, or acetone and lubricate the breaker cam with contact breaker lubricant. Never use oil or common grease; they break down under high temperature and frictional load and are likely to find their way to the contacts.

A weak breaker spring will allow the points to bounce at high engine speeds and cause misfiring. Usually, however, the spring will last for the life of the contacts.

Close the contacts on a piece of clean white paper, such as a business card, and pull it through the contacts. Continue to do this until no discoloration or residue remains on the card. Finally, rotate the engine and watch the contacts as they open and close. If they do not meet squarely, and the condition cannot be corrected by shimming or carefully bending the movable contact, replace them.

Contact Breaker Replacement

1. Remove the right-side cover as discussed in Chapter Four.
2. Unscrew the nut (1, **Figure 4**) and disconnect the leads. Note the location of the insulating washers (2). In addition, there is an insulating collar located inside the post. These 3 pieces must be installed correctly during reassembly to prevent the contacts from shorting to ground. Unscrew the contact lock/mounting screw (3) and remove the contact breaker assembly.
3. Reverse the above steps to install a new breaker assembly. Grease the pivot shaft with contact breaker lubricant (Bosch Ft 1 v4 or an equivalent) before installing the breaker arm. Apply contact breaker lubricant to the groove in the rubbing portion of the arm. Be sure the terminals are clean and tight and that there is no oil or grease between the contact carrier and the stator baseplate.

Condenser Replacement

The condenser should be routinely replaced with the points. Unsolder the condenser leads and remove the 2 screws from the condenser mounting bracket (**Figure 5**). Set the new condenser in place and install the screws. Resolder the leads.

Ignition Timing

Contact gap, 0.012-0.016 inch (0.3-0.4mm), on the Maico ignition is self setting when the

ignition is correctly timed, provided the contacts are not worn or eroded beyond the service limit.

1. Remove the spark plug from the cylinder and rotate the crankshaft to line up the scribe on the rotor with the center of the inspection hole (**Figure 6**). If the "E" gap of the ignition is correct, the rotor scribe will be centered in the stator hole just as the points begin to open. If not, loosen the stator mounting bolts and carefully rotate the stator—without moving the rotor—until the aligment is correct. Then tighten the stator mounting bolts securely.

> NOTE: *Correct "E" gap is essential in that it represents the precise point at which the electrical energy from the magneto primary is the most intense.*

2. Screw a timing gauge into the spark plug hole in the head and connect a continuity light to the contact breaker (**Figure 7**).

3. Rotate the crankshaft clockwise to bring the piston to correct position specified in **Table 1**, as shown by the timing gauge.

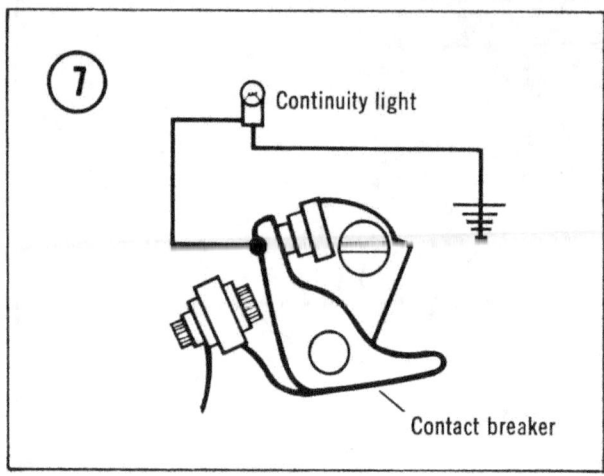

Table 1 FIRING POINT

Model	Firing Point, BTDC
250cc	2.75-3.0mm (0.108-0.118 in.)
360cc	3.5-3.8mm (0.138-0.150 in.)
400cc	3.8-4.0mm (0.150-0.158 in.)
450cc	3.5mm (0.138 in.)
501cc	3.5-3.8mm (0.138-0.150 in.)

4. Loosen the lock screw in the fixed contact (**Figure 8**) and move the plate so that the points just begin to open (indicated by the continuity light going out). When the firing point has been set, tighten the lock screw and double check the adjustment by slowly rocking the crankshaft back-and-forth over the firing point as shown on the gauge. Each time the piston reaches the firing point with the crankshaft rotated clockwise, the continuity light should go out. If necessary, repeat the adjustment procedure until it is absolutely correct.

5. When the "E" gap and firing point have been adjusted, rotate crankshaft slowly to bring contacts to their widest opening and check their serviceability with a flat feeler gauge. The contact gap should be 0.012-0.016 in. (0.3-0.4mm).

Ignition Coil

The ignition coil is a step-up transformer which increases the low voltage produced by the magneto to a high voltage required to jump the spark plug gap. The only service required is periodic inspection of the electrical leads to make sure they are clean and tight, and checking to see that the coil is mounted securely.

If the condition of the coil is in doubt, there are several checks which should be made.

1. Using an ohmmeter, measure the resistance between the primary wire and ground as shown in **Figure 9**. Resistance should be about 1 ohm.
2. Measure the resistance between the high tension lead and ground as shown in **Figure 10**. It should be 3,000 ohms.

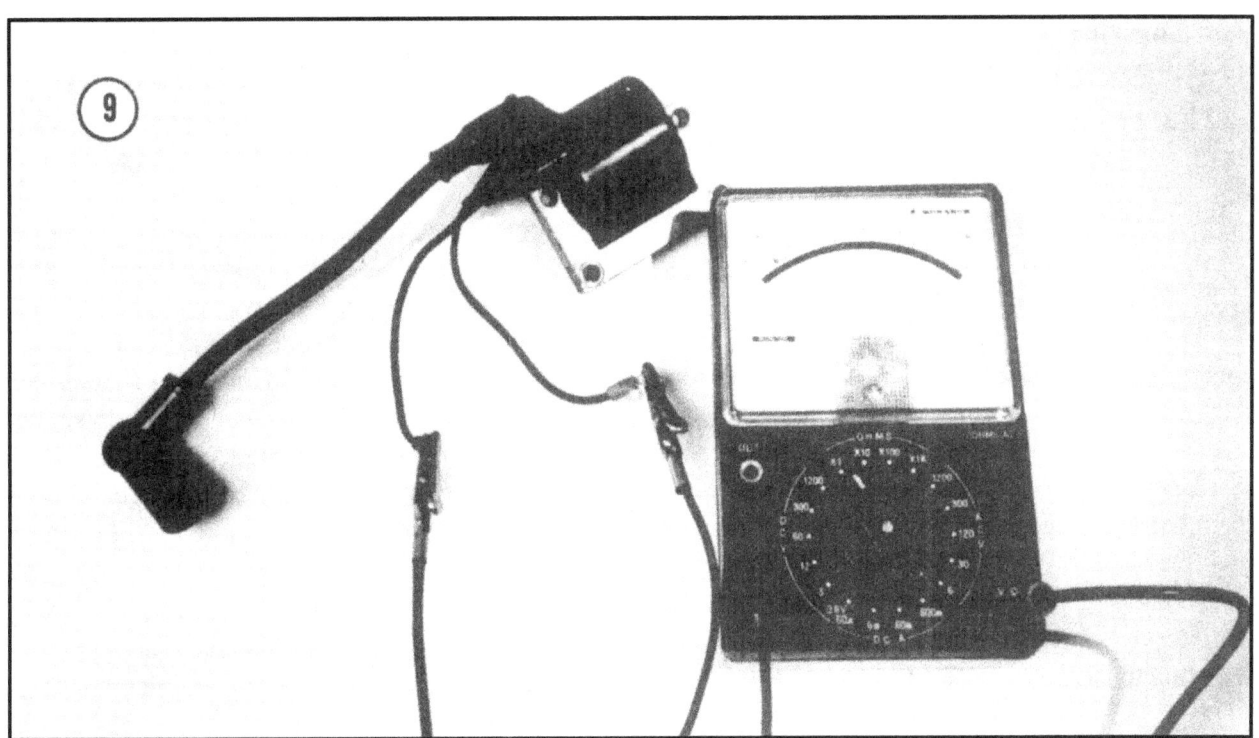

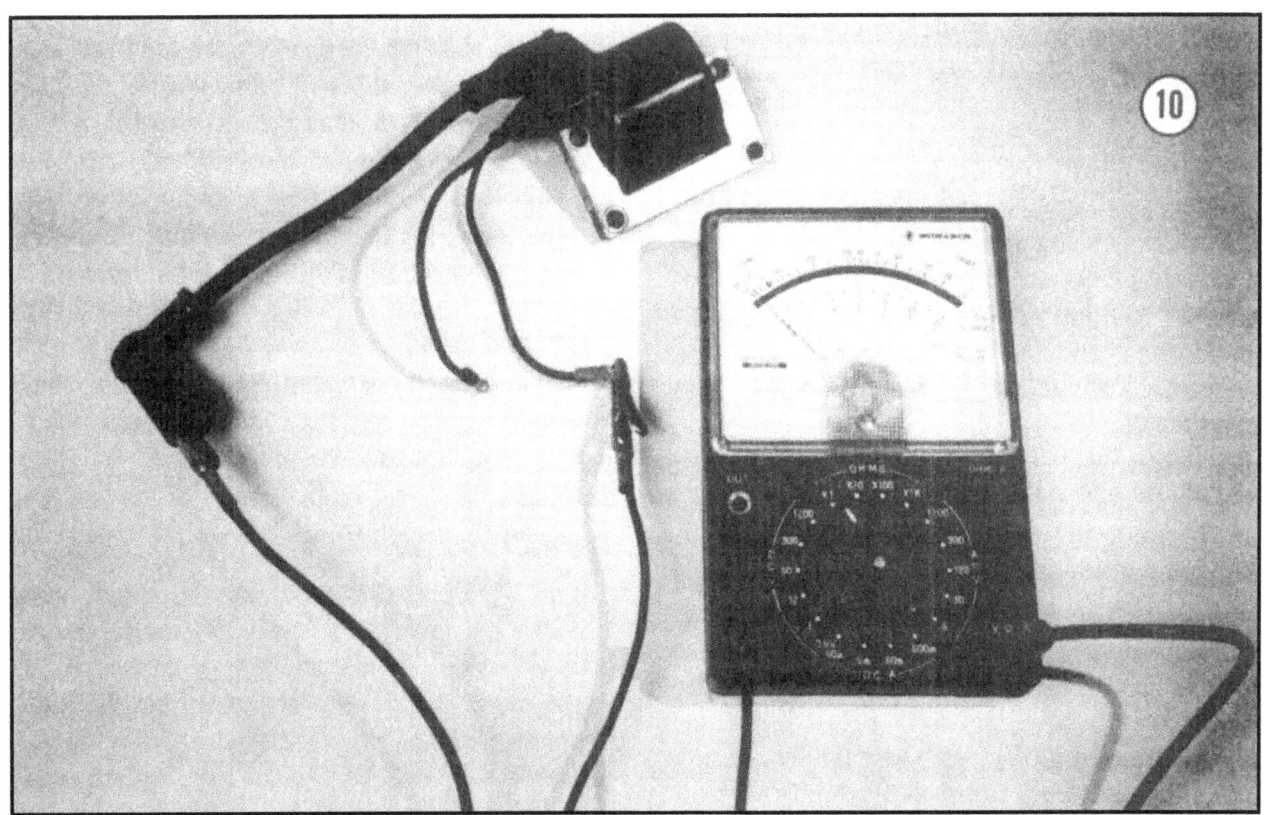

3. If the meter indicates an open circuit (no continuity) in Step 2, unplug the high tension lead from the coil and connect the test lead directly to the post in the coil. If the resistance is now correct, the trouble is in the high tension lead. It may be a bad connection at the spark plug cap or an internal break in the wire. Make sure the connection is good and check the lead for continuity, and if an open cricuit is still indicated, replace the high tension lead. However, if an open circuit is indicated between the primary and high tension leads of the coil itself, the coil is defective and must be replaced.

Condenser

The condenser requires no service other than checking to see that its connections are clean and tight. It should be routinely replaced each time the contact breaker is replaced (see *Condenser Replacement*). To test the condenser, connect it to a battery—negative to negative, positive to positive—and allow it to charge for a few seconds. Then quickly disconnect it and touch one condenser lead to the other. If there is a spark, the condenser may be assumed to be all right.

Troubleshooting

The magneto is a simple device which should give little trouble. If problems are suspected, perform the following checks with all the wiring disconnected.

1. Block the contact breaker open with a business card or similar piece of paper.
2. Disconnect both of the contact leads and, with an ohmmeter set at its highest range, check that the movable breaker is not shorted to ground. If the ohmmeter registers at all, replace the points.
3. Check the condenser and replace it if there is any doubt about its condition.
4. Examine the armature coils for chafing and check them individually for shorts and continuity. Replace any coils that are faulty (see *Electrical System Testing*).
5. Check the flywheel for cracks or movement at the point where the cam is pressed into it. If the cam moves, the "E" gap (which ensures maximum energy from the primary ignition pulse) will not be correct and the flywheel must be replaced.

LIGHTING/CHARGING SYSTEM (ENDURO MODELS)

The lighting/charging system on Maico Enduro models incorporates a battery as well as headlight, taillight, stoplight, and horn. A typical system is shown schematically in **Figure 11**.

Service of the lighting/charging system is simple and straightforward; however, a volt-ohmmeter is required to determine minimum performance standards and is extremely helpful in isolating trouble. Before any electrical system work is undertaken, it's important that the battery be at full operation capacity.

The generator is rated to maintain the battery at an acceptable charge level and power the lights under normal service conditions. However, it's incapable of fully restoring the charge level of a weak battery.

Battery

The battery is the heart of the electrical system. Its condition can greatly affect the performance of the rest of the electrical system. It should be checked regularly—at least each time the motorcycle is ridden—to make sure the electrolyte level is correct, the connections are clean and tight, and case is not damaged in any way.

If the motorcycle has been sitting for a long period of time prior to being ridden, or if tests are to be conducted on the electrical system, the charge level of the battery should be checked with a hydrometer and corrected if necessary.

Battery Testing

1. Clean the top of the battery and the terminals with a solution of baking soda and water, flushing the residue away with clear water.
2. Check the level of the electrolyte. It should be about 0.24 inch (6mm) above the top of the plates. Top up any cells that are low with distilled water; never add electrolyte to a battery that has been in service.
3. Measure the specific gravity of the electrolyte with a hydrometer. To use the hydrometer, squeeze the rubber bulb, insert the tip of the hydrometer into one of the battery cells and

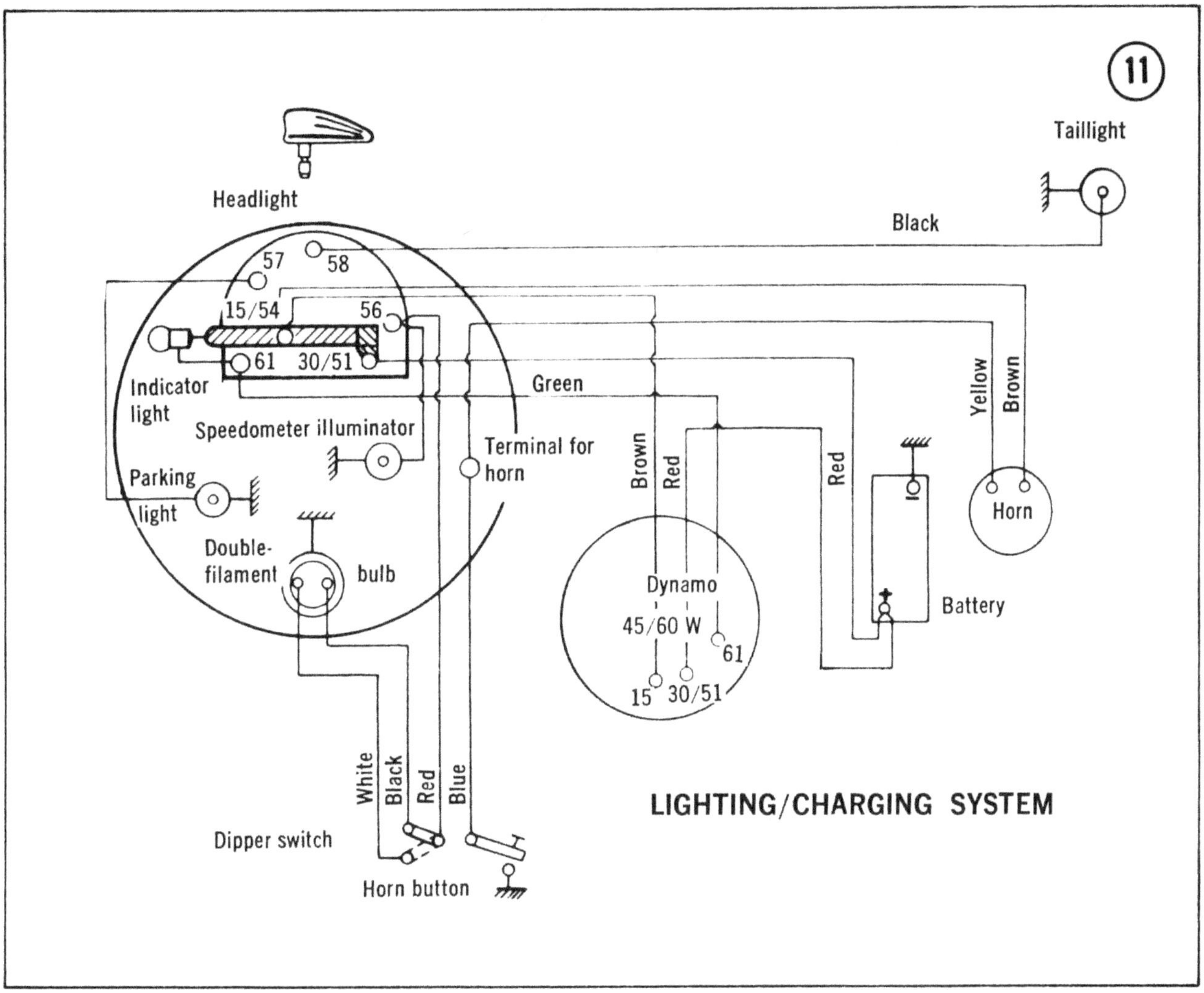

LIGHTING/CHARGING SYSTEM (Figure 11)

release the bulb. Draw enough electrolyte out of the cell to float the weighted float inside the hydrometer. Read the hydrometer as shown in **Figure 12**. This is the specific gravity for the cell being tested. When you have made your reading, return the electrolyte to the cell from which it was taken and check the next cell.

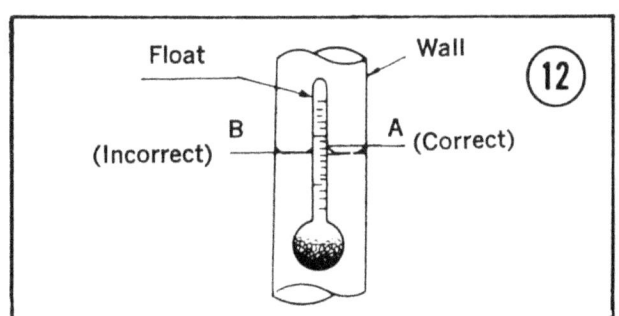

Generally, the specific gravity should be between 1.26 and 1.28. If it is less than 1.225, the battery should be charged.

Charging

A trickle charger is recommended for restoring a low-voltage battery. Most inexpensive automotive type chargers have a charging rate between 2 and 6 amperes.

A "quick charge" should never be applied to a fully discharged battery, and only seldom to one that's partially discharged; the heat resulting from a quick charge is harmful to the battery.

WARNING
During charging, highly explosive hydrogen gas is released from the battery. The battery should be charged only in a well-ventilated area, and open flames should be kept away. Never check the charge of a battery by arcing across the terminals; the resulting spark can ignite the hydrogen gas.

1. Connect the positive charger lead to the positive battery terminal, and the negative lead to the

negative terminal. Reversing the leads can result in damage to both the charger and the battery.

2. Remove the vent caps from the battery, select 6 volts on the charger, and switch it on. The battery should remain on charger for about 10 hours, and not less than 8 if it is to receive a full charge. If the output of the charger is adjustable, it's best to select a low setting—1½ to 2 amps.

3. After a suitable charging period (8 to 10 hours), switch off the charger, disconnect the battery, and check the specific gravity. It should be within 1.26 to 1.28. If it is, and if after an hour's time the reading is the same, the battery is charged.

Battery Installation

1. Make sure battery terminals, cable clamps, and case are free of corrosion. Check the rubber pad in the battery case and replace it if it is excessively compressed or rotted.

2. Install the battery in reverse order of removal. Be careful to route the vent tube so that it is not crimped. Connect the positive terminal first, then the negative terminal. Don't overtighten the clamp bolts, but make them snug enough so the clamps can't be rotated on the terminals.

3. Coat the terminals with a silicon spray, or Vaseline, to retard decomposition of the lead.

Electrical System Testing

1. Refer to Figure 11 and check the wiring and connectors to be sure they are correctly connected and tight.

2. Check fuses and replace any that are blown.

3. Connect a DC voltmeter to the battery (positive to positive, negative to negative) and record the reading.

4. Start the engine and run it at about 1,500 rpm. Turn on the headlight. If the generator is operating correctly, the meter should indicate from 1-1½ volts higher than it did in Step 3. In such case, no further testing of the generator is necessary.

If the meter reading is unsatisfactory, and if all the connections are clean and tight, the lighting/charging coil in the generator can be assumed to be faulty and should be replaced. When a new coil has been installed, repeat each of the tests to confirm that the system is operating correctly.

FAULT TRACING

Refer to the system schematics (Figure 1, Motocross, and Figure 11, Enduro) for electrical system fault tracing. Continuity checks using an ohmmeter should be performed between each pair of connections and terminals so that any system faults can be isolated.

CHAPTER EIGHT

FRONT SUSPENSION, AND STEERING

The front suspension is a spring-controlled telescopic fork with oil damping on compression and rebound. Damping characteristics depend to a great extent on damping oil viscosity. Handling characteristics can be altered appreciably by a change from one weight oil to another. Chapter Two explains changing damping oil.

If the fork legs contain the correct amount of a recommended weight oil and the damping is inadequate, check seals for wear or damage.

FORKS

Fork Seal Replacement

The only service operation normally required on the front suspension is seal replacement. Seals may be replaced without removing the fork tubes from the clamps.

1. Support the motorcycle on a workstand or block so that the front wheel is off the ground.
2. Disconnect the brake cable from the arm and remove it from the backing plate (**Figure 1**). Remove brake anchor nut from the backing plate.
3. Loosen the pinch bolt on the axle side, unscrew the axle (**Figure 2**), and pull it out of the wheel and the forks. There is no need to loosen the pinch bolt on the nut side.
4. Pull the wheel out of the forks, noting the location of spacers and seals.

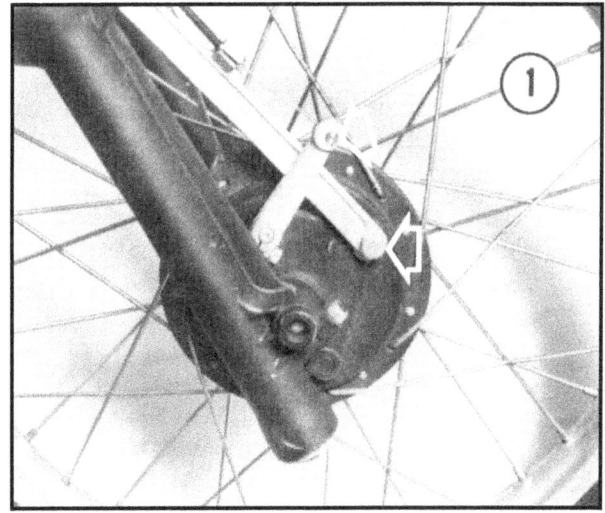

5. Place a drip pan beneath one of the fork legs and unscrew the large bottom plug. Allow the leg to drain. Loosen the lower clamp screw on the fork boot (**Figure 3**).
6. Attach a tie-down strap between the handlebar and the axle mounting lug on the fork slider and draw the slider up against spring pressure to expose the damper rod. Grip the damper rod with Vise Grips and unscrew the bottom plug (**Figure 4**). Release the strap and pull the slider down off the tube. The sliders should be removed, serviced, and reinstalled one at a time to prevent mixing of the parts.
7. Carefully pry the seal out of the top of the

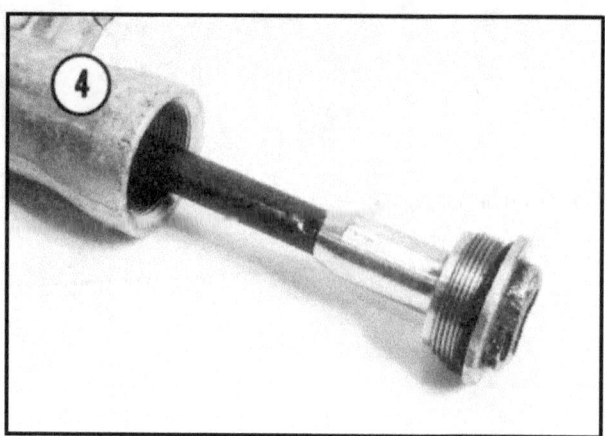

slider (**Figure 5**). A simple protector (**Figure 6**) which will prevent damage to the top of the seal bore can be made from a strip of aluminum. Flush the slider with clean solvent.

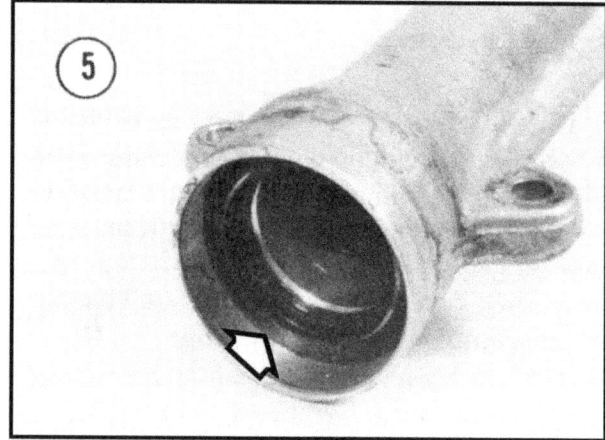

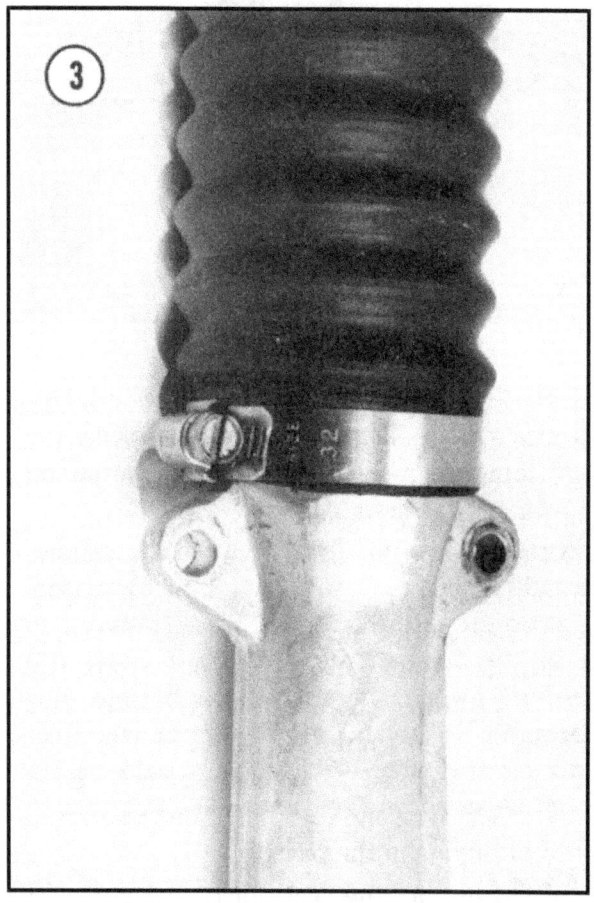

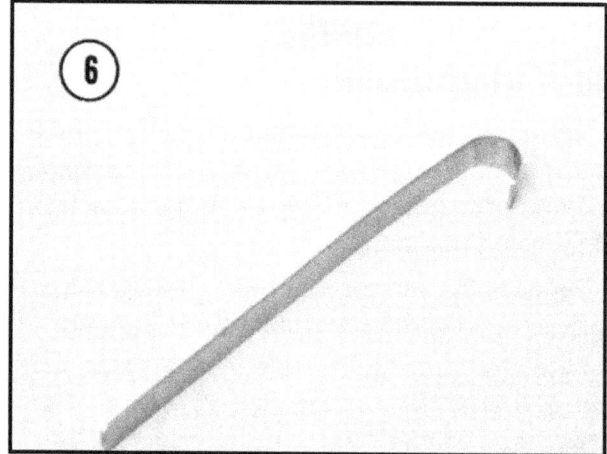

8. Wipe the seal bore to remove any foreign matter or fragments of seal rubber and press in a new seal, open end down, using a suitably sized socket as a driver. Set the spring contact washer on top of the seal.

NOTE: *Service life of the new seals can be extended by setting the old seals on top of the new ones; they work as wipers and will keep a lot of dirt out of the new seals.*

9. Lightly oil the fork tube and install the slider. Pull it up against spring pressure and screw the bottom plug onto the damper rod. Release the slider and screw the bottom plug into it and tighten it securely.

10. Repeat the procedure for the other fork leg. Reinstall the front wheel. Fill the forks with damping oil and adjust the front brake. See Chapter Two.

Fork Damper Service

The fork damper assemblies rarely require service other than changing oil. However, if the fork legs contain the correct amount and grade of damping oil, seals are in good condition, yet damping is inadequate, the damper pistons may be worn or scored. Remove damper assemblies, inspect them, and replace any parts that are unserviceable.

1. Refer to *Changing Fork Seals* and remove the sliders.

2. Remove the circlip from the bottom of one of the fork tubes (**Figure 7**) and pull out the damper assembly. The dampers should be serviced one at a time to prevent mixing the parts.

3. Thoroughly clean and dry the damper assembly. Check the pistons for signs of wear and galling (**Figure 8**). If one or both pistons are unsatisfactory, replace them.

4. Carefully clamp the damper in a vise fitted with jaw protectors. Tighten the vise enough to prevent the damper from rotating but not so tight to collapse it. Remove the cotter key and unscrew the castellated nut (**Figure 9**).

5. Remove the washer, piston, circlip, spring, valve plate, valve, and bottom piston. Replace the defective parts with new ones and reassemble the damper assembly.

6. Thoroughly clean the inside of the fork tube

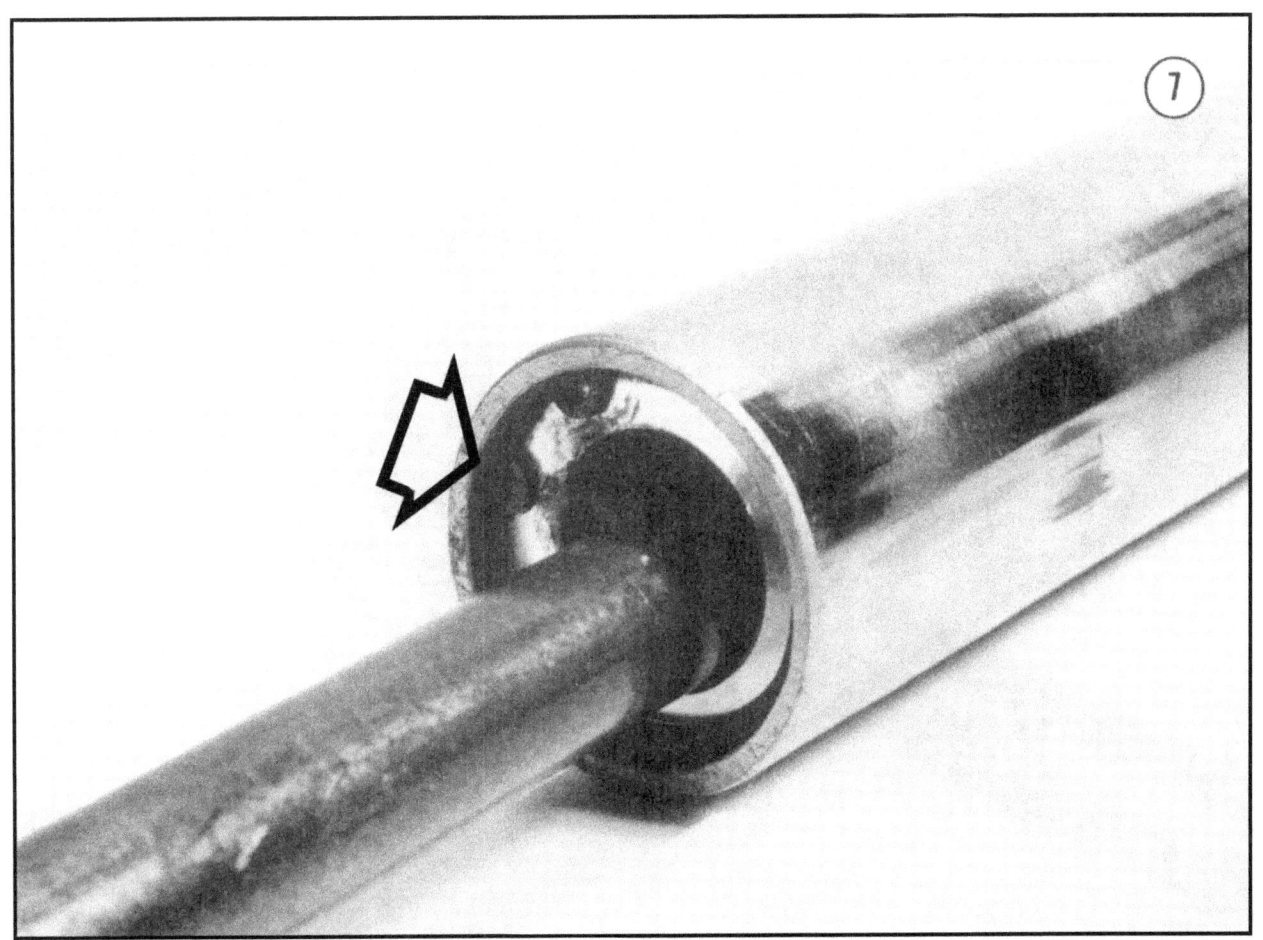

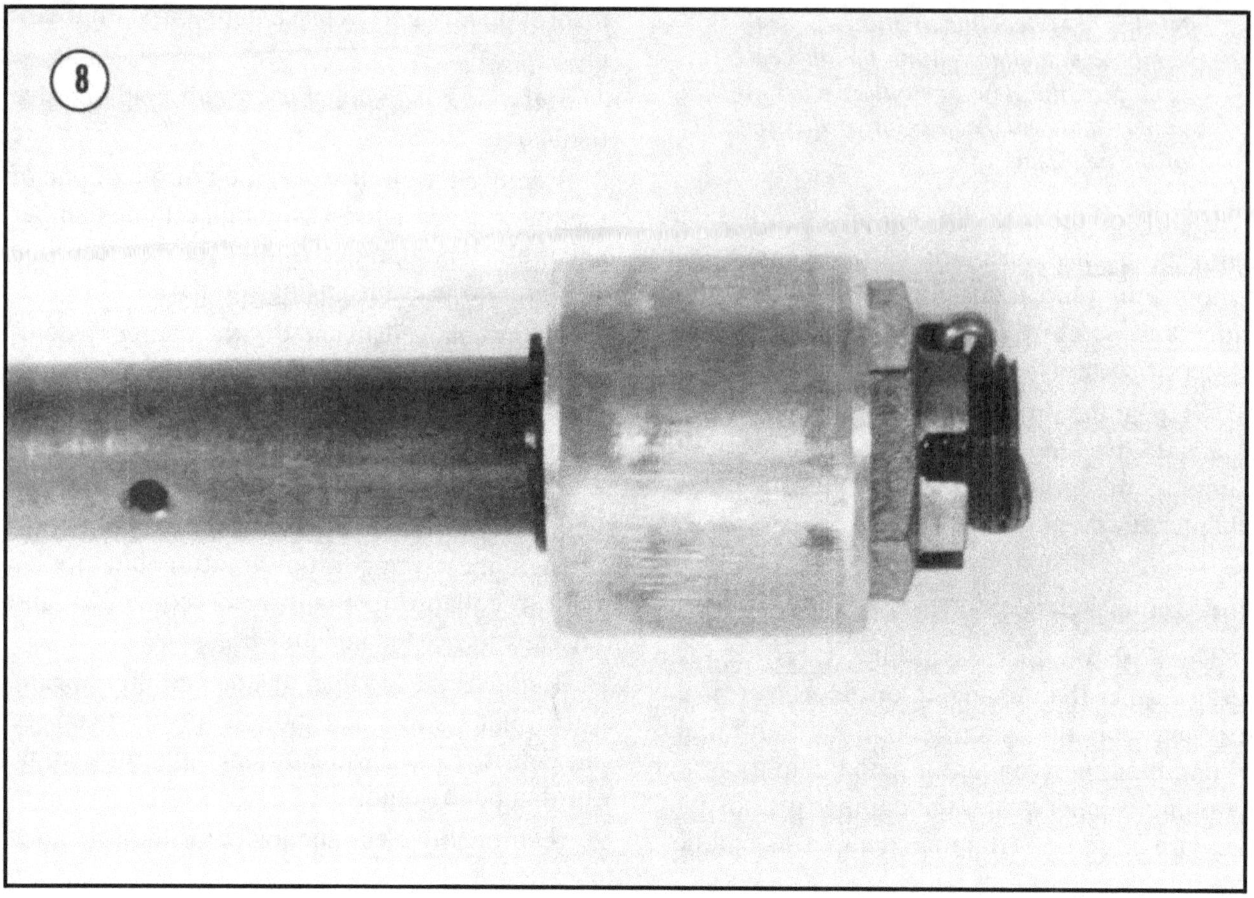

74

and lightly oil it. Reinstall the damper assembly in the tube and fit the circlip securely in the groove at the bottom. Rotate the clip with the end of a small screwdriver to make sure it is seated all the way around.

7. Remove and service the other damper in the same manner. Reassemble the suspension and install the wheel. See *Fork Seal Replacement*.

Fork Tube Replacement

If the fork tube is bent or a slider is dented, replace the affected components. Never attempt to straighten a tube; bending and straightening severly weakens it and makes it prone to failure.

1. Refer to *Fork Seal Replacement* and *Fork Damper Service* and remove sliders, dampers, and springs from the fork tubes.

2. Loosen the pinch bolts in the top and bottom fork clamps (**Figure 10**) and pull the tubes down and out of the clamps.

3. If bending damage is suspected but not readily apparent, support the fork tube in a lathe, V-blocks, or another suitable centering device and check it with a dial indicator (**Figure 11**). If the runout (bending) is greater than 0.0039 inch (0.1mm), the fork tube should be replaced.

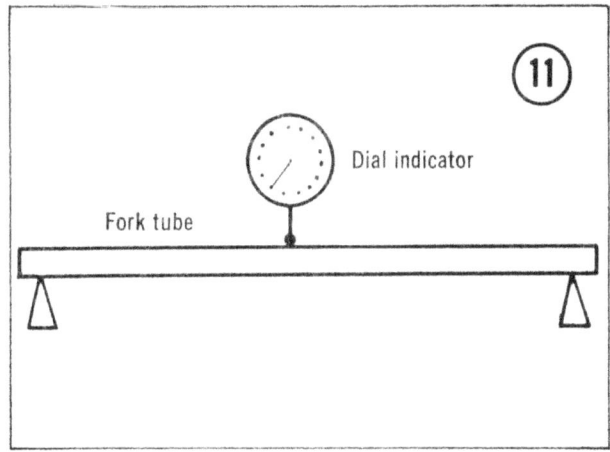

4. Install the fork tubes in the clamps and tighten only the pinch bolts in the bottom clamp. Refer to the earlier procedures in this chapter,

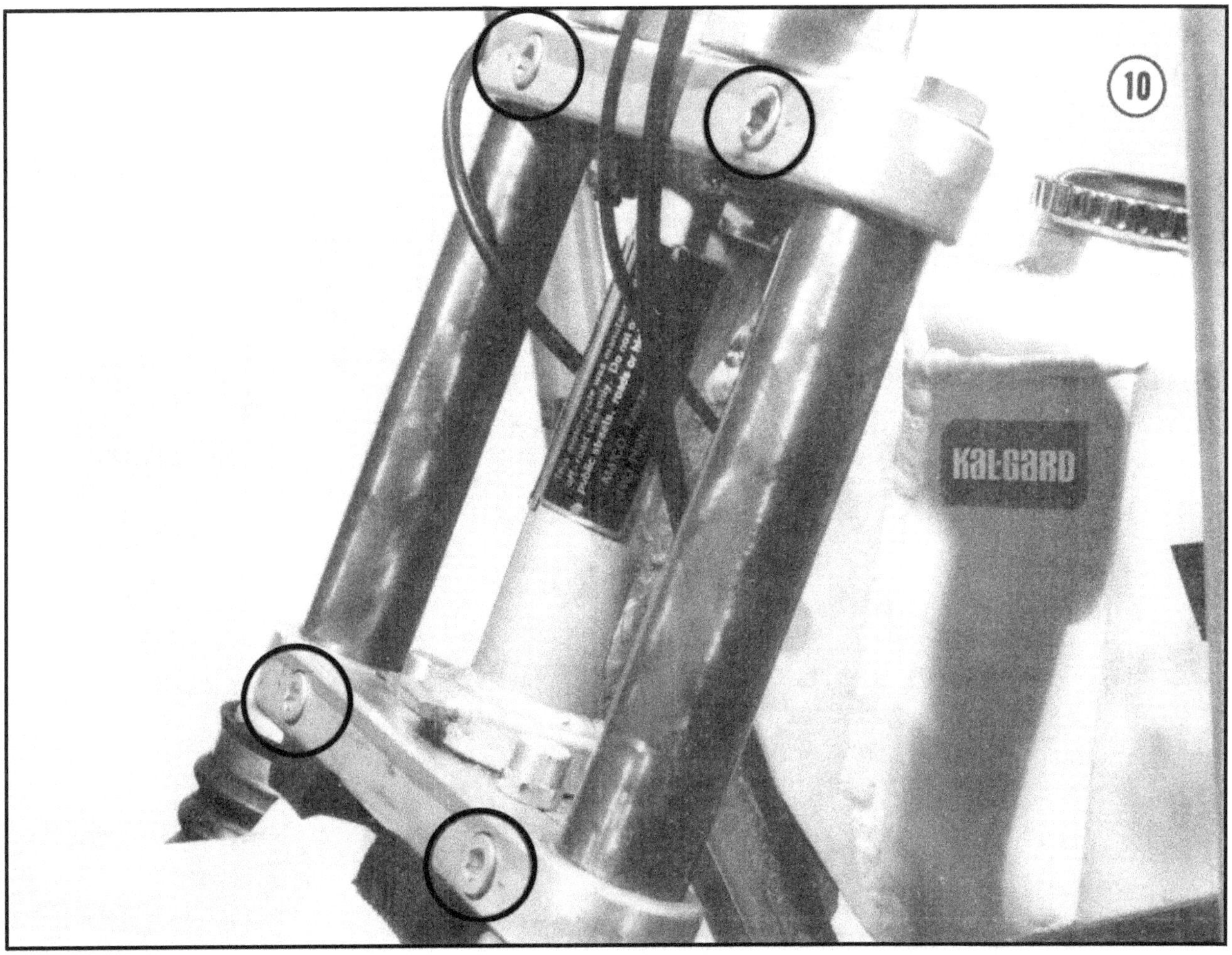

reassemble the suspension, install the front wheel, and fill the forks with damping oil.

5. Remove the motorcycle from the workstand or block. Apply the front brake and compress the front suspension several times to permit the tubes and sliders to align. Then tighten the axle pinch bolt and the pinch bolts in the top clamp.

Fork Springs

In time, the front fork springs lose resiliency and must be replaced. To check their condition, lock the front brake and quickly depress and release the front end. If the springs are in good condition, the suspension will extend fully so that lifting on the handlebar will not raise the motorcycle any farther without lifting the front wheel off the ground. If after depressing and releasing the front end the suspension can be extended farther by lifting on the handlebar, the springs are unserviceable and must be replaced.

Refer to *Fork Seal Replacement* and remove the sliders. Loosen the clamping band on the rubber fork cover and pull the cover and spring off the fork tube. Install the new springs by reversing this procedure. Refer to the earlier procedures in this chapter and reassemble the rest of the front end.

STEERING

Service to the steering involves checking for looseness, lubrication, and replacement of the bearings and races.

Checking for Looseness

1. Support the front of the motorcycle so the wheel is off the ground. Grasp the fork sliders firmly and attempt to move the wheel backward-and-forward. If movement can be felt, it's likely that the steering head bearings are loose.

2. Loosen the pinch bolts in the bottom fork clamp (**Figure 12**). Loosen the top locknut and tighten the stem nut (**Figure 13**) until no move-

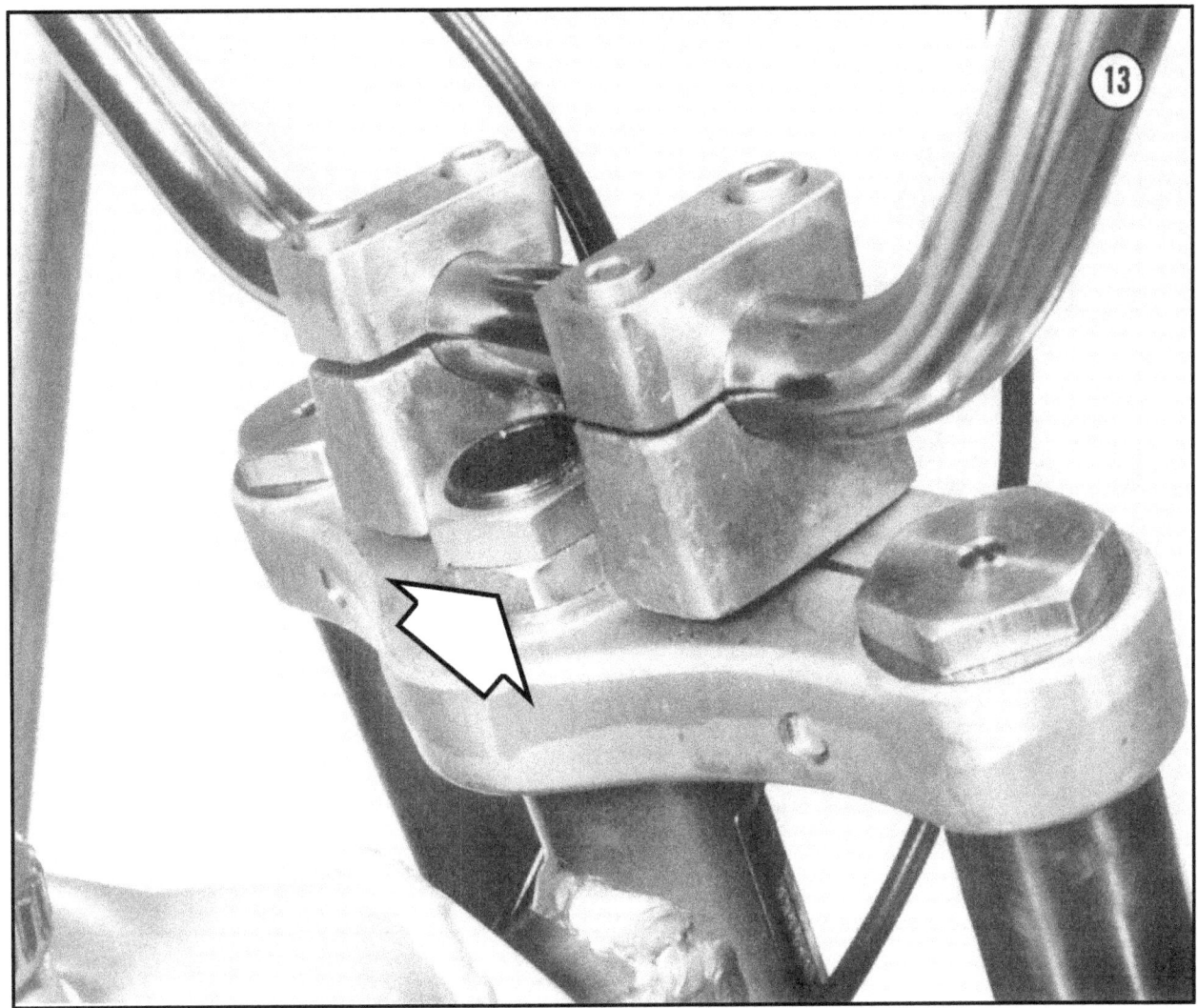

ment can be felt in the forks. The front end must still turn to each side from center under its own weight. If there is any resistance to turning after the stem nut has been tightened, it is too tight and is preloading the steering bearings. In actual use, under load, the preload will be compounded and make steering imprecise and difficult.

3. When the adjustment is correct, tighten the pinch bolts in the bottom fork clamp and the top stem locknut.

Bearing Lubrication and Replacement

The steering assembly should be disassembled, checked for wear and damage, and lubricated every few months.

1. Remove the front wheel and the handlebar.
2. Loosen the pinch bolts in the top fork clamp and unscrew the steering stem nuts. Remove the top clamp and pull the complete fork assembly down and out of the steering head.
3. Thoroughly clean the bearings and races, inspect them for damage or wear, and replace them if necessary.
4. Thoroughly grease the bearings and races and reassemble the steering assembly and forks.

NOTE: *One of the bearing races is deeper than the other to accomodate the offset of the bearings in the cage* **(Figure 14)**. *Make certain the deeper race* **(Figure 15)** *is installed on the side of the cage where the bearings are more exposed.*

Referring to earlier procedures in this chapter, reassemble the front end and adjust the steering.

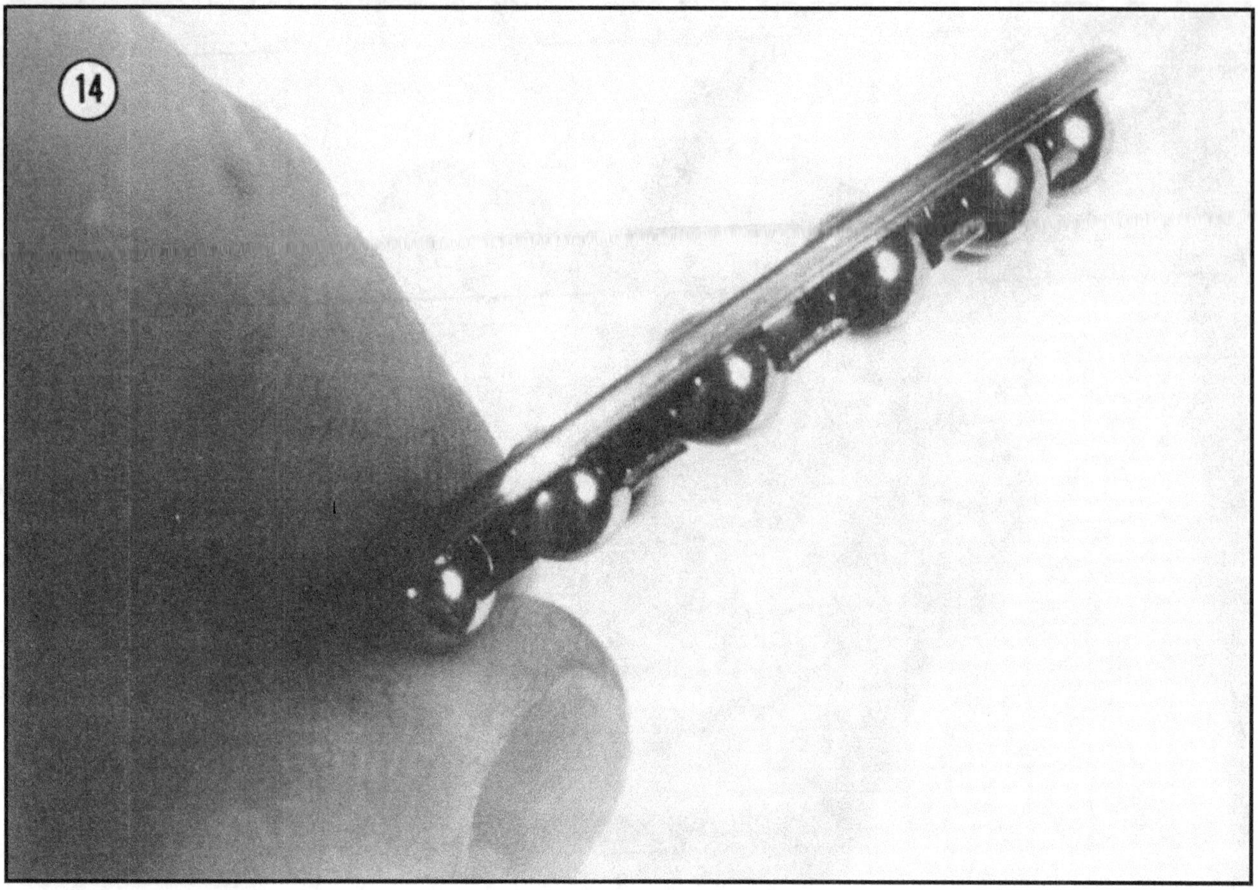

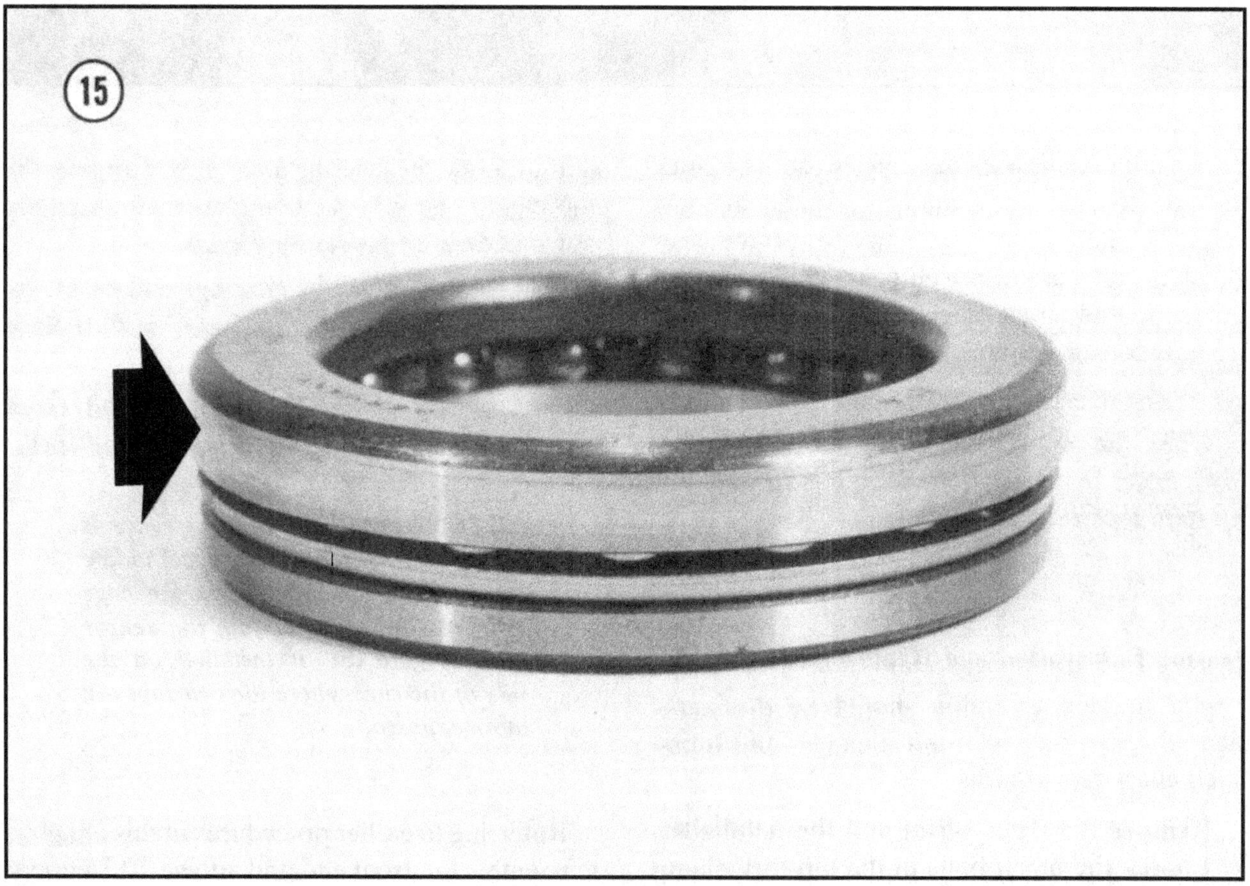

CHAPTER NINE

REAR SUSPENSION

The rear suspension consists of a pivoted fork, or swinging arm, supported by 2 spring-controlled, hydraulically dampened struts. Service to the rear suspension consists of periodically tightening the pivot bolts, replacing the pivot bushings, and checking the condition of the spring/shock units and replacing them as necessary.

SWINGING ARM

Pivot Bolts

The swinging arm pivot bolt (**Figure 1**) should be tightened routinely before each race or prior to a long trail ride. Tighten the bolt to 100 ft.-lb. (13.8 mkg). The bolt should be removed, cleaned, and greased at least once a month.

Bushing Replacement

Maico swinging arm bushings are silent bloc type and require no lubrication. In time, the bushings will wear beyond service limits and must be replaced. The condition of the bushings can greatly affect handling performance. Worn bushings produce erratic handling. Common symptoms are wheel hop, pulling to one side under acceleration and pulling to the other side during braking. If the condition of the bushings is doubtful, check them (after carrying out

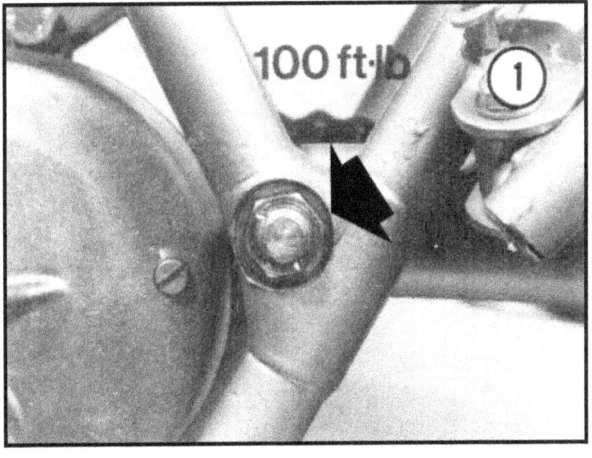

Steps 1 through 6 below) by grasping the ends of the swinging arm and attempting to move it from side-to-side in a horizontal arc. If more than a very slight movement is felt, and the pivot bolt is correctly tightened as described above, replace the bushings. See **Figure 2**.

1. Place the motorcycle on a workstand with the rear wheel off the ground.
2. Disconnect the rear brake rod (**Figure 3**).
3. Disconnect the rear chain and remove it.
4. Disconnect the brake anchor from the brake backing plate and the swinging arm (**Figure 4**).
5. Unscrew the axle nut, pull out the axle and remove the rear wheel.
6. Remove the bottom bolts from the suspension

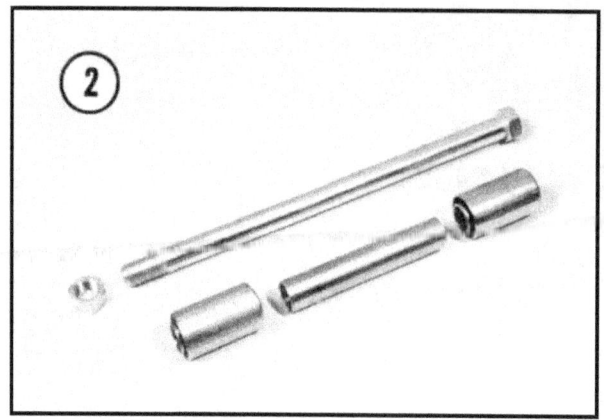

units, loosen the top bolts, swing the units up, and tighten the top bolts to hold the units out of the way.

7. Check the play in the swinging arm pivot (see introductory paragraph in this section).

8. Unscrew the nut from the left end of the pivot bolt (**Figure 5**) and carefully drive the bolt out with a soft drift. Remove the swinging arm from the motorcycle.

9. Heat the pivot tube of the swinging arm. Drive the bushings out from the inside using a long drift. Displace the spacer tube to one side so the drift can be applied to the bushings.

> NOTE: *If the bushings have been in service for a long time, it may be necessary to burn the rubber portion of the bushings out of the arm with a torch and remove the outer sleeve by first cutting it with a chisel. Be careful not to damage the bushing bores in the swinging arm.*

10. Press a new bushing into the left end of the swinging arm pivot until the bushing material is flush with the end of the pivot tube. Insert the pivot bolt through the bushing and install the spacer tube over the bolt and into the arm from the right side.

11. Press a new bushing into the right end of the pivot tube until it is stopped by the spacer. The bushing material should be flush with the right end of the swinging arm pivot tube.

12. Remove the bolt and install the swinging arm in the motorcycle, reversing the removal steps. Continue until the motorcycle is completely reassembled. Refer to Chapter Two to adjust the rear brake and drive chain.

SPRING/SHOCKS

Service to the original equipment rear spring/shocks is limited to inspection for damage to the damper rod, checking the damping rates, and replacing worn mounting bushings and unserviceable springs.

Rear spring/shocks are at least as important as the front suspension. Almost without exception, they are the first components to be blamed for poor handling performance. While sophisticated laboratory test machines are required to evaluate the true overall performance capability of a shock absorber unit, there are some simple common-sense tests to determine if a unit meets the basic standards.

1. Place the motorcycle on a workstand with the rear wheel off the ground. Unscrew the top (**Figure 6**) and bottom (**Figure 7**) bolts from one of the spring/shock units and remove it from the motorcycle.

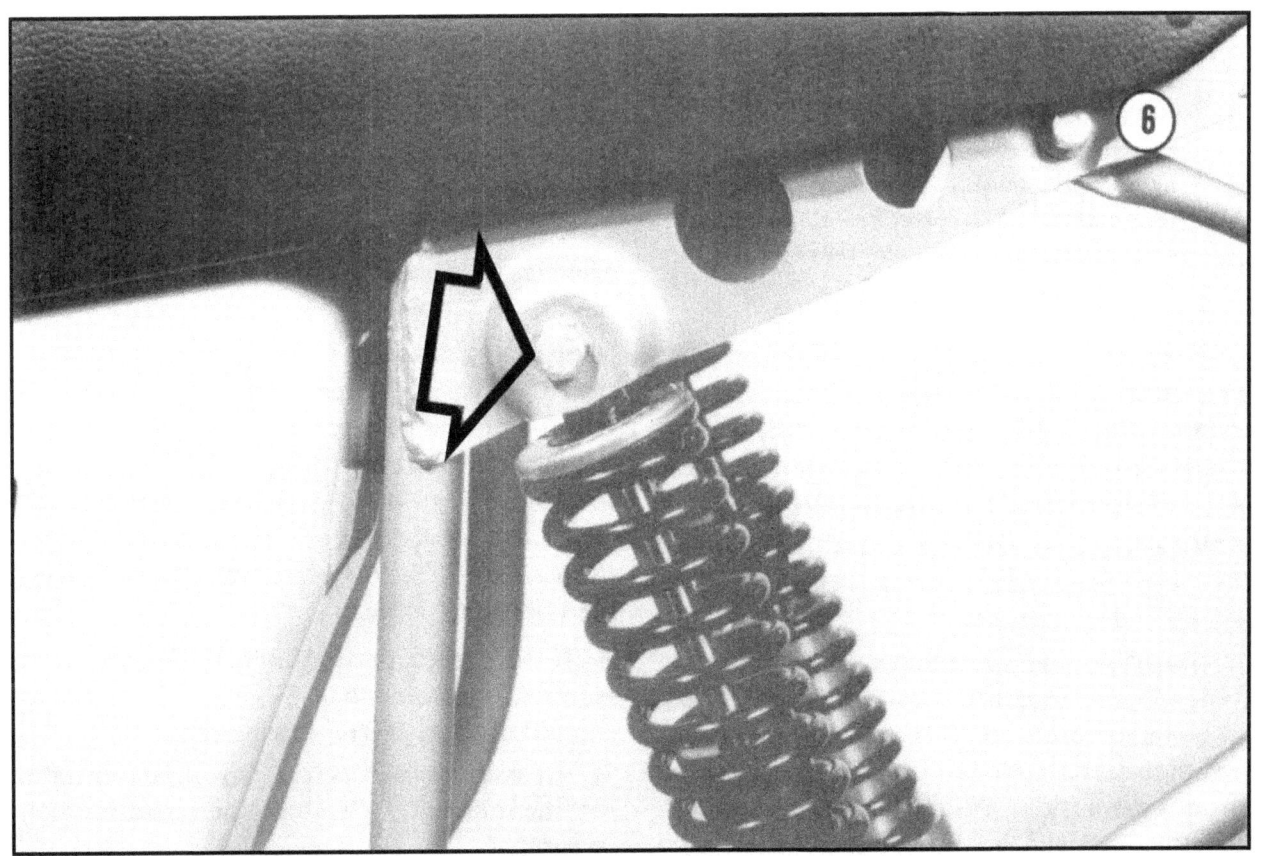

NOTE: *Removal and installation of one unit at a time makes the task easier. The unit that remains in place will maintain the correct relationship of the swinging arm to the frame.*

2. Clamp the lower eye of the shock absorber in a vise fitted with jaw protectors. With assistance, compress the spring and remove the spring keepers from the top of the unit (**Figure 8**). Remove the spring and the cover (if fitted).

3. Visually check the damper rod for bending. If bending is apparent, the unit is unserviceable and should be replaced.

4. Grasp the upper mounting eye and repeatedly compress and extend the damper rod to check for damping resistance. Resistance during extension of the rod should be noticeably greater than during compression. Also, the resistance in both directions should be smooth throughout the stroke. If the shock absorber fails on either of these points, it is unsatisfactory and should be replaced.

5. Check the rubber mounting eye bushings for damage or deterioration and replace them if necessary.

6. Before reassembling the spring/shock, accurately measure the free length of the spring and write it down so it may be compared to the free length of the other spring; while it's unlikely that one spring will lose resiliency faster than the other, the situation does occur. Handling performance suffers greatly and the cause is difficult to assess.

If the free length difference between the springs is greater than 1/8 inch (3.2mm) they should probably be replaced as a set.

7. Reassemble each spring/shock and install it on the motorcycle. Tighten the mounting bolts securely.

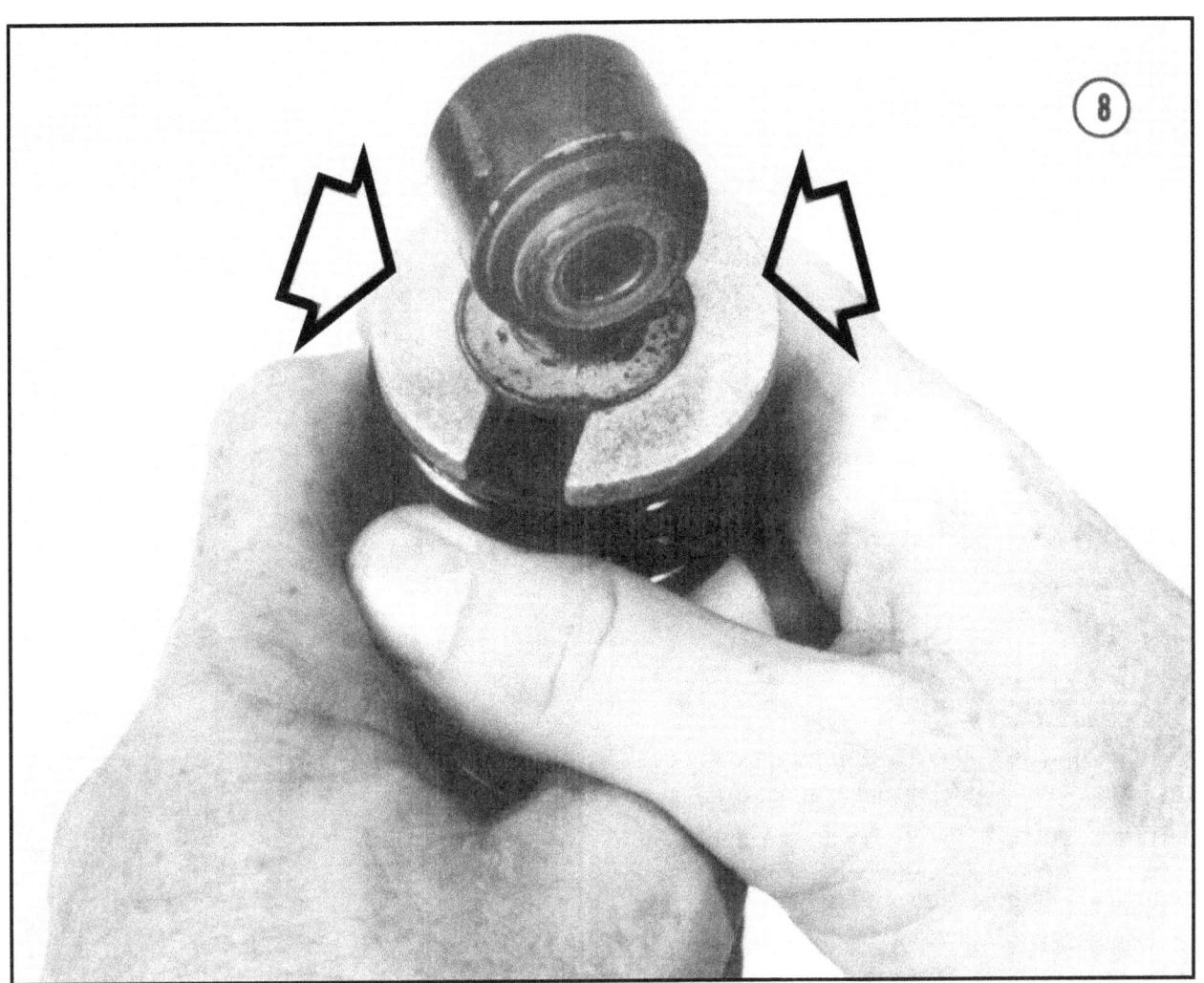

CHAPTER TEN

WHEELS, TIRES, AND BRAKES

Both Maico Motocross and Enduro models are fitted with 21-inch front rims and 18-inch rear rims. Tire cross-section sizes are largely a matter of individual preference; however, the original equipment tire sizes and patterns are recommended for most track and trail conditions. If the rims are fitted with rim locks (**Figure 1**), they should be checked periodically for tightness.

SPOKES

Spokes should be checked for tightness before each race or long trail ride. The "tuning fork" method for checking spoke tightness is simple and works well. Tap each spoke with a spoke wrench or the shank of a screwdriver and listen to the tone. A tightened spoke will emit a clear, ringing tone, and a loose spoke will sound flat. All of the spokes in a correctly tightened wheel will emit tones of similar pitch but not necessarily the same precise tone.

Bent or stripped spokes should be replaced as soon as they are detected. Unscrew the nipple from the spoke and depress the nipple into the rim far enough to free the end of the spoke, taking care not to push the nipple all the way in (**Figure 2**). Remove the damaged spoke from the hub and use it to match a new spoke of identical

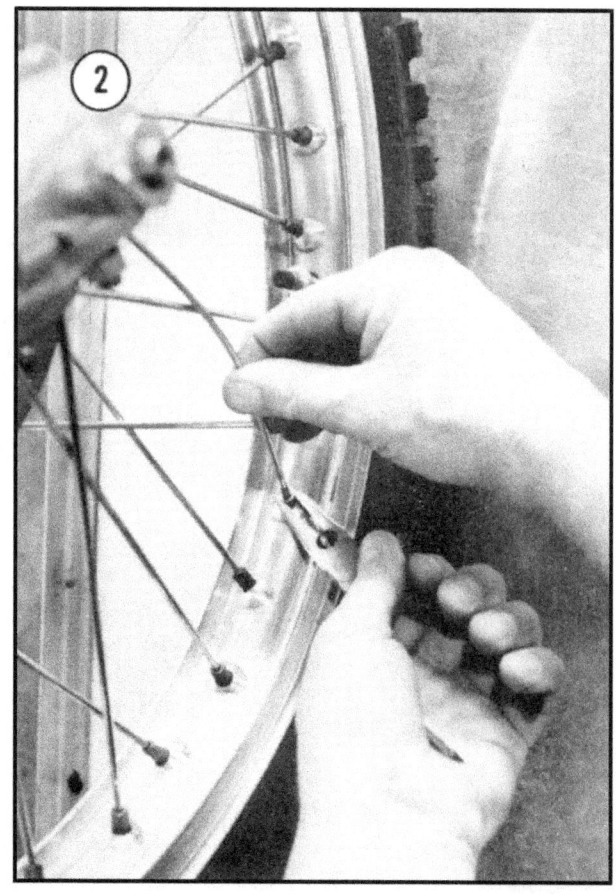

length. If necessary, trim the new spoke to match the original and dress the end of the threads with a die. Install the new spoke in the hub and screw on the nipple, tightening it until the spoke's tone

is similar to the tone of other spokes in the wheel. Periodically check the new spoke; it will stretch and must be retightened several times before it takes its final set.

WHEEL BALANCE

An imbalanced wheel can adversely affect handling performance. Balance weights applied to the light side of the wheel will correct imbalance. Before attempting to balance a wheel, check to make sure the wheel bearings are in good condition and properly lubricated, and the brake does not drag and prevent the wheel from turning freely. Before balancing the rear wheel, disconnect and remove the drive chain.

Place the motorcycle on a workstand so the wheel being balanced is off the ground. Spin the wheel slowly and allow it to come to rest by itself. Mark the lower-most point of the wheel and spin it again. If it does not come to rest at the same position, the balance of the wheel may already be acceptable. If you're unsure, spin it and check it again. If the wheel comes to rest at the same position, however, imbalance is indicated. In this case, add a weight to the top-most spoke and spin the wheel to check the effect. Balance weights are available in ⅓, ⅔, and 1 ounce (10, 20, and 30 grams). Begin with the lightest weight and increase the size as necessary. If more than 1 ounce is required to balance the wheel, add weight to adjacent spokes; never put 2 or more weights on the same spoke. When the wheel comes to rest at a different point each time that it is spun, consider it balanced and tightly crimp the weights so they won't be thrown off.

WHEEL INSPECTION

1. Refer to Chapter Eight and Nine. Remove, inspect, and install the wheels one at a time.

2. Support each axle in a lathe, V-blocks, or other suitable centering device as shown in **Figure 3**, and check its concentricity with a dial indicator. Straighten or replace the axle if it is bent more than 0.028 inch (0.7mm).

3. Check the inner and outer races of the wheel bearings for cracks, galling, or pitting. Rotate the bearings by hand and check for roughness. Replace the bearings if they are worn or damaged (see *Wheel Bearings and Seals*).

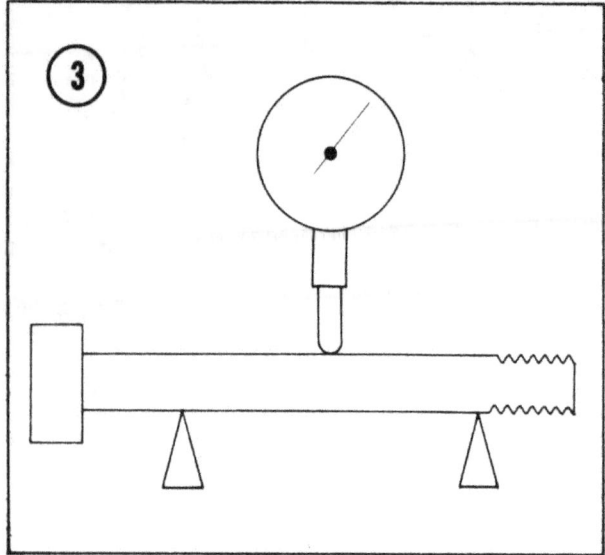

1. Draw the high point of the rim toward the centerline of the wheel by loosening the spokes in the area of the high point and on the same side as the high point, and tightening the spokes on the side opposite the high point. (See **Figure 5**).

2. Rotate the wheel and check it with the indicator. Continue adjusting until the runout is within specification. Be patient and thorough, adjusting the position of the rim a little at a time. If you loosen 2 spokes at the high point ½ turn, loosen the adjacent spokes ¼ turn. Tighten the spokes on the opposite side equivalent amounts (**Figure 6**).

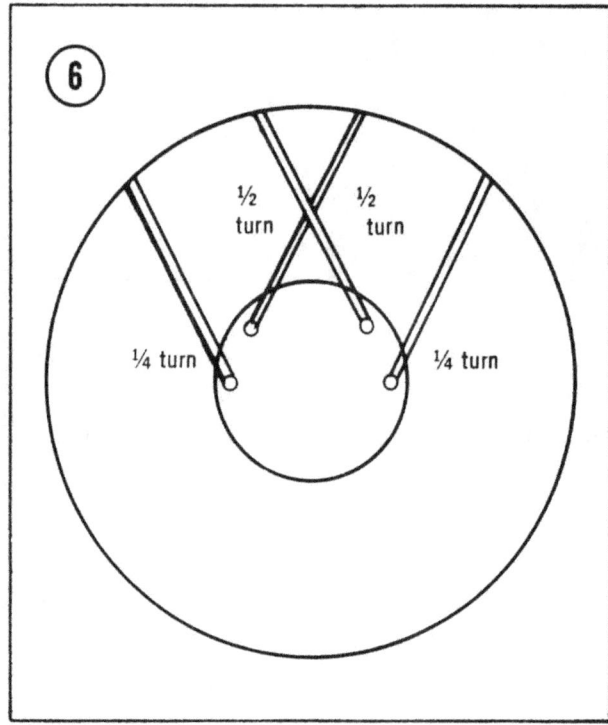

4. Inspect all oil seals for wear or damage and replace as necessary.

5. Check the rims for bending or distortion. Minor distortion can often be corrected by adjusting the spokes. Severe bends or dents cannot be satisfactorily repaired; in such case the rim should be replaced. Unless you are experienced in wheel lacing, this job should be entrusted to an expert.

WHEEL RUNOUT

To measure runout of the rim, support the wheel so that it is free to rotate. Position a dial indicator as shown in **Figure 4**. Observe the indicator as you rotate the wheel through a complete revolution. Runout should not exceed 0.12 inch (3mm). To correct runout, proceed as follows.

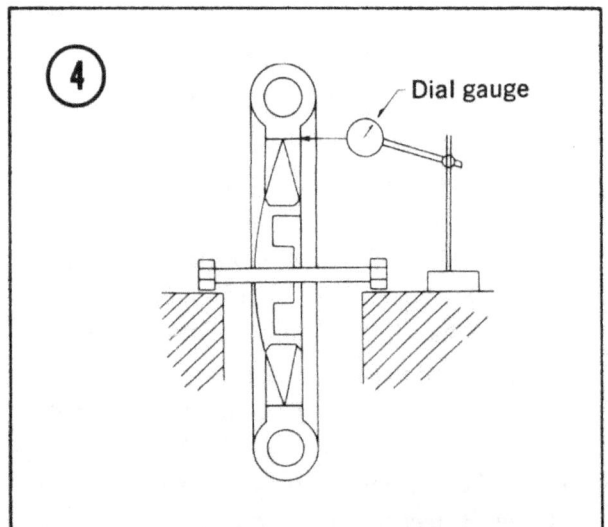

WHEEL BEARINGS AND SEALS

Hub components are nearly identical for all Maico models. Differences are confined to bearing type (sealed and open), interior spacer lengths, and the use of seals (seals are not required on hub fitted with sealed bearings). Service and inspection procedures are the same for all hubs. **Figures 7** (front) and **8** (rear) show typical arrangement of components.

Inspection

Support the motorcycle so that the wheel being checked is off the ground. Steady the fork or rear suspension unit with one hand, and rock

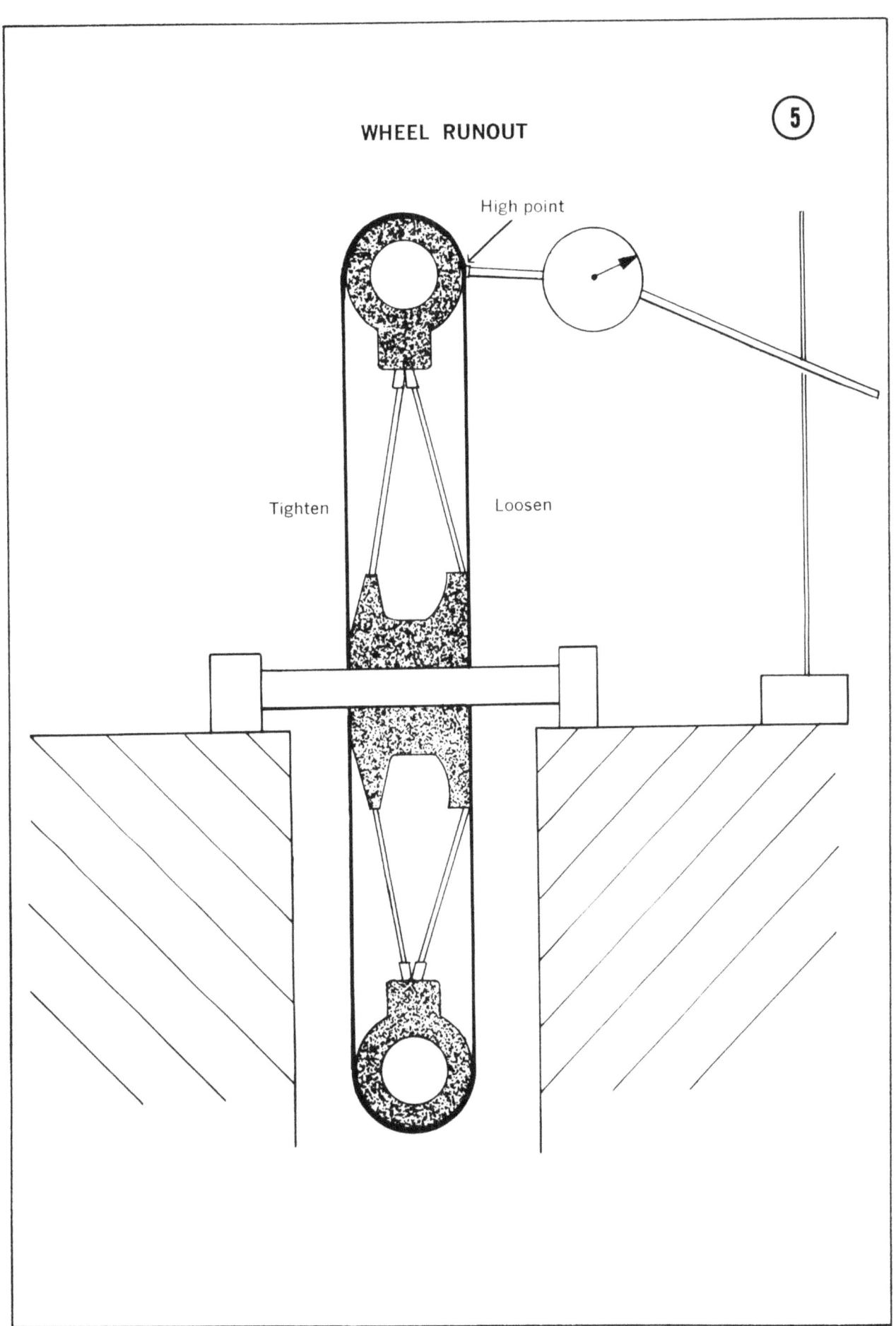

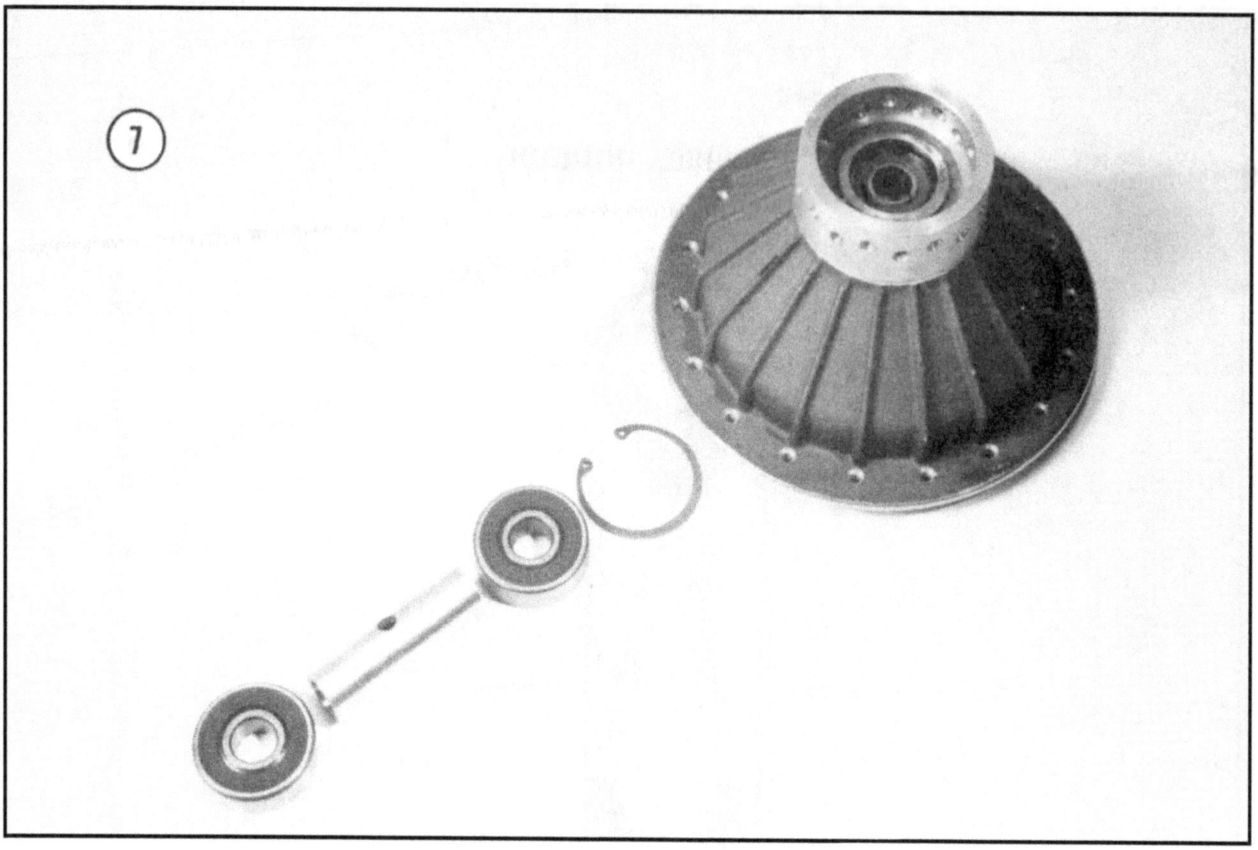

⑦

⑧

the wheel with the other hand. The movement of the wheel should be almost imperceptible. Any movement that can be seen or easily felt is an indication that the bearings are no longer serviceable and should be replaced.

Disassembly and Service

1. Remove the wheel to be serviced as described in Chapter Eight or Nine.
2. From the front wheel, remove the spacers, seals, and circlip (if fitted—**Figure 9**).
3. Insert a long, soft drift into one side of the hub. Displace the interior spacer to the side so that the drift can be applied to the inner race of the bearing (**Figure 10**). Tap the bearing out of the hub by working around the diameter of the inner race.
4. Remove the spacer and tap out the opposite bearing.

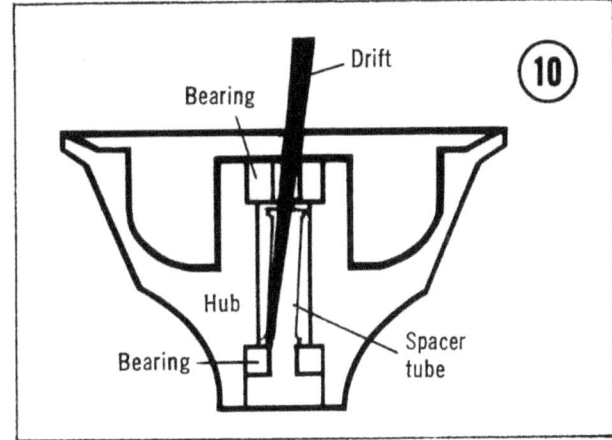

5. Thoroughly clean and dry all of the parts including the hub. Check the seals (if used) for wear and damage and replace them if necessary. Rotate the bearings by hand and check for roughness and radial play (some axial play is normal). The bearings should turn smoothly.
6. Before reassembling the hub, thoroughly grease unsealed bearings and the seals.

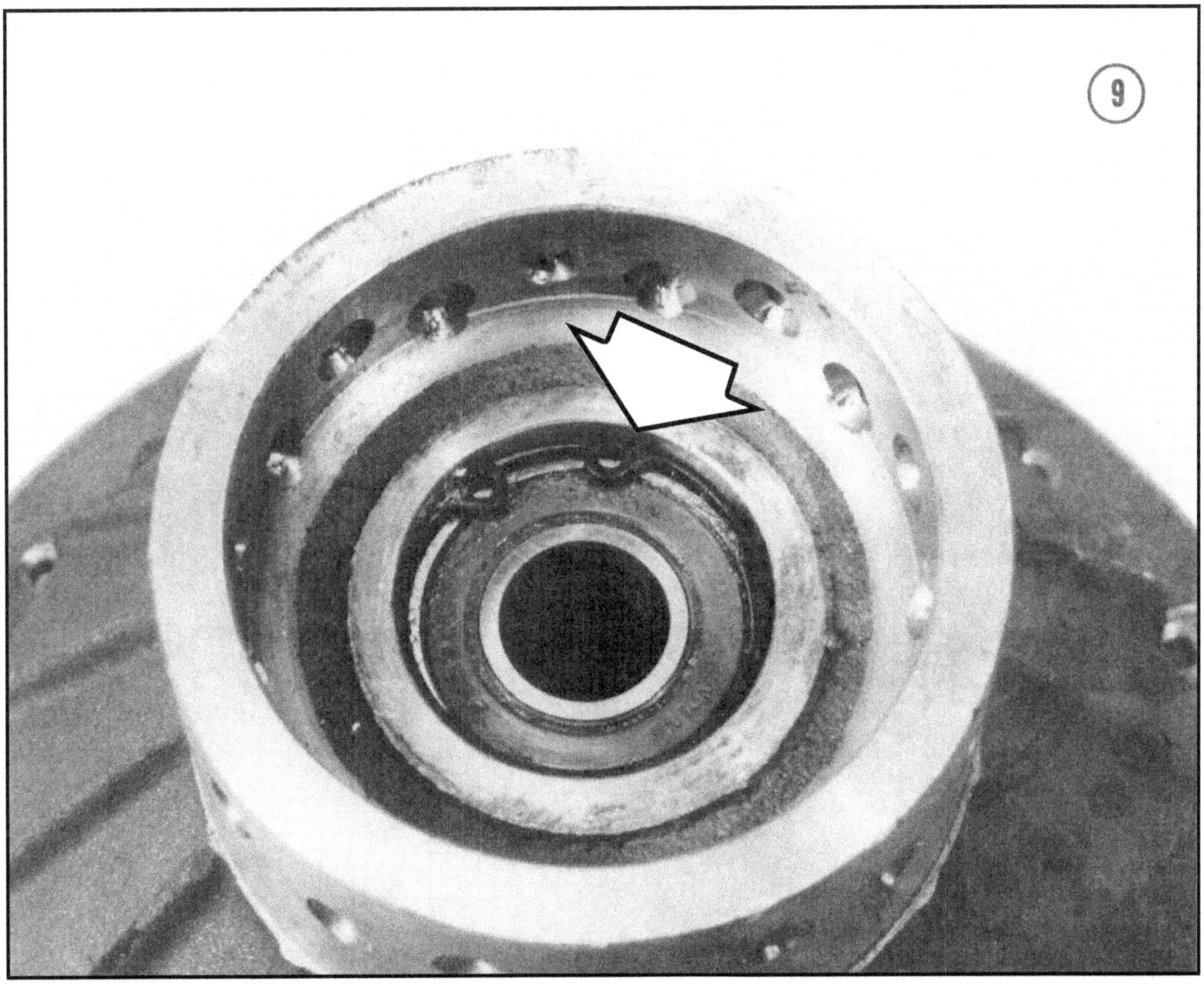

7. Carefully drive one of the bearings into its bore, tapping evenly around the outer race. Invert the hub and set the spacer in place. Install the other bearing on the axle and insert the axle through the spacer and the bearing that has been installed. Carefully tap the other bearing into its bore, tapping evenly around the outer race.

8. Install the seals (if used), spacers, and circlip (if used), then install the wheel in the motorcycle by reversing the removal procedure.

BRAKES

Both front and rear brakes are single-leading shoe type. Shoes, springs, cams, and pivots are identical for both units. The components are shown in **Figure 11**.

Inspection

Periodically check the brakes for wear and the presence of foreign matter. Grooves in the drum deep enough to snag a fingernail are an indication that the drum should be turned down on a lathe and new shoes fitted. This type of wear can be avoided to a great extent if the brakes are disassembled and thoroughly cleaned after the motorcycle has been ridden in mud or deep sand.

Examine the brake linings for oil, grease, or dirt. Oil-soaked linings cannot be satisfactorily rejuvenated; they should be replaced. Dirt imbedded in the lining may be removed with a wire brush.

Measure the thickness of the lining at its thinnest part. Replace both shoes when any portion of the lining is worn to about 1/16 in. (1.5mm).

Check the brake shoe return springs for tension. If the springs are stretched and weak, they won't fully retract the shoes from the drum, resulting in a power-probing drag on the drums and premature wear of the lining. In such case, replace the springs.

During periodic inspection and when installing new shoes, lube the brake cam and pivot

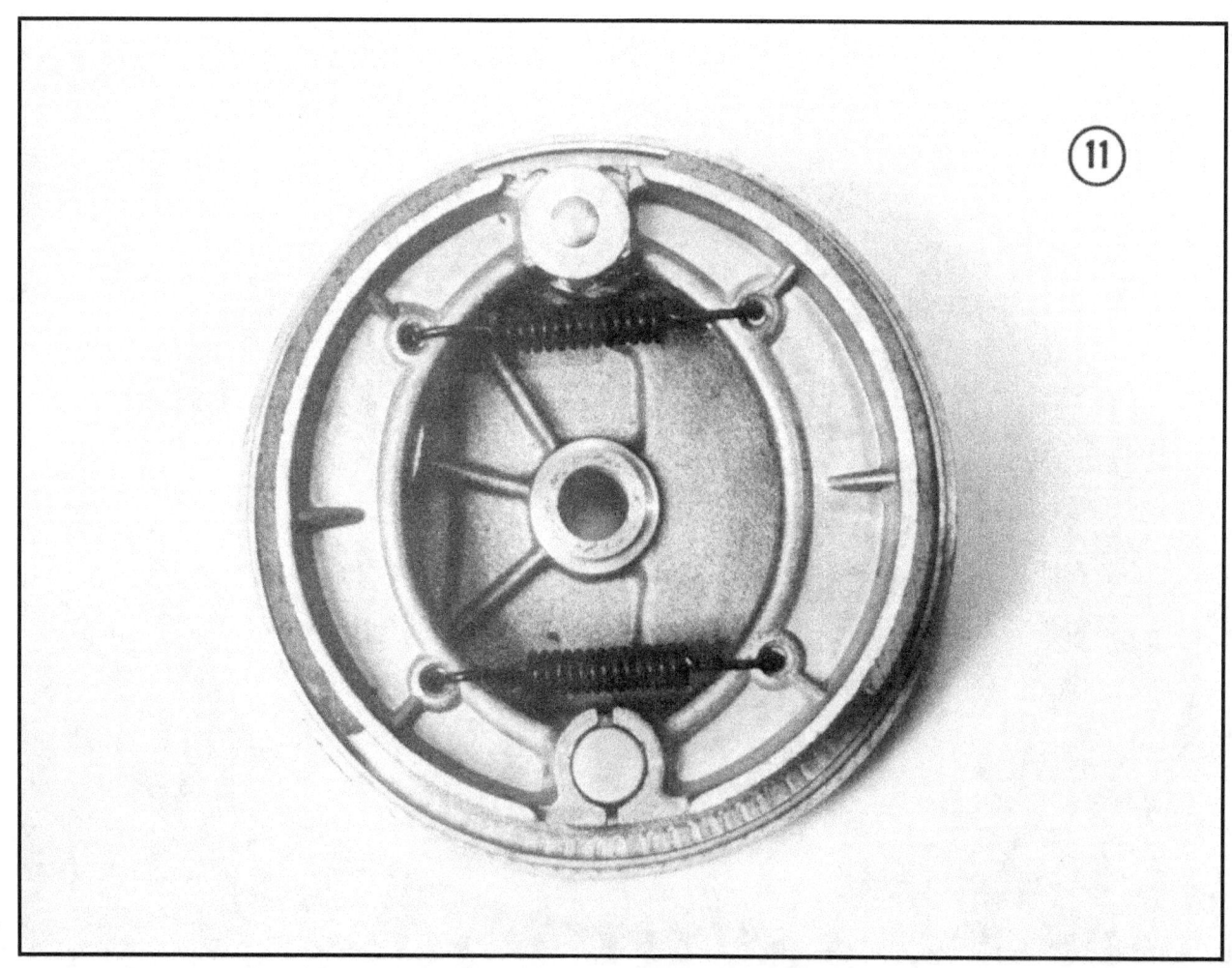

with high-temperature grease (**Figure 12**). Apply it sparingly; excess grease could find its way onto the lining.

Adjustment

Brake adjustment is largely a matter of personal preference. Adjustment of the front brake is covered earlier, under handlebar controls. The rear brake is adjusted by turning the wing nut on the end of the brake rod in or out to achieve the desired brake feel.

NOTE: *A new or newly lined rear brake should be adjusted loose at first and then bedded in gradually. Tighten the adjuster periodically until it suits your riding style. It's not a good idea to to ride the motorcycle strenuously until the bedding in is complete and the adjustment satisfactory.*

If all the brake adjustment has been "used up" and the shoes still have serviceable lining, it may be necessary to reposition the brake arms on the brake camshafts.

1. Slacken the brake adjuster and remove it from the arm.
2. Remove the nut and washer from the end of the camshaft. Pull off the arm and rotate it 15-20 degrees in the direction opposite to that in which it moves when the brake is applied (**Figure 13**). Reinstall the arm on the shaft making sure the return spring is correctly located, and screw on and tighten the nut.
3. Reinstall the cable or rod and adjust the brake action as desired.

REAR SPROCKET

The nuts and bolts which mount the sprocket to the rear hub (**Figure 14**) should be checked

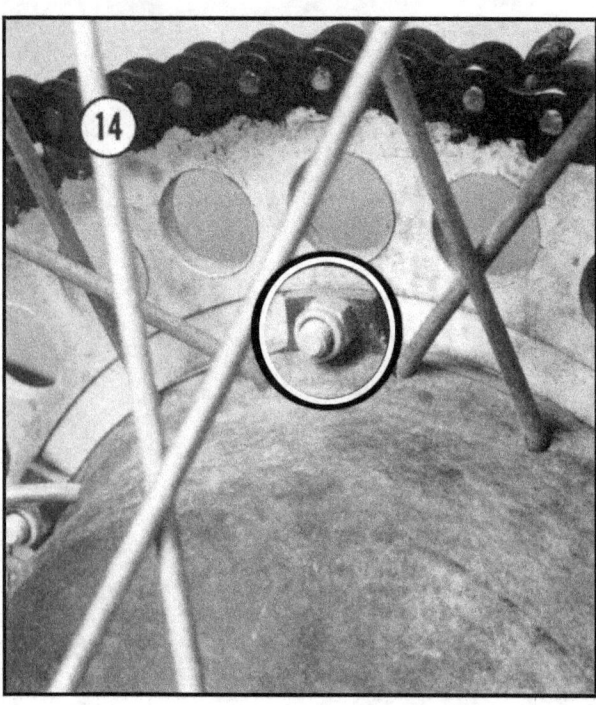

periodically for tightness. If non-locking nuts are used, replace collapsed lockwashers and apply a drop of liquid locking compound, such as Loctite, to the threads of the bolts prior to installing the nuts.

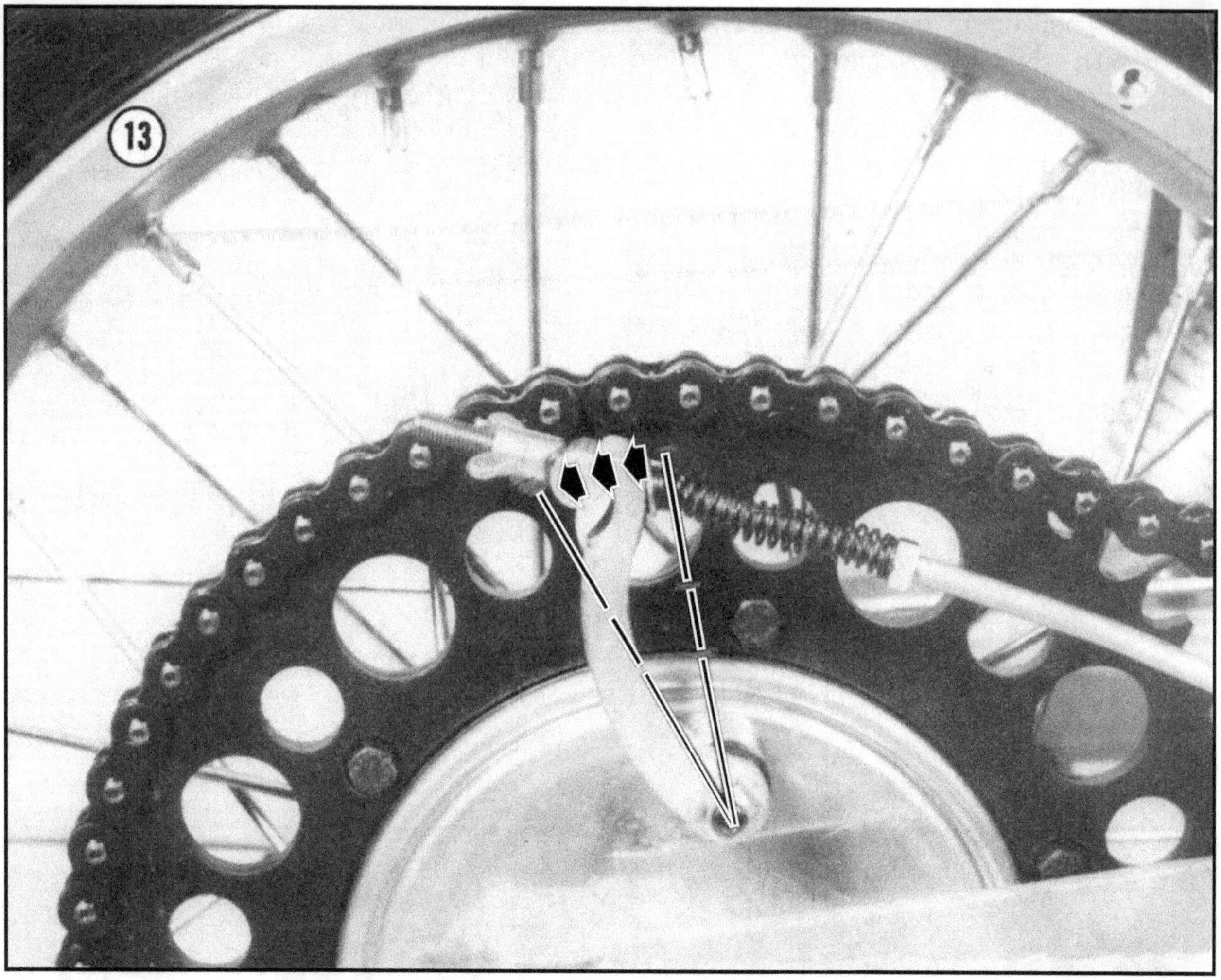

CAUTION
The bolt holes in the hub are threaded. Tighten the bolts firmly and then hold them to prevent them from backing out and tighten the locknuts. IF THE BOLTS ARE TURNED FURTHER THEY WILL STRIP THE THREADS IN THE HUB.

DRIVE CHAIN

Service and adjustment of the drive chain is presented in Chapter Two.

CHAPTER ELEVEN

FRAME

Maico frames are made from welded steel tubing. Service is limited to inspection and repair of bent frame members and cracked or broken welds. Examine the frame carefully if the motorcycle has suffered a collision or hard spill.

Frame repair should be entrusted to a specialist. Alignment of the steering head, engine mounts, and swinging arm pivot is critical for the motorcycle to handle correctly. Misalignment or incorrect weld repairs can result in further damage and possibly unsafe handling.

Service of related chassis components are covered elsewhere in this book.

Front Suspension	Chapter Eight
Steering	Chapter Eight
Rear Suspension	Chapter Nine
Wheels and brakes	Chapter Ten
Controls	Chapter Two

CHAPTER TWELVE

COMPETITION PREPARATION

Maico motorcycles are designed and built primarily for motocross competition. As such, they are rugged and reliable and will handle difficult terrain with relative ease. Like any complex piece of machinery, however, they must be periodically inspected for loose fasteners, worn components, and depleted lubricants and checked for general race-worthiness.

The suggestions for set-up and preparation presented in this chapter apply to virtually all off-road motorcycles under most conditions of use. Altogether, the tasks represent a couple of hours of time in preparation. Measured against failing to finish a race, or having a day of trail riding cut short by a lost bolt or failed parts, it's a very small price to pay.

One of the keys to successful race preparation is having a plan. Most experienced riders carry their plan in their heads. Their experience has shown them what they must do, what they must look for, and how they must prepare their motorcycle before each race. While the details of each successful rider's plan may vary, the important elements are invariably the same and they can be outlined like the check list below.

Specific service and repair procedures are covered in the appropriate chapters in this manual. Refer to the instructions for even the most routine operation until you have performed it so many times and know it so well it becomes second nature.

CHECK LIST

1. Clean and inspect the entire motorcycle.
2. Service the wheels, brakes, and hubs.
3. Service the suspension, swinging arm, and steering.
4. Service and adjust drive chain and sprockets.
5. Clean the fuel tank and fuel feed system.
6. Check the exhaust system for damage.
7. Check the fenders.
8. Check the seat.
9. Check the coil mount.
10. Clean the air filter and air box.
11. Inspect and lubricate the control cables.
12. Check and adjust the clutch.
13. Inspect the cylinder, piston, and connecting rod bearings.
14. Clean and adjust the carburetor.
15. Check, adjust, and time the ignition.
16. Change the transmission oil.
17. Inspect, straighten, and tighten control levers and pedals.
18. Check *every* fastener for tightness.
19. Test ride the motorcycle.

Cleaning and Inspection

Clean the motorcycle thoroughly. Don't just give it a quick shampoo with soapy water; use solvent and a stiff brush to scour away grease and grime in crevices on the engine, frame, and cycle parts. If you discover a correctable malfunction on the trail or in the pits, your work will be a lot easier if you don't have to dig through a thick layer of grime to get to it.

And while you're cleaning it, inspect every inch of it closely, as though your life depended upon it being in good condition; it very well may. Look for cracks and fractures in the engine cases and covers, in the frame and swinging arm, the suspension, and the wheel hubs. Don't assume that everything's OK just because you haven't had any trouble so far. Many parts, particularly those which are heavily stressed, will fatigue through normal use and should be repaired or replaced before they fail completely.

Wheels, Brakes, and Hubs

Periodically remove the wheels and disassemble the brakes and hubs. Check the serviceability of the drums, shoes, and linings and correct any conditions which may lead to trouble. There's no harm in cleaning and repacking the wheel bearings even before you think they need it. A grit-locked bearing could cost you an expensive aluminum hub, to say nothing of the power that's consumed by a stiff-turning wheel.

Check the spokes for tightness; a loose spoke is prone to failure and it places a greater strain on the other spokes in the wheel. Bent or broken spokes should be replaced as soon as they are found.

Check the wheels for trueness and carefully correct any deviations from normal. A bent or warped wheel can severely degrade the handling performance of your motorcycle.

Check the tires for tread condition and cracking of the sidewalls. If the traction blocks or knobs are worn down to more than ⅓ their original height, the tire should be replaced. Deep cracks in the sidewalls of a tire are also reason to replace it. A severely worn or damaged tire will degrade handling performance as much as a damaged or severely worn suspension component. Be very critical of patching a punctured inner tube; at best, a patch is a compromise remedy and the few dollars saved are small compensation for having the tire go flat a second time. And on top of all this, consider the time and effort required to change the tube. A punctured tube will find better use when it's cut into a couple of dozen strong rubber-band ties which can be used for all sorts of things such as holding on a front number plate, or fastening a spark plug wrench to the frame for a trail ride, or holding a damaged fender in place until you get home.

Frequently check and maintain good tire pressure. As a rule of thumb, 12 psi in the front tire and 16 psi in the rear provide good all-around tire performance. A small tire pump is good insurance but it's wise to overinflate your tires to about 20 psi at a service station when you're unsure of the surface conditions where you intend to ride; it's much easier to deflate to an acceptable pressure after you know what's required. Don't guess at tire pressure. Invest a couple of dollars in a pressure gauge and use it before you begin riding.

Check the rim locks to be sure they are tight.

Suspension, Swinging Arm, and Steering

In addition to the periodic maintenance (seal replacement, etc.) of the suspension units, it's a good idea to change the damping oil at frequent intervals. Front forks and rear shock units can't be simply topped up. In normal operation, a certain amount of the damping oil will get past the seals and not be returned to the reservoirs. As a result, the amount of oil in a damping component will gradually decrease until the unit no longer has sufficient oil to dampen properly. In addition to providing hydraulic resistance, damping oil also lubricates the suspension components and must therefore occasionally be changed to remove the microscopic bits of material which are worn away and become suspended in the oil.

Fork seal failure is usually an obvious malfunction. Large quantities of damping oil will seep out of the forks or rear units and the damping will degrade rapidly after the units have been drained and refilled. When this happens don't hesitate; replace the seals immediately. The problem only gets worse if it's not corrected.

Periodically remove the swinging arm pivot bolt and grease it to ensure its continued easy removal. When the swinging arm bushings become worn, replace them; no amount of tightening will cure the problem. However, when they are in good condition, tighten the bolt frequently.

Occasionally disassemble the steering head and clean and regrease the bearings and races. The steering head bearings experience high impact loads which extrude the grease, and there's virtually no way of excluding dirt and water. Water-resistant marine grease works well in the steering head. The preload on the bearings should always be firm but not so tight that the forks can't be turned easily with the front end unloaded. Excessive preload of the steering head will result in stiff and imprecise steering.

Drive Chain and Sprockets

Few motorcycle components experience as much mechanical abuse and service neglect as the drive chain. The operating environment of the drive chain is as bad as any that might be imagined for a mechanical component—high frictional and temperature loads, constant exposure to abrasive and corrosive foreign matter—and for these reasons it deserves more attention than it usually gets. The drvie chain should be removed, cleaned, checked, and lubricated after every race or long trail ride. Its adjustment should be checked and corrected at every opportunity. If it's too tightly adjusted, not only will it be overstressed, but it will also stress the transmission countershaft and bearings. If the chain is too loosely adjusted, you run the risk of it coming off its sprockets and severely damaging the rear hub or the transmission and engine, or all of them. It's not uncommon for a broken or thrown chain to damage a sprocket or hub or engine case beyond repair.

The sprockets are no less important than the chain. Frequently check to see that they are tight and inspect them for wear. When sprocket teeth show signs of undercutting, the sprocket should be replaced at once. Retaining bolts on the rear wheel sprocket should be checked for tightness and collapsed lockwashers should be replaced.

Fuel Tank and Fuel Feed System

The fuel tank should be removed, drained, flushed with clean gasoline, and inspected for cracked seams and brackets after each time the motorcycle has been subjected to strenuous use. Condensation, contaminated fuel, and manufacturing swarf can clog the fuel feed system and bring an end to a trail ride or race as certainly as a blown engine.

Each time the tank is cleaned, the fuel taps should also be removed, disassembled, and cleaned. In addition to being on-off fuel valves, the taps are fuel filters which must be frequently cleaned of the foreign matter they have filtered out of the fuel supply.

Exhaust System

The exhaust system on a 2-stroke motorcycle engine is much more than a means of routing exhaust gases to the rear of the motorcycle. It's a vital performance component and frequently, because of its design, it is a very vulnerable piece of equipment. Check the exhaust system for deep dents and fractures and repair them. Check the expansion chamber mounting for fractures and loose bolts and bushings. Check the cylinder mounting flange or collar for tightness. A loose headpipe connection will not only rob the engine of power, it could also damage the piston and the cylinder.

Fenders

Check the fender mounts for tightness and the fenders themselves for cracks. Small cracks in steel and aluminum fenders can be repaired with gussets held in place with pop rivets. Small cracks and fractures in fiberglass fenders can be repaired with strips of fiberglass cloth laminated in place with resin. Vacuum-formed fenders, such as the front fender on 1974 models, are difficult to repair and should be replaced.

Don't overlook the importance of fenders. Not only do they keep wheel-thrown dirt and mud out of your eyes and off your goggles, but they also keep it out of the engine cooling fins, the chain, and countershaft sprocket. A loose fender, particularly a steel one, which comes in contact with either of the wheels can damage the tire or the spokes.

Seat

Check the seat mount to be sure the brackets are not fractured and that the hold-down nut is tight. Also check the underside of the seatbase for cracks and fractures and repair them with riveted gussets or with resin-impregnated fiberglass tape.

Coil Mount

Check the coil mount on the frame for fractures and repair them at once. Also check the mounting bolts to be sure they are tight and make certain coil connections won't come loose.

Air Filter and Air Box

Check the brackets on the air filter box for fractures and make sure the mounting bolts are tight. The filter unit should be cleaned without fail after each time the motorcycle is ridden. If you use your motorcycle in competition that has scheduled maintenance breaks, such as motocross or enduro, have an extra, fresh, clean filter element on hand for each competition period and change the element even if you think that it's not required; a filter that's only slightly used will have collected enough foreign particles to degrade engine performance.

Make sure the filter element is correctly seated on the intake opening and that the cover plate fits tightly. Secure the mounting nut and if it's not a self-locking type, add a cotter key or piece of tubing to the threaded shaft to ensure the filter won't come off and the nuts find their way into the engine.

Control Cables

Carefully examine the control cables and sheaths for crimping, fraying, and separation and replace any that are less than perfect. Thoroughly lubricate the cables, either with a positive cable lubricator or by removing them, hanging them up, and allowing oil to flow down between the cable and sheath.

Clutch

Carefully adjust the clutch so that it engages fully but does not drag. If it has been in service for a long time and if it tends to slip, rotate the clutch spring retainer collars so their shallowest grooves line up with the locking pins.

Head, Cylinder, Piston, and Big-End Bearing

The engine upper end needn't be looked into before each time the motorcycle is ridden, but it should be checked periodically for scoring and wear, and the carbon should be removed from the combustion chamber, the piston crown, and the exhaust port. Carefully measure the bore and the piston, the ring clearance, and check the wrist pin and upper end bearing for wear and damage. Check the condition of the big-end bearing by pulling up on the rod, tapping it with your free hand, and listening for that sharp metallic sound that warns of excessive wear.

Always use a fresh cylinder base gasket when reassembling the upper end and tighten the head and cylinder nuts to the specified torque. Never begin a race or long trail ride with a fresh bore or fresh rings unless the engine has been run in.

Carburetor

Remove, disassemble, and clean the carburetor frequently. Adjust it carefully and don't try to anticipate the jetting you will need; have a range of jets on hand and tune the engine as best you can where you will be racing. When the jetting and adjustments are correct, wrap the carburetor in polythylene and secure it with tape to keep out dirt and water.

Ignition

The ignition should be serviced prior to every race. Check the condition of the points, check and set the contact gap, check the timing and the E-gap and correct any condition that's not absolutely perfect. There's no margin for error in the ignition system.

Check the spark plugs for condition and gap. Never begin a race on a brand new plug; a hairline fracture in the spark plug's ceramic insulation may open up as the plug is heated by the engine, resulting in the plug discharging directly to ground rather than across the electrode gap. Such a plug will usually function well for a couple of minutes, until the engine warms up, and then cease to function at all until the engine and the plug itself cool down. Don't take chances; this type of malfunction can commonly occur when the plug is being installed and won't be detected until it's too late.

Transmission

About the only attention a transmission requires is frequent oil change. It's a good idea to change the oil after each race to remove the microscopic particles produced as gears wear in.

Controls

Controls should be checked for cracks and fractures, and pivot points should be lubricated and tightened. Straighten bent levers or pedals and inspect them closely for fatigue.

Fasteners

When all of the checks, tests, and services have been completed, check the tightness of every nut, bolt, screw, and clevis on the motorcycle. Replace any lockwasher that has become flattened and all self-locking nuts whose inserts have become extruded through repeated tightening and unscrewing.

Don't reuse cotter keys or safety wire; once they have been removed, discard them and replace them with new pieces. Use Loctite where appropriate, such as on threaded fasteners which are not frequently removed. And each time a Loctited fastener is removed or turned, clean the threads thoroughly and apply fresh Loctite before reinstalling it.

Test Riding

When all of the preparation work has been completed, test ride the motorcycle to make sure it is in correct working order. If any adjustment is not quite right, redo it until it is.

MODIFICATIONS AND UPDATING

While the differences between the earliest and the latest Maicos covered in this handbook may at first appear to represent very different motorcycles, close examination shows that the latest is really only a refinement of the early models. Many of the tricks incorporated in the 1975 Maicos and in the factory racing motorcycles are readily adaptable to the 1968's. And as refined as the 1975 models are, they can also benefit from some changes in suspension components and cycle parts.

Engine

Engine output can always be increased, on the latest Maicos as well as the early models. However, the consequences of altering porting, increasing compression ratio, and changing the expansion chamber should be examined carefully before any work is undertaken. The engines have been designed to provide the very broadest possible powerband with good specific horsepower on the top end. Alterations that will improve engine output in one range will almost certainly compromise it in another area.

Performance modifications to the radial series engines are not recommended nor are they required. The radials are highly refined racing engines which require no "help" other than careful maintenance and assembly. Radial engine models benefit most from chassis improvements which help the rider to exploit the engines already good characteristics.

Square barrels models can be improved substantially by updating the porting and head to later specifications. This is a job for an expert. Not only does it require special skills and tools, but it also requires exact dimensional and contour information. Your Maico dealer should have this information and if he's not able to perform the work, he can refer you to a specialist who can.

Transmission/Clutch

Modifications to the late transmission and clutch are not required. The oil should be changed after every race and the drain plug magnet carefully "read" as described in Chapter Two.

For early square barrel models, modifications to the shifter and some of the clutches can be made by most Maico dealers to improve shifting response and eliminate clutch slip and drag. As with the engine work, this is a task that is best entrusted to a Maico dealer or a specialist who has the tools, experience, and information to correctly perform the required work.

Suspension

Rear suspension on early models can be updated to the forward-mounted shock design of the 1975's. Like engine modifications, this job requires skill, experience, tools, and information that take it out of the realm of do-it-yourself work. While few Maico dealers will undertake the rear suspension modification, virtually all can arrange to have it done.

Front suspension requires no modification. It's important that the damping oil be changed at regular and frequent intervals and the seals be periodically changed as described in Chapters Two and Eight.

Wheels, Hubs, and Brakes

Another major gain in handling performance can be realized through modification of the wheels and hubs to reduce unsprung weight. On the latest models which are equipped with lightweight aluminum hubs and brake components, the unsprung weight can be further reduced through a change to aluminum rims and a substitution of screw-type rim locks in place of the heavy bolt and friction types.

There are several aluminum rims available. The most common are Akront and D.I.D., both of which are drilled for the 36-hole continental spoke pattern suitable for the Maico hubs. Rear hubs should be laced with heavy duty spokes, while the front hub should have standard weight spokes. The spoke holes in the rear hub (**Figure 1**) must be countersunk deeper for the larger heads on the heavy-duty spokes.

Holes for the rim lock screws in the rear wheel should be drilled 90 degrees apart on both sides (8 screws) and 120 degrees apart on the front (6 screws).

An additional weight savings can be realized on the rear wheel by drilling the final drive sprocket. This can amount to as much as a pound of unsprung weight saved without sacrificing the strength of the sprocket. **Figure 2** illustrates the extent to which an earlier model can be modified and updated.

On early models equipped with a full-width front hub, a large weight saving can be gained through a change to a late-model conical hub. For economy, a Yamaha MX front hub (**Figure 3**) can be purchased for about half the cost

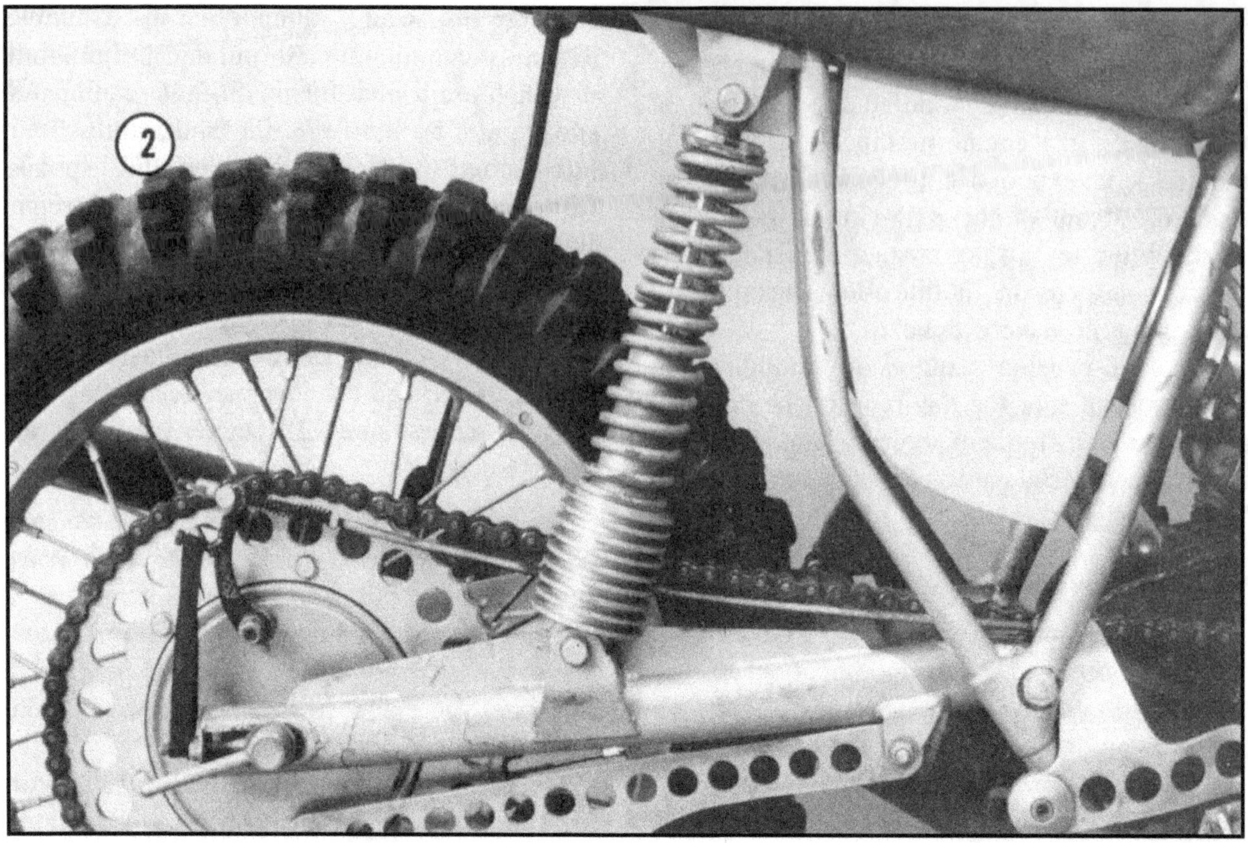
2

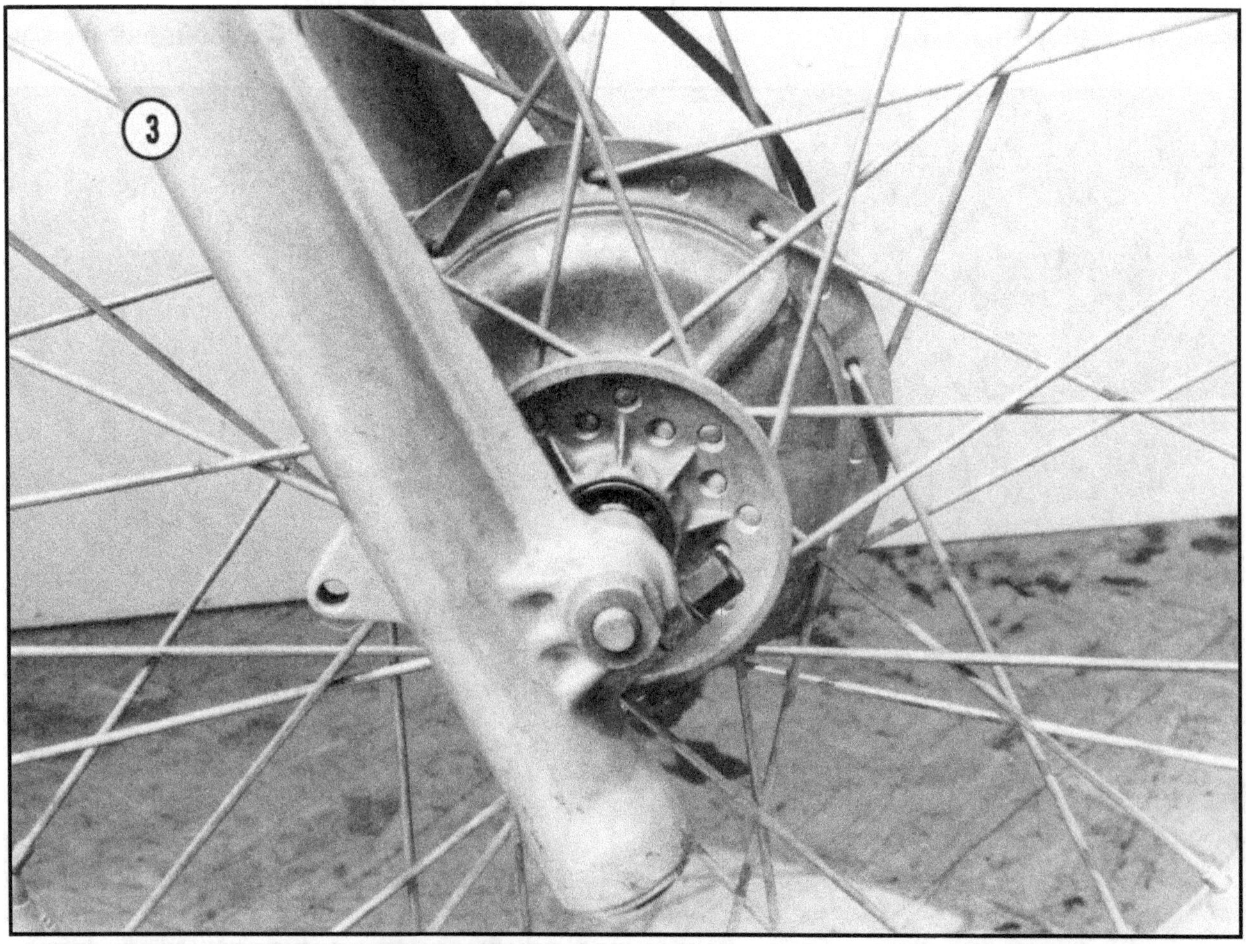
3

of a new Maico hub. The Yamaha hub and the Maico forks and axle require no modification. Used with an aluminum rim, this hub results in a front wheel that is one of the lightest available.

ADDITIONAL MODIFICATIONS

There are any number of little tricks that can help to ensure success in racing. Here are just a few that, along with the careful pre-race preparation and modifications described earlier, help to make a winning motorcycle.

Rear Brake Return

The rear brake return spring can be given a big assist by a band of innertube stretched between the axle adjuster and a bolt brazed to the brake arm (**Figure 4**). The added tension ensures that the brake is fully released when the pedal is released.

Front Brake Cable Guard

When the front suspension is fully compressed the brake cable will bow and can snag on the right handlebar mounting block. When the front suspension fully extends, the snagged cable can lock the front wheel. This situation is most likely to occur upon landing off a jump. The result is obvious. An inner tube band stretched between the mounting blocks (**Figure 5**) will prevent this potentially hazardous situation.

Carburetor Mount

The carburetor mount on radial models has a tendency to come loose, particularly on rough courses. This trouble can be virtually eliminated with innertube bands wrapped around the carburetor and held to the cylinder with nails bent into hooks and installed in holes drilled in the third fin from the bottom (**Figure 6**).

Water- and Dirt-Proofing the Air Box

The openings between the air box and the frame should be sealed with duct tape, both beneath the seat and on the outside (**Figure 7**). In addition, an apron of tape should be placed over the top of the front half of the opening in the box.

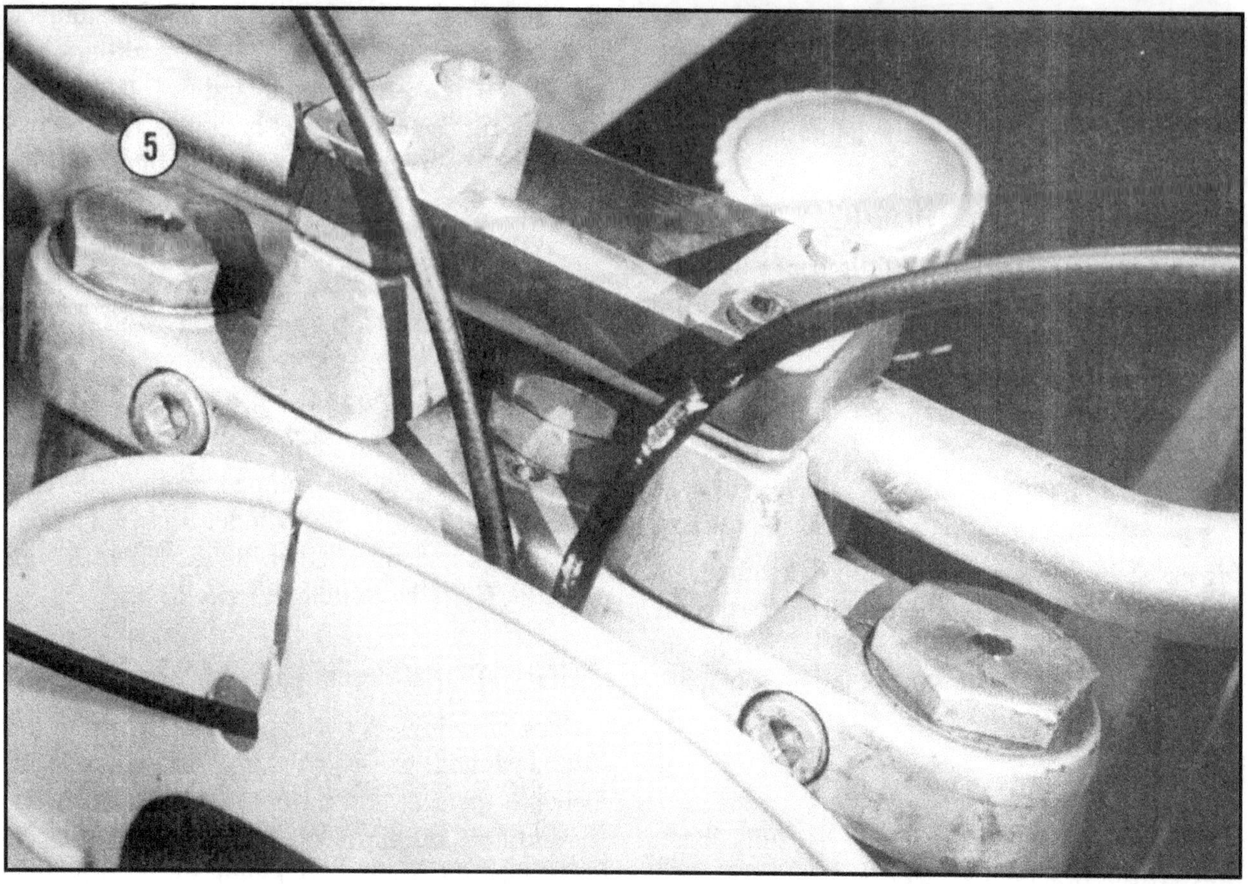
5

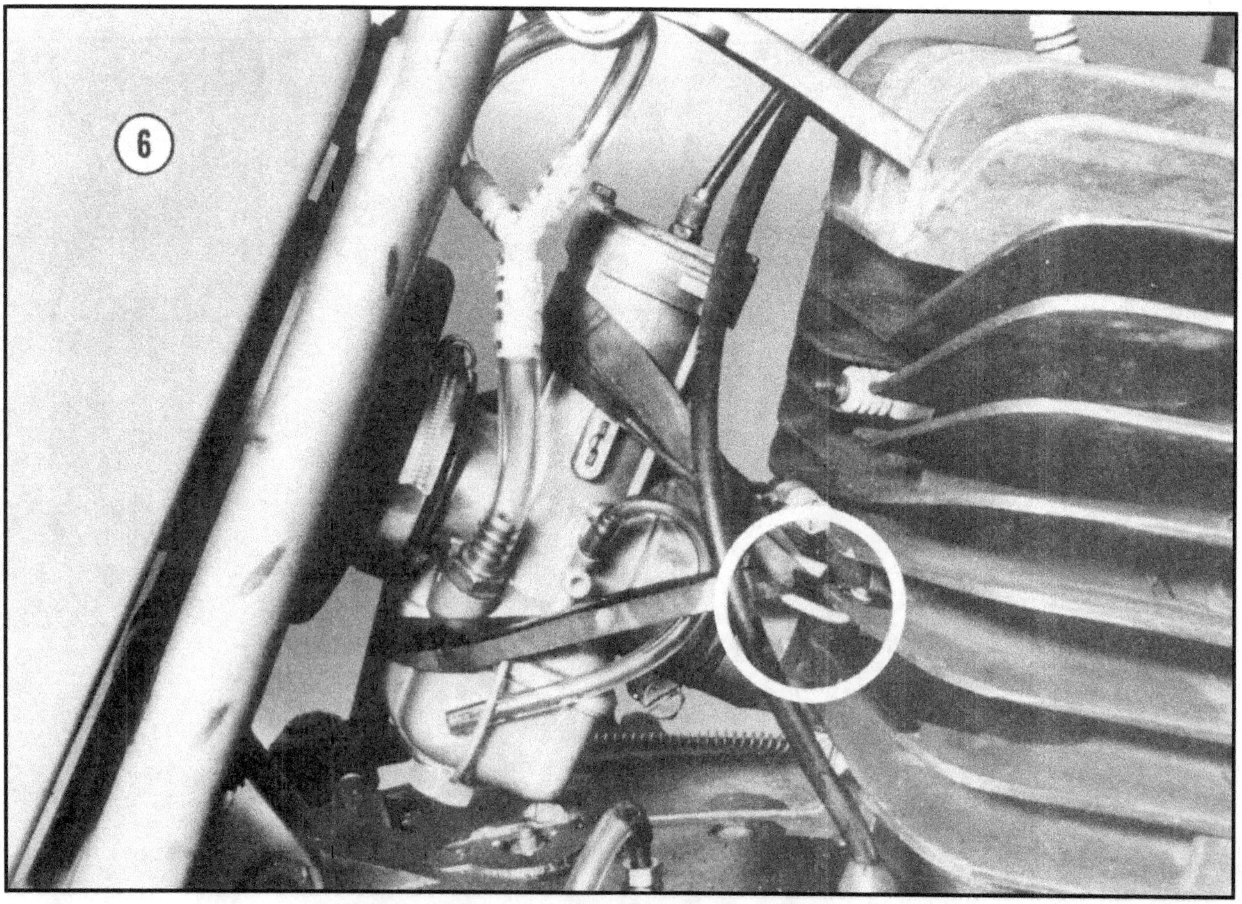
6

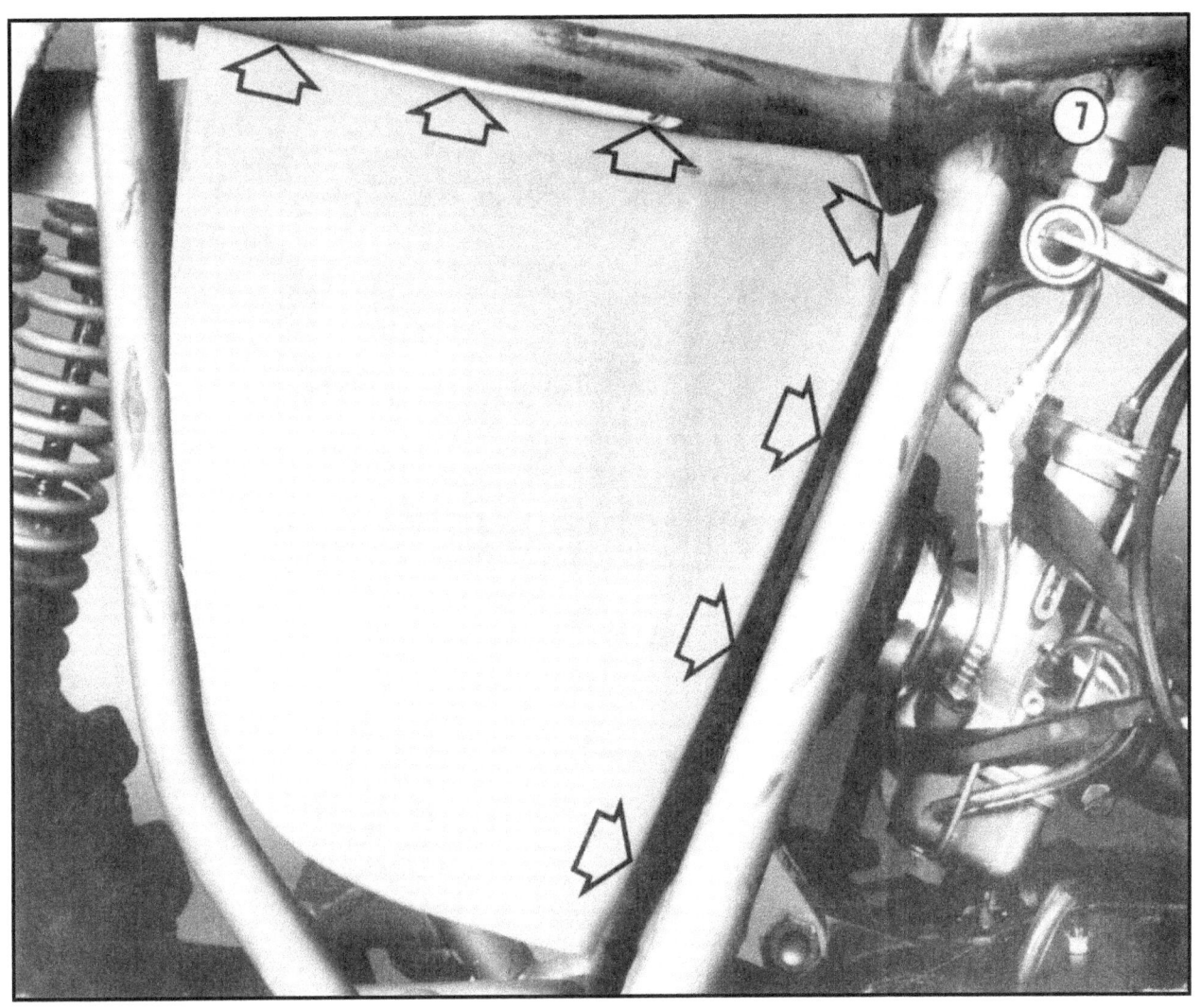

CHAPTER THIRTEEN

USEFUL FORMULAS AND TABLES

It is often necessary to convert metric to American dimensions or vice versa. This chapter contains formulas for doing so, with typical examples worked out. Also in this chapter are other useful tables and formulas.

CONVERSIONS

Multiply	by	To obtain
Volume		
Cubic centimeters	0.061	Cubic inches
Cubic inches	16.387	Cubic centimeters
Liters	0.264	Gallons
Gallons	3.785	Liters
Liters	1.057	Quarts
Quarts	0.946	Liters
Cubic centimeters	0.0339	Fluid ounces
Fluid ounces	29.57	Cubic centimeters
Length		
Millimeters	0.03937	Inches
Inches	25.4	Millimeters
Centimeters	0.3937	Inches
Inches	2.54	Centimeters
Kilometers	0.6214	Miles
Miles	1.609	Kilometers
Meters	3.281	Feet
Feet	0.3048	Meters
Millimeters	0.10	Centimeters
Centimeters	10.0	Millimeters
Weight		
Kilograms	2.205	Pounds
Pounds	0.4536	Kilograms
Grams	0.03527	Ounces
Ounces	28.35	Grams
Other		
Metric horsepower	1.014	Brake horsepower
Brake horsepower	0.9859	Metric horsepower
Kilogram-meters	7.235	Foot-pounds
Foot-pounds	0.1383	Kilogram-meters
Kilometers per liter	2.352	Miles per gallon
Miles per gallon	0.4252	Kilometers per liter
Square millimeters	0.00155	Square inches
Square inches	645.2	Square millimeters
Square inches	6.452	Square centimeters
Square centimeters	0.155	Square inches
Kilometers per hour	0.6214	Miles per hour
Miles per hour	1.609	Kilometers per hour
Foot-pounds	0.1383	Kilogram-meters
Kilogram-meters	7.233	Foot-pounds
Pounds per square inch	0.0703	Kilograms per square centimeter
Kilograms per square centimeter	14.22	Pounds per square inch
Miles per hour	88	Feet per minute
Feet per minute	0.01136	Miles per hour
Miles per hour	1.467	Feet per second

EXAMPLES OF CONVERSIONS

1. To convert 250 cubic centimeters to cubic inches, multiply 250 cubic centimeters by 0.061:

$$250 \times 0.061 = 15.25 \text{ cubic inches}$$

2. To convert 0.65 inch to millimeters, multiply 0.65 inch by 25.4:

$$0.65 \times 25.4 = 16.51 \text{ millimeters}$$

3. To convert 76 kilograms to pounds, multiply 76 kilograms by 2.205:

$$76 \times 2.205 = 167.58 \text{ pounds}$$

4. To convert 41 miles per gallon to kilometers per liter, multiply 41 miles per gallon by 0.4252:

$$41 \times 0.4252 = 17.43 \text{ kilometers per liter.}$$

5. To convert 50 miles per hour to feet per second, multiply 50 miles per hour by 1.467:

$$50 \times 1.467 = 73.35 \text{ feet per second}$$

TEMPERATURE

It is sometimes specified in a service manual to perform a repair operation at a certain temperature, such as heating crankcase halves to 150 degrees C before installing bearings. There are two basic formulas for converting degrees F to degrees C and vice versa:

$$C = 5/9 \, (F - 32)$$
$$F = 9/5 \, (C + 32)$$

Example 1

Measurement temperature for the electrolyte in a battery is specified as 68 degrees F. What is that temperature in degrees C?

$$\begin{aligned}
C &= 5/9 \, (F - 32) \\
&= 5/9 \, (68 - 32) \\
&= 5/9 \times 36 \\
&= \frac{180}{9} \\
&= 20 \text{ degrees C}
\end{aligned}$$

Example 2

A motorcycle service manual specifies that main bearings be heated to 200 degrees C before installing them onto the crankshaft. What is that temperature in degrees F?

$$\begin{aligned}
F &= 9/5 \, C + 32 \\
&= (9/5 \times 200) + 32 \\
&= 360 + 32 \\
&= 392 \text{ degrees F}
\end{aligned}$$

PISTON DISPLACEMENT

The formula for finding piston displacement can be expressed as:

$$D = \pi \times R^2 \times S \times N$$

$D =$ Piston displacement

$\pi = 3.1416$ (a constant)

$S =$ Piston stroke

$N =$ Number of cylinders

$R =$ Radius of one cylinder (one-half of bore)

(R^2, read "R squared", means R multiplied by itself)

Example 1

A single cylinder engine has a bore of 70 millimeters, stroke of 62 millimeters. What is its displacement?

First convert 70 millimeters (bore) and 62 millimeters (stroke) to centimeters by dividing each by 10, which is equivalent to multiplying each by 0.10. This step is necessary so that our answer will come out in cubic centimeters. Then using bore and stroke figures expressed in *centimeters* in the formula:

$R =$ one-half of bore $= 3.5$

$S = 6.2$

$N = 1$

$$\begin{aligned}
D &= \pi \times R^2 \times S \times N \\
&= 3.1416 \times (3.5)^2 \times 6.2 \times 1 \\
&= 3.1416 \times 12.25 \times 6.2 \\
&= 238.6 \text{ cubic centimeters}
\end{aligned}$$

Example 2

A 3-cylinder engine has a bore of 60 millimeters and a stroke of 58.8 millimeters. What is its piston displacement?

First convert both bore and stroke into centimeters by multiplying by 0.10:

R = one-half of bore = 3 centimeters

S = 5.88 centimeters

N = 3

$$D = \pi \times R^2 \times S \times N$$
$$= 3.1416 \times (3.0)^2 \times 5.88 \times 3$$
$$= 3.1416 \times 9 \times 5.88 \times 3$$
$$= 498.75 \text{ cubic centimeters}$$

Note that the formula will work equally well if bore and stroke are expressed in inches or millimeters. If they are expressed in inches, the answer will come out in cubic inches. The answer will come out in cubic millimeters if millimeters are used in the formula.

COMPRESSION RATIO

To determine compression ratio of an engine, it is first necessary to know piston displacement (of one cylinder) and combustion chamber volume. The formula can be expressed as:

Compression ratio =

$$\frac{\text{Piston Displacement} + \text{Combustion chamber vol.}}{\text{Combustion chamber volume}}$$

Example

An engine has a piston displacement of 244.6 cubic centimeters and a combustion chamber volume of 41.5 cubic centimeters. What is its compression ratio?

$$\text{Compression ratio} = \frac{244.6 + 38.2}{38.2}$$
$$= \frac{282.8}{38.2}$$
$$= 7.4 \text{ to } 1 \text{ (rounded off)}$$

HORSEPOWER AND TORQUE

There is sometimes confusion about horsepower and torque. Horsepower is a measure of how much work can be done in a given length of time. One horsepower is equal to the work done when a weight of 550 pounds is lifted one foot in one second, or 33,000 pounds lifted one foot in one minute. Torque is merely twisting force developed by an engine, and is not indicative of how much work can be done, unless engine speed is known. The relationship between horsepower, torque, and engine speed can be expressed as:

$$\text{Horsepower} = \frac{\text{rpm} \times \text{Torque}}{5,252}$$

Example 1

A motorcycle engine develops 30 foot-pounds torque at 6,000 rpm. How much horsepower does it produce at that speed?

$$= \frac{6,000 \times 30}{5,252}$$
$$= \frac{180,000}{5,252}$$
$$= 34.3 \text{ horsepower (rounded off)}$$

It is sometimes desired to know how much torque is developed by an engine when horsepower and rpm are known. The formula can then be written as:

$$\text{Torque} = \frac{\text{Horsepower} \times 5,252}{\text{rpm}}$$

Example 2

During a dynamometer test, an engine developed 14.7 horsepower at 3,500 rpm. How much torque did it produce?

$$= \frac{14.7 \times 5,252}{3,500}$$
$$= \frac{77,204}{3,500}$$
$$= 22.06 \text{ foot-pounds (rounded off)}$$

PISTON SPEED

It is at times desirable to know the maximum speed pistons reach as they move in their cylinders. This peak speed is reached when the piston is midway between top dead center and bottom dead center. The formula for finding piston speed is:

$$\text{Piston speed} = \frac{\text{Stroke length (in inches)} \times 2 \times \text{rpm}}{12}$$

Example

An engine has a stroke of 2.5 inches. What is its piston speed at 5,000 rpm?

$$\text{Piston speed} = \frac{2.5 \times 2 \times 5{,}000}{12}$$

$$= \frac{25{,}000}{12}$$

$$= 2{,}083 \text{ feet per minute}$$

GEAR RATIO

Gear ratio is defined as the number of revolutions a driving gear makes to turn a driven gear through one complete revolution. By convention, a 4 to 1 gear ratio is said to be lower than a 2.5 to 1 ratio. Note that it is possible to have a gear ratio of less than unity. For a pair of gears, the ratio is found by dividing the number of teeth on the driven gear by the number of teeth on the driving gear. The same formula works equally well for engine and rear wheel sprockets.

Example 1

There are 27 teeth on the primary drive gear on a certain motorcycle, and 60 teeth on the primary driven gear. What is its primary reduction ratio?

$$\text{Gear ratio} = \frac{\text{Teeth on driven gear}}{\text{Teeth on driving gear}}$$

$$= \frac{60}{27}$$

$$= 2.22 \text{ to } 1 \text{ (rounded off)}$$

Example 2

In a certain transmission, there are 27 teeth on 5th input (driving) gear, and 26 teeth on 5th output (driven) gear. What is the gear ratio?

$$\text{Gear ratio} = \frac{\text{Teeth on driving gear}}{\text{Teeth on driven gear}}$$

$$= \frac{27}{26}$$

$$= 0.96 \text{ to } 1 \text{ (rounded off)}$$

Example 3

There are 15 teeth on the engine sprocket on a certain bike, and 49 teeth on the rear wheel sprocket, What is the final reduction ratio?

$$\text{Reduction ratio} = \frac{\text{Number of teeth on driven sprocket}}{\text{Number of teeth on drive sprocket}}$$

$$= \frac{49}{15}$$

$$= 3.27 \text{ to } 1 \text{ (rounded off)}$$

BOLT TORQUE

The table on the following page lists nominal tightening torque for various metric thread sizes.

BOLT TIGHTENING TORQUES

Diameter (Millimeters)	Pitch (Millimeters)	Torque Foot-pounds	(Meter-kilograms)
Coarse thread			
5	0.90	2.53-3.47	(0.35-0.48)
6	1.00	4.56-6.37	(0.63-0.88)
8	1.25	11.6-15.9	(1.6-2.2)
10	1.50	22.4-30.4	(3.1-4.2)
12	1.75	39.1-54.2	(5.4-7.5)
14	2.00	60.0-83.2	(8.3-11.5)
16	2.00	94.0-130	(13-18)
18	2.50	130-181	(18-25)
20	2.50	188-253	(26-35)
Fine thread			
5	0.50	2.53-3.47	(0.35-0.48)
6	0.75	3.98-5.57	(0.55-0.77)
8	1.00	9.76-13.4	(1.35-1.85)
10	1.25	18.4-25.3	(2.55-3.5)
12	1.50	32.5-44.8	(4.5-6.2)
14	1.50	53.5-73.8	(7.4-10.2)
16	1.50	83.2-116	(11.5-16)
18	1.50	123-166	(17-23)
20	1.50	166-239	(23-33)

APPENDIX - 1973 AND LATER 250cc, 400cc, 440cc AND 501cc MODELS

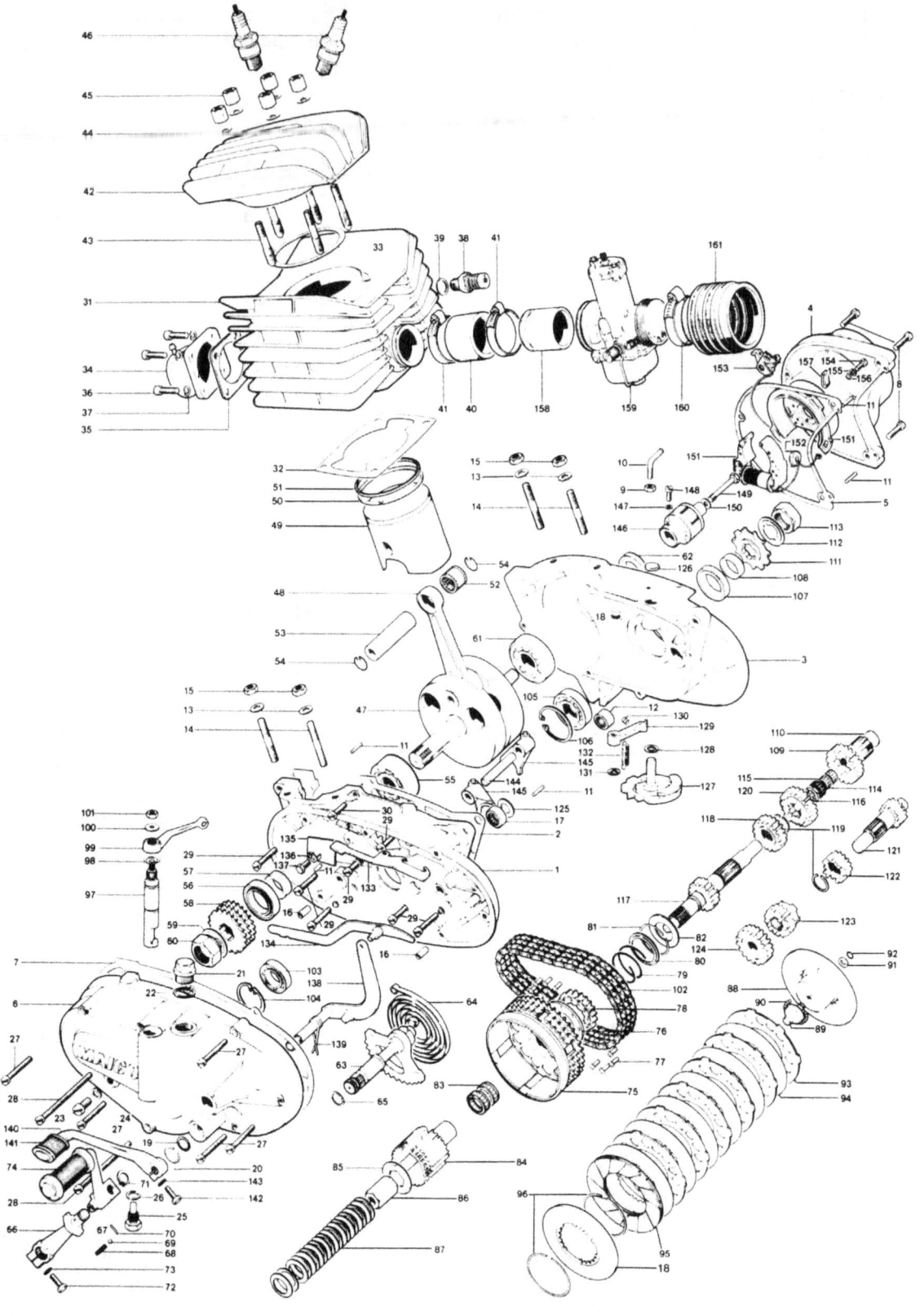

110

Engine/gearbox unit, 250, 400, 440 and 501 models

1	Left hand crankcase half	82	Thrust washer
2	Gasket	83	Bearing, needle roller
3	Right hand crankcase half	84	Clutch centre
4	Right hand engine cover	85	Washer, tab
5	Gasket	86	Nut
6	Left hand engine cover	87	Cup springs
7	Gasket	88	Clutch pressure plate
8	Screw - 3 off	89	Clutch thrust pin
9	Nut	90	Ball bearings - 14 off
10	Breather tube	91	Washer
11	Dowel pin - 3 off	92	Circlip
12	Bearing, needle roller	93	Clutch plate, driving
13	Washer - 4 off	94	Clutch plate, driven
14	Stud - 4 off	95	Clutch plate faced
15	Nut - 4 off	96	Wire circlip
16	Hollow dowel pin - 2 off	97	Clutch operating spindle
17	Bearing, needle roller	98	Oil seal
18	Clutch backing plate	99	Clutch operating lever
19	Felt washer	100	Washer
20	Wire circlip	101	Nut
21	Oil filler bolt	102	Primary drive chain
22	Washer, fibre	103	Bearing, ball
23	Screw	106	Circlip
24	Washer, fibre	107	Oil seal
25	Oil drain plug	108	Spacer
26	Washer, fibre	109	Final drive gear
27	Screw - 4 off	110	Blanking off plate
28	Screw - 2 off	111	Gearbox final drive sprocket
29	Screw - 7 off	112	Washer, tab
30	Screw	113	Nut
31	Cylinder barrel complete with liner	114	Bearing, needle roller - 2 off
32	Gasket	115	Bearing, needle roller
33	Gasket	116	Spacer
34	Exhaust manifold	117	Mainshaft and gear
35	Gasket	118	Gear
36	Screw - 4 off	119	Circlip - 2 off
37	Washer - 4 off	120	Gear
38	Decompressor	121	Layshaft and gear
39	Washer	122	Gear
40	Induction hose	123	Gear
41	Hose clip - 2 off	124	Gear
42	Cylinder head	125	Thrust washer
43	Stud - 5 off	126	Blanking off plate
44	Washer - 5 off	127	Selector cam plate
45	Nut - 5 off	128	Thrust washer
46	Spark plug - 2 off	129	Selector plate stop
47	Flywheel assembly	130	Spring
48	Connecting rod	131	Circlip
49	Piston	132	Spring
*50	Piston ring	133	Hook selector lever
*51	Piston ring	134	Selector pull rod
52	Bearing, needle roller	135	Plate
53	Gudgeon pin	136	Tab washer
54	Circlip	137	Bolt
55	Bearing, ball	138	Gear operating lever and spindle
56	Oil seal	139	Gear lever return spring
57	Spacing collar	140	Gear lever
58	Primary drive sprocket	141	Gear lever rubber
59	Washer	142	Bolt
60	Nut	143	Washer
61	Bearing, ball	144	Gear selector fork spindle
62	Oil seal	145	Gear selector fork - 2 off
63	Kickstart spindle and quadrant	146	Rotor
64	Kickstart return spring	147	Washer
65	Oil seal	148	Screw
66	Kickstart lever	149	Bolt
67	Kickstart swivel pedal	150	Washer
68	Spring	151	Stator
69	Ball bearing	152	Condenser
70	Pin	153	Contact breaker
71	Circlip	154	Screw
72	Bolt	155	Washer
73	Washer	156	Washer
74	Kickstart rubber	157	Felt oiler
75	Clutch housing	158	Induction hose sleeve
76	Kickstart ratchet plate	159	Carburettor
77	Rivets - 8 off	160	Hose clip
78	Kickstart ratchet gear	161	Connecting rubber hose
79	Spring		
80	Spring locating washer		
81	Wire circlip	*	Current models have only one piston ring

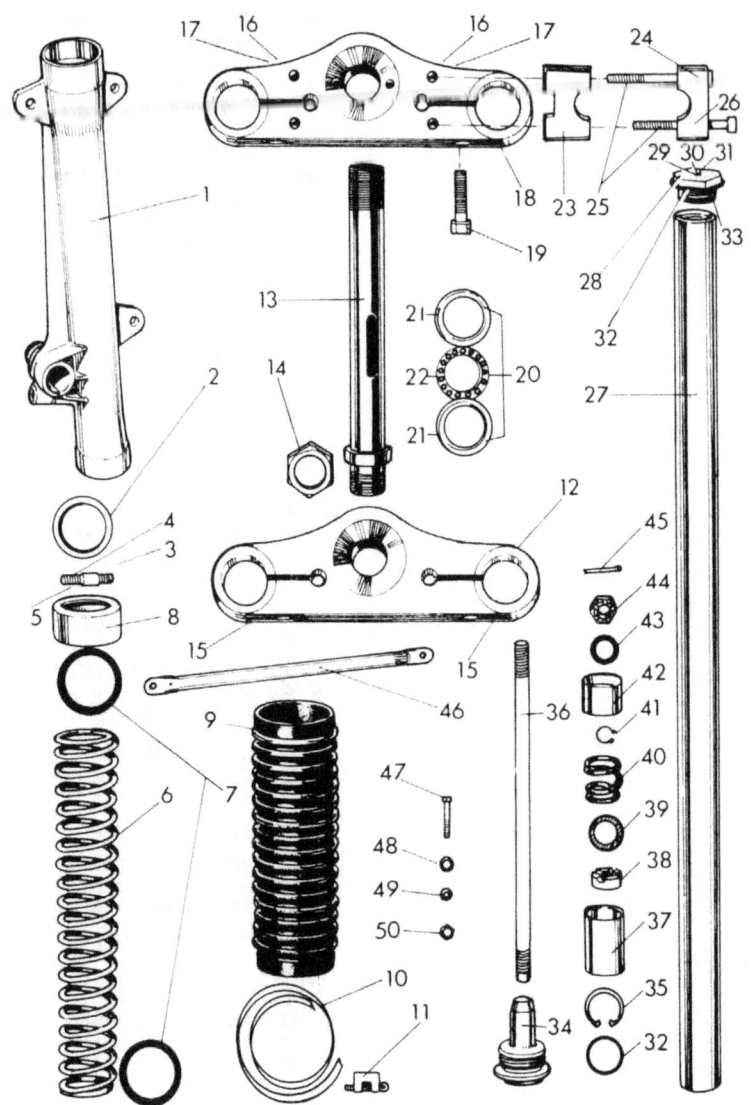

Front forks

1. Slider - 2 off
2. Oil seal - 2 off
3. Stud - 2 off
4. Nut - 2 off
5. Washer, spring - 2 off
6. Spring - 2 off
7. Spring seat - 4 off
8. Gaiter securing cap - 2 off
9. Rubber gaiter - 2 off
10. Hose, clip - 4 off
12. Bottom yoke
13. Steering column tube
14. Nut - 3 off
15. Allen screw - 2 off
16. Steering stop screw - 2 off
17. Rubber buffer - 2 off
18. Top yoke
19. Allen screw - 2 off
20. Bearing assembly complete 2 off
21. Bearing cups - 4 off
22. Ball bearings, caged - 2 off
23. Handlebar clamp, lower - 2 off
24. Handlebar clamp, upper - 2 off
25. Allen screw - 4 off
26. Washer, spring - 4 off
27. Fork tube - 2 off
28. Top nut - 2 off
29. Ball - 2 off
30. Spring - 2 off
31. Stud - 2 off
32. 'O' ring - 2 off
33. Washer - 2 off
34. Bottom nut and damper cone - 2 off
35. Circlip - 2 off
36. Damper tube - 2 off
37. Damper collar - 2 off
38. Valve - 2 off
39. Washer - 2 off
40. Damper spring - 2 off
41. Circlip - 2 off
42. Damper piston - 2 off
43. Washer - 2 off
44. Castle nut - 2 off
45. Split pin - 2 off
46. Front brake torque arm
47. Bolt
48. Washer - 2 off
49. Washer, spring
50. Nut - 2 off

112

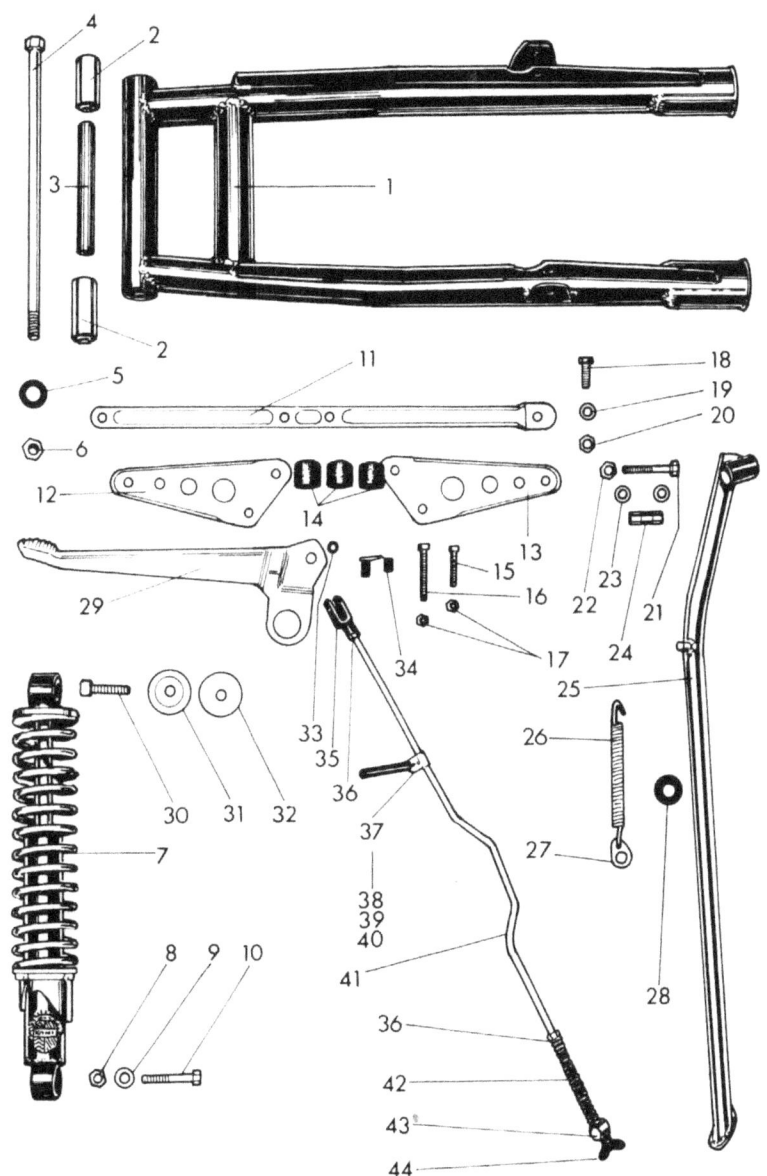

Swinging arm and prop stand

1. Swinging arm rear fork
2. Silentbloc bushes - 2 off
3. Spacing tube
4. Swinging arm pivot bolt
5. Washer
6. Swinging arm pivot nut
7. Rear suspension unit - 2 off
8. Nut 8 mm
9. Washer - 8 off
10. Bolt 8 mm - 4 off
11. Torque arm
12. Right hand chain guard halve
13. Left hand chain guard halve
14. Sliding rollers - 3 off
15. Screw 6 mm - 2 off
16. Screw 6 mm
17. Nut 6 mm - 2 off
18. Bolt 8 mm
19. Washer - 2 off
20. Nut 8 mm - 2 off
21. Bolt 8 mm
22. Nut 8 mm
23. Washer
24. Spacer bush
25. Prop stand
26. Stand return spring
27. Spring shackle
28. Rubber washer
29. Rear brake pedal
30. Allen screw 8 mm
31. Brake pedal collar
32. Washer
33. Bush
34. Security clip
35. Yoke
36. Nut 6 mm - 2 off
37. Brake rod return spring
38. Brake rod return spring clamp
39. Nut 4 mm - 2 off
40. Washer, spring
41. Rear brake rod
42. Spring
43. Trunnion
44. Nut, wing

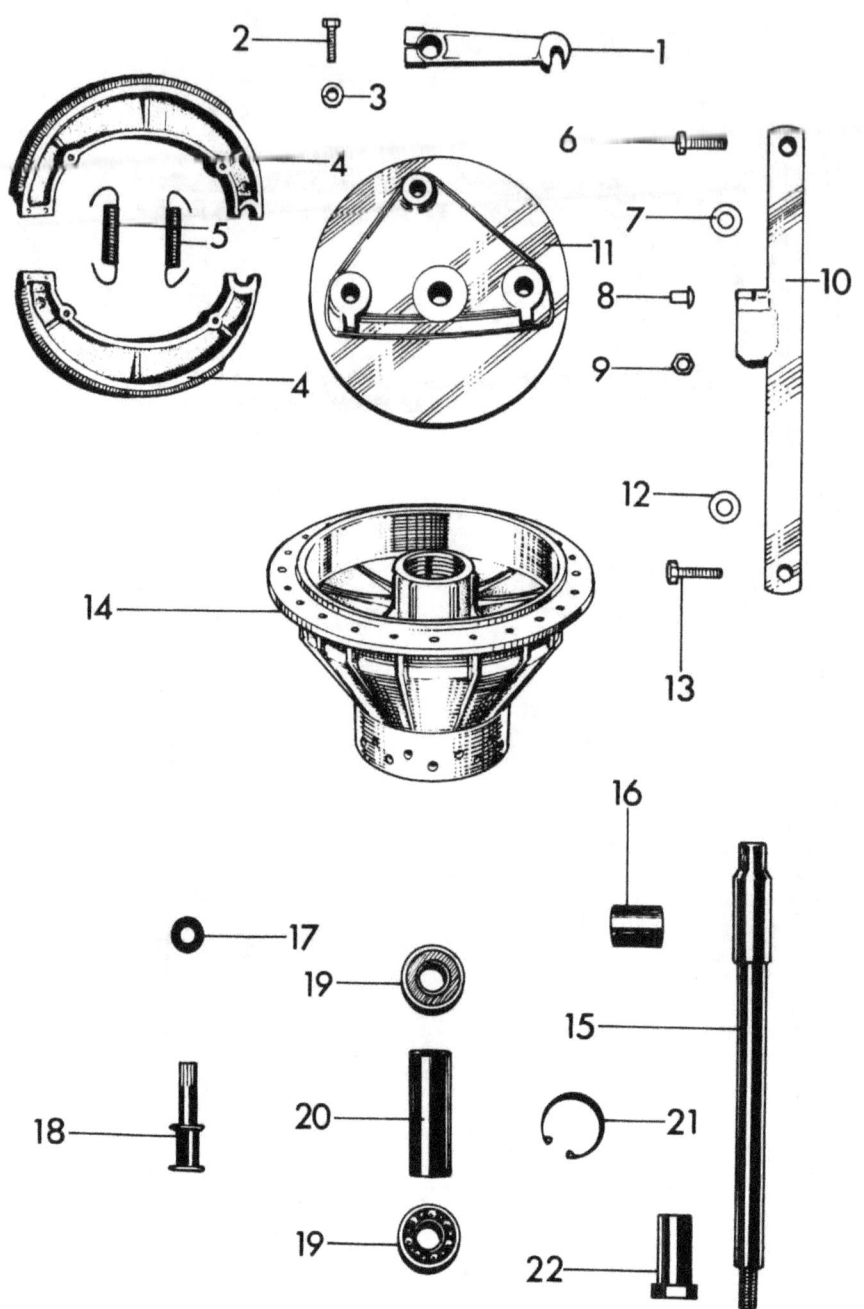

Front hub and brake - all models

1	Brake lever		12	Washer
2	Bolt 6 mm		13	Bolt 8 mm
3	Washer, spring		14	Front hub
4	Brake shoe - 2 off		15	Wheel spindle
5	Brake shoe spring - 2 off		16	Spacer
6	Bolt 8 mm		17	'O' ring
7	Washer		18	Operating cam
8	Cable outer holder		19	Bearing - 2 off
9	Nut 8 mm		20	Spacer tube
10	Torque arm		21	Circlip
11	Brake plate		22	Wheel spindle nut

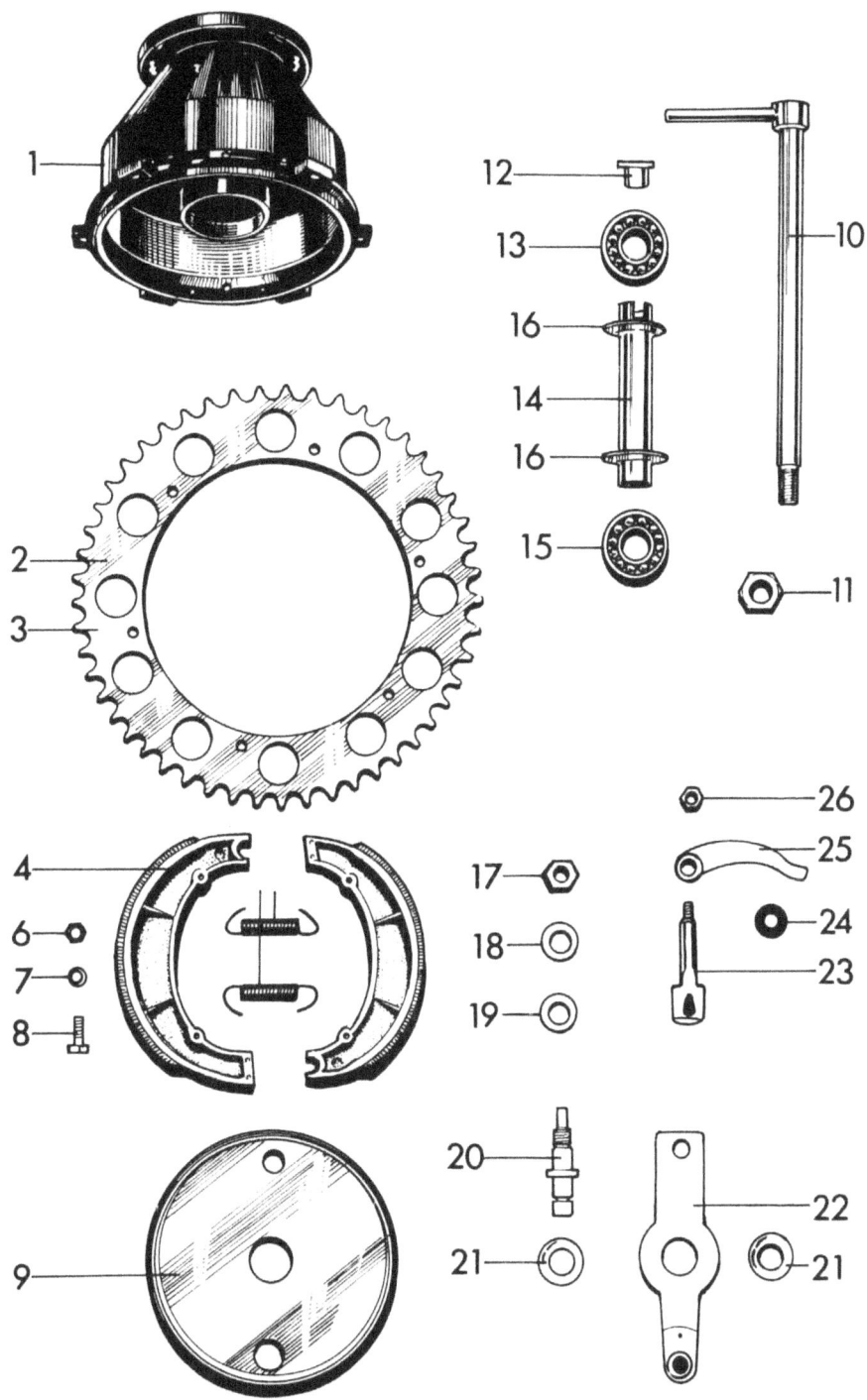

Rear hub and brake, 250, 400, 440 and 501

1	Rear hub	14	Spacer tube
2	Sprocket, 52T or 59T	15	Bearing, 6303RS
3	Sprocket, 52T or 59T	16	Shim - 2 off
4	Brake shoe - 2 off	17	Nut - 12 mm
5	Brake shoe spring - 2 off	18	Washer, spring
6	Nut 7 mm - 6 off	19	Washer
7	Washer, spring - 6 off	20	Brake shoe pivot
8	Bolt 7 mm - 6 off	21	Spacer
9	Brake plate cover	22	Brake plate
10	Wheel spindle	23	Operating cam
11	Wheel spindle nut	24	'O' ring - 2 off
12	Reducing collar	25	Brake lever
13	Bearing, 6204RS	26	Nut 8 mm

SPECIFICATIONS

Model	250 cc	400 cc	440 cc	501 cc
Type	Air cooled, piston port, two stroke engine			
Bore (mm)	67	77	82	91.6
Stroke (mm)	70	83	83	76
Capacity cc	247	386	438	501
Brake horsepower (Din)/rpm	33/7000	43/6700	47/6900	51/6900
Compression ratio	12 : 1	12 : 1	12 : 1	12 : 1
Gear ratio: 1	Moto Cross		Cross Country	
First	1.99		2.78	
Second	1.52		1.79	
Third	1.23		1.29	
Top	1		1	
Primary drive reduction	1.86 : 1			

Dimensions and wear limits:

Cylinder liner to bore interference (new)	0.013 in.
Cylinder liner to bore interference (replacement)	0.004 - 0.006 in.
Cylinder bore wear limit	0.004 in.
Cylinder bore to piston clearance	0.002 in.
Piston ring end gap	0.010 in.
Piston ring end gap wear limit	0.016 in.
Piston oversizes	Approx. 0.15 mm (X8) intervals
Flywheel alignment: max. out of true	0.002 in.
Big end play (new)	0.001 - 0.0015 in.
Connecting rod side play	0.019 - 0.020 in.
Connecting rod side play wear limit	0.024 in.
Big end eye thickness (new)	0.665 - 0.670 in.
Distance across flywheels (reference only since the connecting rod side clearance is the determining factor)	2.475 - 2.490 in.
Crankshaft end float	0.004 - 0.012 in.
First gear side clearance	0.004 - 0.008 in.
Gear selector fork to camplate clearance	0.010 - 0.025 in.
Clutch cup spring height	0.075 in.
Clutch cup spring height wear limit	0.070 in.
Clutch plate thickness (plain driven)	0.050 in.
Clutch plate thickness (plain driven) wear limit	0.045 in.
Clutch plate thickness (driving with holes)	0.085 in.
Clutch plate thickness (driving with holes) wear limit	0.080 in.

Fuel system:

Fuel tank capacity	9½ or 15 pints (5.5 or 8.5 litres)
Gearbox/clutch oil capacity	1.7 pints (1 litre)

Carburettor

Make	Bing			
Engine capacity c.c.	250	400	440	501
Choke size m.m	36	36	36	38
Main jet	175-180	185	185	185
Needle jet	280-285	285	285	285
Pilot jet	35	40	40	40
Needle position (numbered from bottom groove)	As required............			
Mixture adjustment screw (turns off seat)	1½	1½	1½	1½
Throttle needle	—	—	—	—
Throttle slide	—	—	—	—

Wheels, brakes and tyres:

Model	250, 400, 440 and 501 cc
Front wheel	Chromed steel or aluminium alloy rim with alloy hub and steel brake drum insert
Brake dia	136 mm
Spokes	18 x M4 x 125 mm
	18 x M4 x 230 mm
Rear wheel	Chromed steel or aluminium alloy rim with alloy hub and steel brake drum insert
Brake dia	160 mm
Spokes	18 x M4 x 143 mm
	18 x M4 x 208 mm
Tyre size: front	3.00 - 3.25 x 21 in.
rear	4.00 - 4.50 x 18 in.
Chain size	5/8 x 1/4 in.
Sprocket size: gearbox (teeth)	11 - 14
rear wheel	52 or 59

continued

SPECIFICATIONS (continued)

Ignition and electrical system

Model — 250 cc

Spark plug
- Make — Champion
- Type — N2 or N2G (Use N3 or N3G for moist or cold conditions)
- Thread size — 14 mm
- Reach — ¾ in
- Gap — 0.018-0.020 in.

*Ignition timing B.T.D.C. — 0.110-0.126 in.

Contact breaker gap — 0.012 in.

*For 400, 440 and 501 cc models all the 250 cc specifications are applicable except for the ignition advance which is as follows:-

Model	400 cc	440 cc	501 cc
Ignition timing B.T.D.C.	0.138-0.146 in.	0.138 in.	0.118 in.

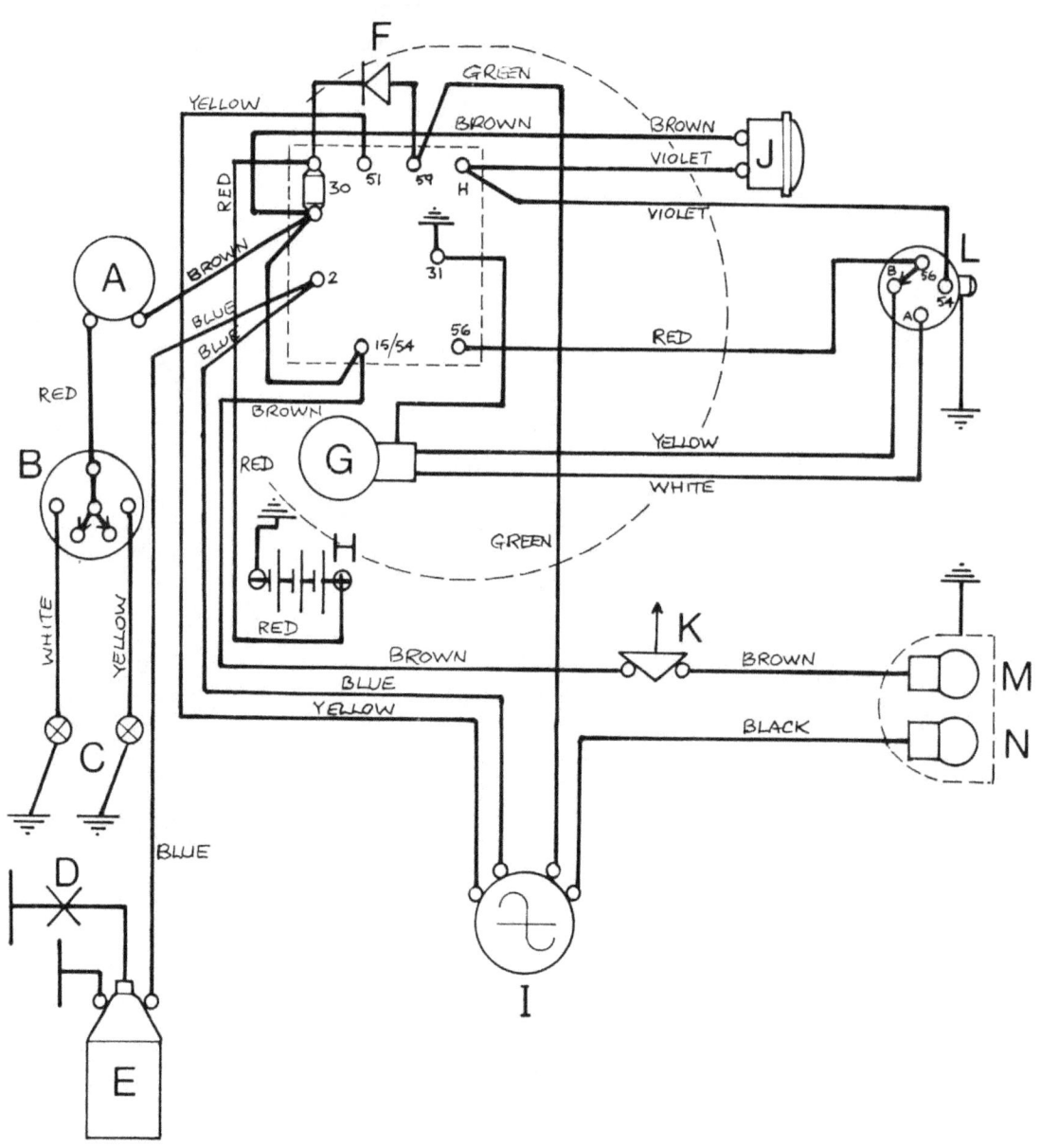

Wiring diagram for Enduro models

A	Flasher unit		I	Flywheel magneto
B	Turn signal switch		J	Horn
C	Flashing indicator lamps		K	Stop lamp switch
D	Spark plug		L	Horn and dip switch
E	Ignition coil		M	Brake light
F	Rectifier		N	Tail light
G	Headlamp			

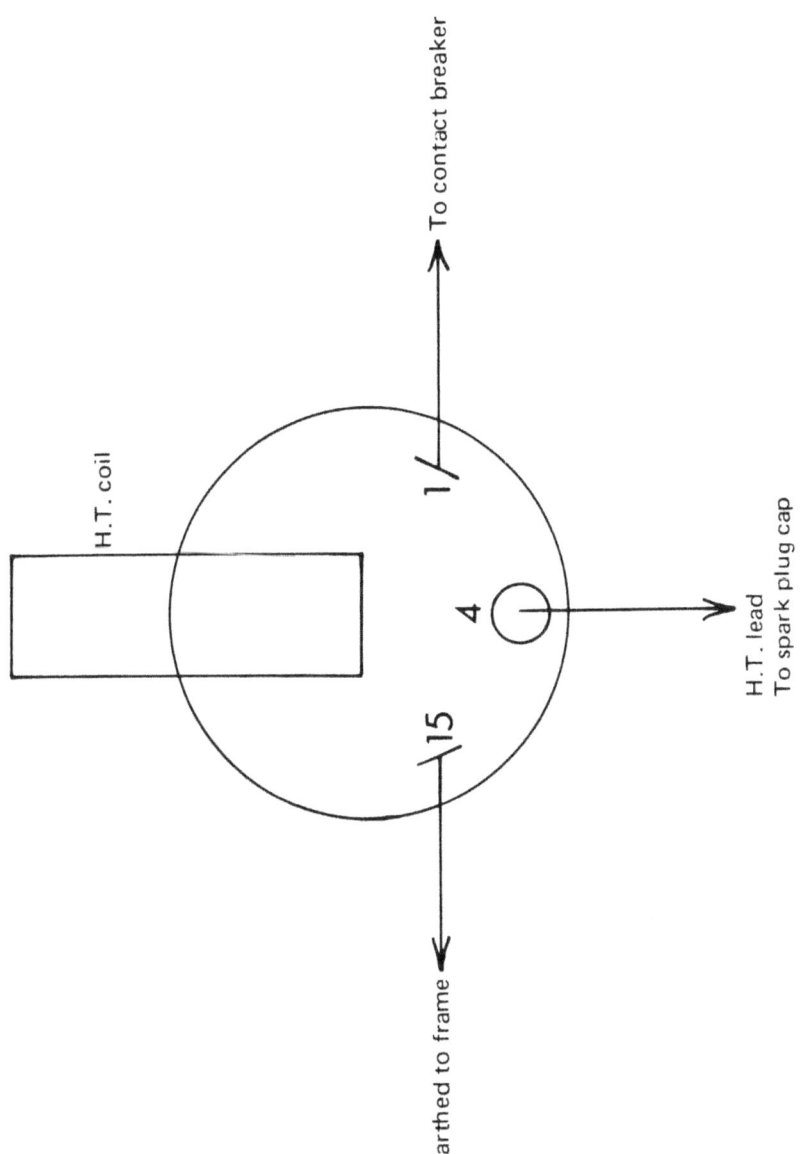

Wiring diagram - all models without lights

INDEX

A

Air box, water-and-dirt-proofing............ 101
Air cleaner................................ 4, 9
Air filter and air box competition, check.... 97
Appendix 1973 and later models.............. 110

B

Backfiring 16
Bolt torques........................... 108-109
Brakes
   Adjustment 9, 91
   Brake cable guard, front................. 101
   Brake return, rear....................... 101
   Competition check........................ 95
   Inspection 90
   Lubrication cable........................ 8
   Modifications for competition............ 99
   Troubleshooting 17

C

Carburetor
   Adjustment 60
   Carburetor mount, competition
     modification 101
   Cleaning and inspection.................. 58
   Competition check........................ 97
   Fuel feed system operation............... 55
   Idling system operation.................. 57
   Main control system operation............ 55
   Maintenance, periodic.................... 12
   Reassembly 59
   Removal and disassembly.................. 57
Charging system (see Lighting/charging
   system)
Charging system troubleshooting............. 22
Clutch
   Adjustment 9
   Clutch (steel) service limits............ 46
   Competition check........................ 97
   Description 42
   Inspection 46
   Lubrication cable........................ 8
   Modifications for competition............ 98
   Removal 43
   Slip or drag............................. 16
   Spring stacking.......................... 48
Coil mount, competition check............... 97
Condenser 97
Competition preparation
   Air box, water-and-dirt-proofing......... 101
   Air filter and air box................... 97
   Brake cable guard, front................. 101
   Carburetor 97

   Carburetor mount........................ 101
   Check list.............................. 94
   Cleaning and inspection................. 95
   Clutch 97
   Clutch modifications.................... 98
   Coil mount.............................. 97
   Controls 98
   Control cables.......................... 97
   Drive chain and sprockets............... 96
   Engine modifications.................... 98
   Exhaust system.......................... 96
   Fasteners 98
   Fenders 96
   Fuel tank and fuel feed system.......... 96
   Head, cylinder, pistons, and big-end bearing 97
   Ignition 97
   Rear brake return....................... 101
   Seat 97
   Suspension modifications................ 99
   Suspension, swinging arm, and steering... 95
   Test riding............................. 98
   Transmission 98
   Transmission modifications.............. 98
   Wheels, brakes and hubs................. 95
   Wheel, hub, and brake modification...... 99
Compression test........................... 19
Connecting rods............................ 43
Contact point replacement.................. 14
Control cables, compression check.......... 97
Control lubrication and adjustment......... 8
Controls, competition check................ 98
Conversion tables.......................... 105
Crankshaft and crankcase
   Solenoid check.......................... 86
   Bearing replacement..................... 40
   Disassembly 34
   Inspection 39
   Removal 29
Crankshaft sprocket and seal............... 30
Cylinder
   Inspection 23
   Installation 25
   Piston-to-cylinder clearance............ 25
   Removal 21
Cylinder head
   Carbon deposits, removing............... 20
   Description 19
   Installation 21
   Removal 20
   Torque settings......................... 21

D

Drive chain
   Adjustment 11
   Cleaning and lubrication................ 10
   Competition check....................... 96

E

Electrical system
   Fault tracing.................................. 70
   Lighting/charging system (Enduro models) 68
   Magneto ignition system.................. 62
Engine
   Carbon removal............................. 13
   Compression ratio......................... 107
   Crankshaft and crankcase............29-41
   Cylinder 21-26
   Cylinder head.............................19-21
   Lubrication 13
   Modifications for competition............ 98
   Noises, unusual............................. 16
   Operating principles....................... 18
   Operating requirements.................. 14
   Pistons and rings........................26-29
   Service timing and adjustment.......... 41
   Torque valves............................... 41
   Upper end, competition check.......... 97
Exhaust system, competition check......... 96

F

Fasteners, competition check................. 98
Fenders, competition check................... 97
Flat spots... 16
Fork, front
   Competition check........................ 95
   Damping oil.................................. 7
   Damper service............................. 73
   Seal replacement........................... 71
   Springs 76
   Tube replacement.......................... 75
Frame 93
Fuel system
   Air filter...................................... 60
   Carburetor operation..................... 55
   Carburetor servicing...................... 57
   Fuel tank.................................... 60
   Tank and feed system, competition check.. 96

G

Gear ratio determination...................... 108
Gearshifting difficulties........................ 17

H

Handling, poor.................................... 17
Horsepower and torque, determining........ 107

I

Idling, poor.. 16
Ignition system, magneto
   Breaker points............................. 62

Competition check............................. 97
Condenser 68
Condenser replacement...................... 64
Contact breaker replacement............... 64
Firing point...................................... 66
Ignition coil..................................... 66
Ignition timing.................................. 64
Magneto operation............................ 62
Maintenance, periodic........................ 12
Troubleshooting 68

K

Kickstarter 50

L

Lighting/charging system (Enduro models)
   Battery installation........................ 70
   Battery testing............................. 68
   Charging 69
   Electric system testing................... 70
Loss of power.............................16, 17
Lubrication (see Maintenance and lubrication, periodic)

M

Magneto ignition system (see Ignition system, magneto)
Maintenance and lubrication, periodic
   Air cleaner.................................. 4
   Carbon removal........................... 13
   Carburetor 12
   Control lubrication and adjustment.... 8
   Damping oil (front suspension)........ 7
   Drive chain................................. 10
   Engine lubrication......................... 13
   Fuel and oil mixtures..................... 13
   Ignition 12
   Transmission oil............................ 4
Misfiring 16

O

Oil, fork... 7
Oil, transmission................................ 4
Overheating 16

P

Piston and rings
   Inspection 27
   Installation 28
   Piston displacement..................... 106
   Piston oversizes.......................... 25
   Removal 26
   Seizure 16

S

Safety hints	2
Seat, competition check	97
Service hints	1
Shock absorbers	81
Specifications and data, general	
Clutch spring stacking	48
Clutch (steel) service limits	46
Cylinder head torque settings	21
Engine torque values	41
Fuel and oil mixtures	13
Ignition firing points	66
Piston-to-cylinder clearance	25
Piston oversizes	25
Speed determination	108
Spokes	84
Spring/shocks	81
Sprocket, rear	91
Starting difficulties	15
Steering	
Bearing lubrication and replacement	77
Competition check	95
Looseness, checking for	76
Troubleshooting	17
Suspension, rear	
Competition check	95
Modifications for competition	99
Spring/shocks	81
Swinging arm	79
Supplies, expendable	2
Suspension, front (see Fork, front)	
Swinging arm	79, 95

T

Test riding	98
Tools	2
Throttle lubrication adjustment	8-9
Transmission	
Description	42
Disassembly	50
Competition check	98
Inspection	52
Modifications for competition	98
Oil changing and checking	4
Troubleshooting	
Backfiring	16
Brake problems	17
Clutch slip or drag	16
Engine noises	16
Excessive vibration	16
Flat spots	16
Lighting problems	17
Misfiring	16
Operating requirements	14
Overheating	16
Power loss	16
Piston seizure	16
Poor handling	17
Poor idling	16
Starting difficulties	15
Troubleshooting summary	17

V

Vibration, excessive	16

W

Wheels and tires	
Competition check	95
Modifications for competition	99
Spokes	84
Sprocket, rear	91
Wheel balance	85
Wheel bearings and seals	86
Wheel inspection	85
Wheel runout	86

VELOCEPRESS MANUALS – MOTORCYCLE BY MAKE

AJS 1932-1948 SINGLES & TWINS 250cc THRU 1000cc (BOOK OF)
AJS 1945-1960 SINGLES 350cc & 500cc MODELS 16 & 18 (BOOK OF)
AJS 1955-1965 SINGLES 350cc & 500cc (BOOK OF)
AJS 1957-1966 FACTORY WSM - ALL SINGLES & TWINS
AJS 1959-1969 FACTORY WSM G80CS G85CS & P11 OFF ROAD
ARIEL UP TO 1932 (BOOK OF)
ARIEL 1932-1939 PREWAR MODELS (BOOK OF)
ARIEL 1933-1951 (WORKSHOP MANUAL)
ARIEL 1939-1960 4 STROKE SINGLES (BOOK OF)
ARIEL 1958-1964 LEADER & ARROW FACTORY WSM & PARTS LIST
ARIEL 1958-1964 LEADER & ARROW (BOOK OF)
BMW R26 R27 (1956-1967) FACTORY WORKSHOP MANUAL
BMW R50 R50S R60 R69S (1955-1969) FACTORY WORKSHOP MANUAL
BMW R50/5 R60/5 R75/5 (1969-1973) FACTORY WORKSHOP MANUAL
BRIDGESTONE 90 SERIES FACTORY WSM & PARTS CATALOGUE
BRIDGESTONE 175 SERIES FACTORY WSM & PARTS CATALOGUE
BRIDGESTONE 350 SERIES FACTORY WSM & PARTS CATALOGUES
BSA SERVICE SHEETS MASTER CATALOGUE ALL MODELS 1945-1967
BSA BANTAM D1 TO D7 1948-1966 FACTORY SERVICE SHEETS MANUAL
BSA BANTAM ALL MODELS FROM 1948 ONWARDS (BOOK OF)
BSA BANTAM D14 FACTORY SERVICE MANUAL
BSA DANDY FACTORY WORKSHOP MANUAL (COMPILATION)
BSA SINGLES & V-TWINS UP TO 1926 inc. 1927 SUPPLEMENT (BOOK OF)
BSA SINGLES & V-TWINS UP TO 1930 (BOOK OF)
BSA SINGLES & V-TWINS UP TO 1935 (BOOK OF)
BSA SINGLES & V-TWINS 1936-1939 (BOOK OF)
BSA C10, C11 & C12 1945-1958 FACTORY SERVICE SHEETS MANUAL
BSA OHV & SV SINGLES 250-600cc 1945-1959 (BOOK OF)
BSA C15 & B40 1958-1967 FACTORY SERVICE SHEETS MANUAL
BSA OHV & SV SINGLES 250cc (ONLY) 1954-1970 (BOOK OF)
BSA B31, B32, B33 & B34 1945-60 FACTORY SERVICE SHEETS MANUAL
BSA OHV SINGLES 350 & 500cc 1955-1967 (BOOK OF)
BSA M20, M21 & M33 1945-1963 FACTORY SERVICE SHEETS MANUAL
BSA TWINS A7 & A10 1948-1962 FACTORY SERVICE SHEETS MANUAL
BSA TWINS A7 & A10 1948-1962 (BOOK OF)
BSA TWINS A50 & A65 1962-1965 FACTORY WORKSHOP MANUAL
BSA TWINS A50 & A65 1962-1969 (SECOND BOOK OF)
BULTACO 125cc to 37cc SINGLES 1968-1979 WORKSHOP MANUAL
CZ 125cc to 380cc SINGLES 1967-1974 WORKSHOP MANUAL
DOUGLAS 1929-1939 PREWAR ALL MODELS (BOOK OF)
DOUGLAS 1948-1957 POSTWAR ALL MODELS FACTORY SHOP MANUAL
DUCATI 160cc, 250cc & 350cc OHC MODELS FACTORY SHOP MANUAL
HODAKA 90cc,100cc & 125cc SINGLES 1964-1978 WORKSHOP MANUAL
HONDA 50cc ALL MODELS UP TO 1970 INC MONKEY & TRAIL (BOOK OF)
HONDA 90cc ALL MODELS UP TO 1966 (BOOK OF)
HONDA TWINS & SINGLES 50cc THRU 305cc 1960-1966 (BOOK OF)
HONDA TWINS ALL MODELS 125cc THRU 450cc UP TO 1968 (BOOK OF)
HONDA C100 50cc SUPER CUB O.H.C. 1959-1962 FACTORY WSM
HONDA C110 50cc SPORT CUB O.H.C. 1960-1962 FACTORY WSM
HONDA 50-65-70-90cc O.H.C. SINGLES 1959-1983 WSM
HONDA 100-125cc SINGLES CB/CD/CL/SL/TL 1970-1984 FACTORY WSM
HONDA 125-150cc TWINS C/CS/CB/CA 1959-1966 FACTORY WSM
HONDA 125-160-175-200cc TWINS 1965-1978 WORKSHOP MANUAL
HONDA 250-305cc TWINS C/CS/CB 1961-1968 FACTORY WSM
HOHDA 250-350cc TWINS CB/CL/SL 1968-1973 FACTORY WSM
HONDA 250-360cc TWINS CB/CL/CJ 1974-1977 FACTORY WSM
HONDA 350F & 400F 4-CYLINDER 1972-1977 FACTORY WSM
HONDA 450cc TWINS CB/CL 1965-1974 K0 TO K7 WORKSHOP MANUAL
HONDA 500cc & 550cc 4-CYL 1971-1978 FACTORY WORKSHOP MANUAL
HONDA 750cc SHOC 4-CYL 1969-1978 K0~K8 WORKSHOP MANUAL
HUSQVARNA 125cc to 450cc SINGLES 1965-1975 WORKSHOP MANUAL
INDIAN PONYBIKE, BOY RACER & PAPOOSE ILL PARTS LIST & SALES LIT

J.A.P. ENGINES 1927-1952 & MOTORCYCLES 1934-1952 (BOOK OF)
MAICO 250cc to 501cc 1968-1978 WORKSHOP MANUAL
MATCHLESS 1931-1939 ALL MODELS 250cc THRU 990cc (BOOK OF)
MATCHLESS 1945-1956 350 & 500cc SINGLES (BOOK OF)
MATCHLESS 1955-1966 350 & 500cc SINGLES (BOOK OF)
MATCHLESS 1957-1966 FACTORY WSM - ALL SINGLES & TWINS
NEW IMPERIAL ALL SV & OHV FROM 1935 ONWARDS (BOOK OF)
NORTON 1932-1939 PREWAR MODELS (BOOK OF)
NORTON 1932-1947 (BOOK OF)
NORTON 1938-1956 (BOOK OF)
NORTON 1945-1963 MODELS 16H, Big4, ES2, 19 & 50 WSM'S & PARTS
NORTON 1955-1963 MODELS 19, 50 & ES2 (BOOK OF)
NORTON 1948-1970 DOMINATOR TWINS FACTORY WSM'S & PARTS
NORTON 1955-1965 DOMINATOR TWINS (BOOK OF)
NORTON 1960-1970 TWIN CYLINDER FACTORY WORKSHOP MANUAL
NORTON 1970-1975 COMMANDO 850 & 750cc FACTORY WSM
NORTON 1975-1978 MK 3 COMMANDO 850 cc FACTORY WSM
PANTHER 1932-1958 LIGHTWEIGHT MODELS 250 & 350cc (BOOK OF)
PANTHER 1938-1966 HEAVYWEIGHT MODELS 600 & 650cc (BOOK OF)
PENTON-KTM-SACHS 1968-1975 100cc & 125cc WORKSHOP MANUAL
PENTON-KTM 1972-1975 175cc, 250cc & 400cc WSM & PARTS MANUALS
RALEIGH MOTORCYCLES 1919-1933 (BOOK OF)
ROYAL ENFIELD 1934-1946 SINGLES & V TWINS (BOOK OF)
ROYAL ENFIELD 1937-1953 SINGLES & V TWINS (BOOK OF)
ROYAL ENFIELD 1946-1962 SINGLES (BOOK OF)
ROYAL ENFIELD 1948-1962 350cc & 500cc PRE-UNIT BULLET WSM
ROYAL ENFIELD 1948-1963 500cc TWINS FACTORY WORKSHOP MANUAL
ROYAL ENFIELD 1952-1963 700cc TWINS FACTORY WORKSHOP MANUAL
ROYAL ENFIELD 1956-1966 250cc CRUSADER & 350cc NEW BULLET WSM
ROYAL ENFIELD 1958-1966 250cc & 350cc SINGLES (SECOND BOOK OF)
ROYAL ENFIELD 1962-1970 INTERCEPTOR WSM'S & PARTS (Compilation)
RUDGE 1933-1939 (BOOK OF)
SACHS 1968-1975 100cc & 125cc ENGINES WSM & M/CYCLE PARTS LIST
SUNBEAM 1928-1939 (BOOK OF)
SUNBEAM 1946-1957 S7 & S8 (BOOK OF)
SUZUKI 50cc & 80cc UP TO 1966 (BOOK OF)
SUZUKI T10 1963-1967 FACTORY WORKSHOP MANUAL
SUZUKI T20 & T200 1965-1969 FACTORY WORKSHOP MANUAL
SUZUKI TWINS 1962 ONWARDS 125-500cc WORKSHOP MANUAL
TRIUMPH 1935-1949 SINGLES & TWINS (BOOK OF)
TRIUMPH 1937-1961 SINGLES SV & OHV 250cc-600cc + TERRIER & CUB
TRIUMPH 1945-1955 PRE-UNIT 350cc, 500cc & 650cc TWINS WSM No.11
TRIUMPH 1945-1959 TWINS (BOOK OF)
TRIUMPH 1956-1969 TWINS (BOOK OF)
TRIUMPH 1956-1962 PRE-UNIT 500cc & 650cc TWINS WSM No.17
TRIUMPH 1957-1963 UNIT CONSTRUCTION 350-500cc WSM No.4
TRIUMPH 1963-1974 UNIT CONSTRUCTION 350-500cc FACTORY WSM
TRIUMPH 1963-1970 UNIT CONSTRUCTION 650cc FACTORY WSM
TRIUMPH 1968-1974 TRIDENT T150 & T150V FACTORY WSM
TRIUMPH 1971-1973 650cc OIL-IN-FRAME FACTORY WSM
TRIUMPH 1973-1978 BONNEVILLE & TIGER FACTORY WSM
TRIUMPH 1979-1983 750cc T140, TR7 & TR65 FACTORY WSM
VELOCETTE 1925-1970 ALL SINGLES & TWINS (BOOK OF)
VELOCETTE 1933-1952 MOV-MAC-MSS RIGID FRAME FACTORY WSM
VELOCETTE 1953-1960 MAC SPRING FRAME WSM & ILL PARTS LIST
VELOCETTE 1954-1971 MSS-VENOM-THRUXTON-VIPER FACTORY WSM
VILLIERS ENGINE UP TO 1959 INC. 3 WHEELERS (BOOK OF)
VILLIERS ENGINE UP TO 1969 (BOOK OF)
VINCENT 1935-1955 (WORKSHOP MANUAL)
YAMAHA 1961-1967 YA5 & YA6 (WORKSHOP MANUAL & ILL PARTS LIST)
YAMAHA 1968-1971 DT1 & MX SERIES Inc. GYT WORKSHOP MANUAL
YAMAHA 1971-1972 JT1& JT2 (WORKSHOP MANUAL & ILL PARTS LIST)

VELOCEPRESS MANUALS – SCOOTERS BY MAKE

BSA SUNBEAM SCOOTER WORKSHOP MANUAL 1959-1965
BSA SUNBEAM SCOOTER 1959-1965 (BOOK OF)
LAMBRETTA 1947-1957 ALL 125 & 150cc MODELS (BOOK OF)
LAMBRETTA 1957-1970 LI & TV MODELS (SECOND BOOK OF)
NSU PRIMA 1956-1964 ALL MODELS (BOOK OF)
TRIUMPH TIGRESS SCOOTER WORKSHOP MANUAL 1959-1965
TRIUMPH TIGRESS SCOOTER (BOOK OF)
VESPA 1951-1961 (BOOK OF)
VESPA 1955-1963 125 & 150cc & GS MODELS (SECOND BOOK OF)
VESPA 1955-1968 GS & SS (BOOK OF)
VESPA 1963-1972 90, 125 & 150cc (THIRD BOOK OF)

VELOCEPRESS MANUALS – MOPEDS & MOTORIZED BICYCLES

CYCLEMOTOR (BOOK OF)
NSU QUICKLY 1953-1963 ALL MODELS (BOOK OF)
PUCH MAXI N & S MAINTENANCE & REPAIR (3 MANUAL COMPILATION)
RALEIGH MOPEDS 1960-1969 (BOOK OF)

VELOCEPRESS MANUALS - THREE WHEELER'S

BOND MINICAR THREE WHEELER 1948-1967 (BOOK OF)
BMW ISETTA FACTORY WORKSHOP MANUAL
BSA THREE WHEELER (BOOK OF)
RELIANT REGAL THREE WHEELER 1952-1973 (BOOK OF)
VINTAGE MORGAN THREE WHEELER (BOOK OF)

VELOCEPRESS TECHNICAL BOOKS – MOTORCYCLE

1930'S BRITISH MOTORCYCLE CARBS & ELEC COMPONENTS (BOOK OF)
1930'S BRITISH MOTORCYCLE ENGINES (OVERHAUL & MAINTENANCE)
1930'S BRITISH MOTORCYCLE GEARBOXES & CLUTCHES (BOOK OF)
CATALOG OF BRITISH MOTORCYCLES (1951 MODELS)
LUCAS ELECTRONICS BRITISH M/CYCLES REPAIR & PARTS (1950-1977)
MOTORCYCLE ENGINEERING (P.E. Irving)
MOTORCYCLE ROAD TESTS 1949-1953 (Motor Cycle Magazine UK)
SPEED AND HOW TO OBTAIN IT (Motor Cycle Magazine UK)
TUNING FOR SPEED (P.E. Irving)
WIPAC (COMBO) MANUAL NUMBER 3 + M/CYCLE & SCOOTER MANUAL

www.VelocePress.com

VELOCEPRESS MANUALS – AUTOMOBILE BY MAKE

ALFA ROMEO GIULIA WORKSHOP MANUAL 1300 TO 2000cc 1962-1975
ALFA ROMEO GIULIA TECH MANUAL CARBURETED CARS FROM 1962
ALFA ROMEO GIULIA TECH MANUAL FUEL INJECTED CARS FROM 1969
ALFA ROMEO GIULIETTA & GIULIA 750 & 101 SERIES 1955-1965 WSM
AUSTIN-HEALEY SPRITE & MG MIDGET WORKSHOP MANUAL 1958-1971
BMW 600 LIMOUSINE FACTORY WORKSHOP MANUAL
BMW 600 LIMOUSINE OWNERS HAND BOOK & SERVICE MANUAL
BMW 2000 & 2002 1966-1976 WORKSHOP MANUAL
BMW 2500, 2800, 3.0 & BARVARIA WORKSHOP MANUAL
CORVAIR 1960-1969 WORKSHOP MANUAL
CORVETTE V8 1955-1962 WORKSHOP MANUAL
FERRARI HANDBOOK ROAD & RACE CARS (SERVICE/SPECS) 1948-1958
FERRARI 250GT SERVICE & MAINTENANCE by JIM RIFF 1956-1965
FERRARI 250GT & 250GTE FACTORY PARTS AND REPAIR MANUALS
FIAT 500 FACTORY WORKSHOP MANUAL 1957-1973
FIAT 600, 600D & MULTIPLA FACTORY WORKSHOP MANUAL 1955-1969
FORD MUSTANG 1965-1973 TRANSMISSION WORKSHOP MANUAL
JAGUAR E-TYPE 3.8 & 4.2 SERIES 1 & 2 WORKSHOP MANUAL
JAGUAR MK 7, 8, 9 & XK120, 140, 150 WORKSHOP MANUAL 1948-1961
MERCEDES-BENZ 230 SERIES 1963-1968
MERCEDES-BENZ 280 SERIES 1968-1972
METROPOLITAN FACTORY WORKSHOP MANUAL
MGA & MGB OWNERS HANDBOOK & WORKSHOP MANUAL
MG MIDGET TC, TD, TF & TF1500 WORKSHOP MANUAL
PORSCHE 356 1948-1965 WORKSHOP MANUAL
PORSCHE 911 2.0, 2.2, 2.4 LITRE 1964-1973 WORKSHOP MANUAL
PORSCHE 911 2.7, 3.0, 3.2 LITRE 1973-1989 WORKSHOP MANUAL
PORSCHE 912 WORKSHOP MANUAL
PORSCHE 914/4 & 914/6 1.7, 1.8, 2.0 LITRE 1970-1976 WSM
TRIUMPH TR2, TR3, TR4 1953-1965 WORKSHOP MANUAL
VOLKSWAGEN TRANSPORTER, TRUCKS & WAGONS 1950-1979 WSM
VOLVO 1944-1968 ALL MODELS WORKSHOP MANUAL

VELOCEPRESS TECHNICAL BOOKS - AUTOMOBILE

HOW TO BUILD A FIBERGLASS CAR
HOW TO BUILD A RACING CAR
HOW TO RESTORE THE MODEL 'A' FORD
MASERATI OWNER'S HANDBOOK
PERFORMANCE TUNING THE SUNBEAM TIGER
SOUPING THE VOLKSWAGEN
SOLEX CARBURETORS (EMPHASIS ON UK & EU AUTOMOBILES)
SU CARBURETORS (EMPHASIS ON UK AUTOMOBILES)
WEBER CARBURETORS (EMPHASIS ON ALFA & FIAT)

VELOCEPRESS BOOKS & GUIDES - AUTOMOBILE

COMPLETE CATALOG OF JAPANESE MOTOR VEHICLES
FERRARI 308 SERIES BUYER'S AND OWNER'S GUIDE
FERRARI BROCHURES AND SALES LITERATURE 1968-1989
FERRARI SERIAL NUMBERS PART I - ODD NUMBERS TO 21399
FERRARI SERIAL NUMBERS PART II - EVEN NUMBERS TO 1050
HENRY'S FABULOUS MODEL "A" FORD
MASERATI BROCHURES AND SALES LITERATURE

VELOCEPRESS BOOKS – AUTO RACING

BOOK OF THE 1950 CARRERA PANAMERICANA - MEXICAN ROAD RACE
DIALED IN - THE JAN OPPERMAN STORY
VEDA ORR'S NEW REVISED HOT ROD PICTORIAL
LIFE OF TED HORN – AMERICAN RACING CHAMPION

www.VelocePress.com